An Ounce of Prevention

Macedonia and the UN Experience in Preventive Diplomacy

Henryk J. Sokalski

UNITED STATES INSTITUTE OF PEACE PRESS
Washington, D.C.

The views expressed in this book are those of the author alone. They do not necessarily reflect views of the United States Institute of Peace.

UNITED STATES INSTITUTE OF PEACE
1200 17th Street NW
Washington, DC 20036-3011

First published 2003

Printed in the United States of America

The paper used in this publication meets the minimum requirements of American National Standard for Information Sciences—Permanence of Paper for Printed Library Materials, ANSI Z39.48-1984.

Library of Congress Cataloging-in-Publication Data

Sokalski, Henryk J., 1936-
    An ounce of prevention : Macedonia and the UN experience in preventive diplomacy / Henryk J. Sokalski
    p. cm.
    Includes bibliographical references and index.
    ISBN 1-929223-46-3 (paper)
    1. Macedonia (Republic)—Politics and government—1992- 2. Albanians—Macedonia (Republic)—Politics and government. 3. Macedonia (Republic)—Ethnic relations. 4. UN Preventive Deployment Force. 5. Intervention (International law) I. Title.

DR2253.S65 2003
949.7303–dc21

2003045289

CONTENTS

LIST OF ACRONYMS

ASNOM: Anti-Fascist Assembly of the National Liberation of Macedonia

CICP: Center for International Crime Prevention

CSCE: Conference on Security and Cooperation in Europe

DA: Democratic Alternative

DPA: Democratic Party of Albanians

EC: European Community

ECRI: European Commission against Racism and Intolerance

EU: European Union

FC: Force Commander

FRY: Federal Republic of Yugoslavia

FYROM: Former Yugoslav Republic of Macedonia

HCNM: High Commissioner on National Minorities

ICFY: International Conference on the Former Yugoslavia

IFOR: Implementation Force

KLA: Kosovo Liberation Army

LDP: Liberal-Democratic Party

LP: Liberal Party

MP: Member of Parliament

NATO: North Atlantic Treaty Organization

NDP: People's Democratic Party

NGO: Nongovernmental organization

NLA: National Liberation Army

NORDBAT: Nordic Battalion

OP: Observation Post

OPT: Temporary Observation Post

OSCE: Organization for Security and Cooperation in Europe

PCER: Party for the Complete Emancipation of Romas

PDD: Presidential Decision Directive

PDP: Party for Democratic Prosperity

PDPA: Party for Democratic Prosperity of Albanians

PfP: Partnership for Peace

PIO: Press and Information Officer

PRC: People's Republic of China

ScanCoy : Scandinavian Company

SCG: Search for Common Ground

SDSM: Social Democratic Alliance of Macedonia

SFRY: Socialist Federal Republic of Yugoslavia

SP: Socialist Party

SRSG: Special Representative of the Secretary-General

UN: United Nations

UNCIVPOL: United Nations Civilian Police

UNDP: United Nations Development Program

UNICEF: United Nations Children's Fund

UNMIK: United Nations Mission in Kosovo

UNMO: United Nations Military Observer

UNPL: United Nations Patrol Line

UNPREDEP: United Nations Preventive Deployment Force

UNPROFOR: United Nations Protection Force

UNTAES: United Nations Transitional Administration in Eastern
Slavonia, Baranja, and Western Sirmium

USBAT: United States Battalion

VMRO-DPMNE: Internal Macedonian Revolutionary Organization
–Democratic Party for Macedonian National Unity

FOREWORD

I N HIS EXCELLENT STUDY OF A UNITED NATIONS MISSION in a small but geopolitically important corner of the Balkans, Henryk Sokalski uses a seemingly curious but apt metaphor from the medical sciences: prevention versus cure.

In this case, "cure" is the reconstruction and reconciliation tasks the international community undertakes in a particular country or region following a protracted, destructive conflict. Such "cure" is costly and takes years, perhaps generations, to restore the buildings, industry, houses, and social relationships that existed before the outbreak of war. We know all too well the course of treatment in these postconflict situations: after nearly seven years of reconstruction work in Bosnia, the country is still heavily dependent on foreign aid and the guidance of myriad international agencies and nongovernmental organizations. We know very little about prevention as a rationale for the international community to intervene in a country or region to bolster its institutional and societal mechanisms that temper the resort to mass violence; yet we can surmise that it is certainly less costly than the "cure."

An Ounce of Prevention is an important work, for it describes the first and, so far, only UN preventive peacekeeping mission—that is, the first mission to be deployed to a country *before* an imminent outbreak of hostilities. When he first convened a series of UN conferences on the matter, Secretary-General Boutros Boutros-Ghali sparked some mild controversy with his notion of preventive action, mainly because in the realm of international politics, prevention runs up against the formidable principle of sovereignty.

Even as much a supporter of preventive diplomacy as Boutros-Ghali's successor, Kofi Annan, acknowledged, a preventive deployment of peacekeeping troops and other international actors is a tough call, for how does the international community know precisely the point at which a country or region is about to fall prey to conflict? What threshold separates international concern and attention from international intervention? Does such a threshold apply to all countries? And after such assessments are made and international actors arrive in the country, how long must they stay before the preventive mission can claim success? In the case of "failed" states whose governments have disintegrated under the crush of nationwide violence, sovereignty suddenly becomes a moot point, and the country essentially becomes a ward of the international community. Regarding the UN Preventive Deployment Force's (UNPREDEP) arrival in Macedonia, the country's leaders at the time agreed to accept the mission—after all, they perhaps knew best that it would be only a matter of time before the rapacious conflicts in the rest of the former Yugoslavia spilled across their newly independent country's borders.

If such agreement is the standard for future UN mandates on preventive deployments, what about other countries that appear to be prey to internal or external conflict whose leaders are not so prescient or not so amenable to having a preventive peacekeeping force operate throughout their national territory? How would the international community justify a mission that seeks to set an entire country aright, especially if the country's leaders believe they can ride out the turbulence and instability? In short, would such missions be considered preventive or premature? As the author of this study expertly acknowledges in his review of the debate on preventive diplomacy, prevention as a peacekeeping modality—much like its practice in the healthcare field—necessarily seeks a "holistic" approach in tackling the fundamental sources of mass violence that lie not so far beneath the surface of society. Using such an approach, a preventive peacekeeping mission can easily become an unwelcome presence—declared as such by a government that sees its basic functions taken over and its political base compromised by the preventive peacekeeping force. Absent the "unity of despair" (as Sokalski dubs it) that has characterized the chaotic and tragically violent environments of recent peacekeeping missions, preventive action is a constantly nuanced and delicate balancing act.

As the Special Representative of the UN Secretary-General and head of

UNPREDEP from 1995 to 1998, Henryk Sokalski was certainly mindful of these concerns, but he and the mission's political and military officials also realized they lacked the benefit of a model for a preventive mission or lessons from previous such missions. Because of UNPREDEP's very novelty as a peace operation, Sokalski and the force's staff members had to rely on a great deal of innovation as they planned and implemented the mission's tasks. That is not to say, however, that the preventive deployment did not borrow some of its components from traditional peacekeeping operations. An outgrowth of the UN peacekeeping mission in other parts of the former Yugoslavia, UNPREDEP had a solid structure and dedicated functions to attempt to diminish the country's increasing external and domestic instability following its independence, along with that of the other former Yugoslav republics at the beginning of the 1990s. UNPREDEP consisted of three "pillars." The first was the traditional stuff of peacekeeping missions: troops and military observers along Macedonia's borders to assist the country's security forces in warding off incursions or hostile acts from neighboring countries that harbored varying degrees of historical animosity to an independent Macedonia. The second pillar went a bit further: political action and "good offices"—the negotiation and mediation services diplomats can provide through their authority and skill; just as important, though, the second pillar also included a contingent of UN civilian police to guard against civil or human rights violations against Macedonia's national minorities—particularly ethnic Albanians—at the hands of the country's overwhelmingly ethnic Macedonian public security forces.

The third pillar—what Sokalski describes as "the human dimension"—was a genuine innovation in the typical peacekeeping mission, but, then again, UNPREDEP was not a typical peacekeeping mission. "The human dimension" in this case touched practically every social institution and government service in the young independent Macedonia, which seems to have not fared as well as its East-Central European counterparts in terms of civil society following independence from a socialist empire. At first blush, UNPREDEP could have garnered much criticism for a portion of its mandate that seemed to be obtrusive and extensive in its supervision of an entire society. Yet it is a testament to the UN's and Sokalski's judgment that these "third pillar" tasks, as Sokalski himself acknowledges, remained at the level of a *catalyst* to reinvigorate and reorient Macedonia's nascent civil society institutions and, in so doing, quell the pent-up frustrations of ethnic Albanians and other minority groups that were threatening to erupt in widespread riots and mass bloodshed.

If UNPREDEP is to serve as a model of future preventive deployments, we must arrive at some criteria of effectiveness in the Macedonian mission. This is a difficult task, obviously, for such missions' success is counterfactual to a large extent. How can one prove that the absence of mass violence or incursions from hostile neighbors was attributable to a preventive intervention on behalf of the international community? Sokalski amasses the evidence in this book's concluding chapter, but perhaps the most telling sign of UNPREDEP's success came two years after the mission left, when the "unfinished war" in Kosovo breached Macedonia's largely unmonitored northern border and swept across much of the country's overwhelmingly ethnic Albanian northern and western regions. As the book's epilogue suggests, the Framework Agreement hammered out between U.S. and European Union envoys and Macedonia's political leaders to put a comprehensive end to the apparently externally triggered insurgency attempts to codify much of what UNPREDEP set out to do with Macedonia's public institutions—that is, to move them in the direction of more representativeness and inclusiveness—albeit in a more unobtrusive and diplomatic fashion.

Of course, such innovation in this unique peace operation leads one to ask whether the model is dependent on the head of the mission. What kind of personal and diplomatic skills did Henryk Sokalski contribute to the success—truncated though it was—of UNPREDEP? After all, there must have been some special reasons why Boutros-Ghali specifically selected Sokalski to head the mission, and if Sokalski himself is too modest to recount them, his colleagues are not: He is the exemplar of the "seasoned" diplomat—politically astute and bureaucratically savvy, which is no surprise, given his years of service in the UN's senior staff. Yet his modesty is but one feature of his unassuming nature; as you will note in the following pages, Henryk Sokalski does not seize the limelight. He is roundly described as soft-spoken, gracious, and sensitive to his colleagues' and interlocutors' concerns—his private demeanor matches his diplomatic persona, which is how he prefers to operate.

Make no mistake about it, though, Sokalski is effective; he knows how to work the diplomatic ropes, and he did so frequently when he had to sell particular UNPREDEP initiatives to the Macedonian government. Some other heads of UN missions would insist on unconditional acceptance of such initiatives in the service of stopping a civil war or preventing the escalation of an interstate imbroglio. Henryk Sokalski had a decidedly different style, preferring to gather the members of the diplomatic community in Skopje and gently, but persuasively, argue his point and then making sure he had diplomatically "collegial" support behind him. His soft-spokenness may have worked to his advantage when he had to be tough, surprising recalcitrant officials when he had to read them the riot act; his careful preparation and strong persuasive abilities, though, kept such episodes to a minimum.

Above all, Henryk Sokalski is an optimist—a quality that can handicap the best of diplomatic stratagems—and readers will note this special trait in his particular concern with Macedonia's youth: through the assignment of peacekeeping commanders to speak at grade schools about the purpose of the UN in Macedonia to the concern with orphans and other young victims of nascent conflict in the country to the prospect of reconciliation he saw after bringing together youth representatives of the country's major ethnic political parties to sign a joint declaration. If there were to be genuine "healing" in Macedonia, Sokalski believed, it was up to the generation that lacked so many years of bitter and hostile attitudes. Indeed, if there is any personal attribute we can ascribe to the success of this preventive mission, it is most likely Sokalski's optimism guiding his seasoned diplomatic pragmatism. His years of service as the UN's director for social development and coordinator of the International Year of the Family perhaps served as the requisite platform for such blending of diplomatic skill and championing the cause of the UN's ultimate clients—innocent parents and children who fall prey to deep poverty or famine, or who are caught up in a voracious and undiscriminating conflict.

The United States Institute of Peace brought Henryk Sokalski to its Jennings Randolph Program for International Peace because his experience and his message obviously fit into the Institute's mandate of exploring new, effective forms of conflict management, conflict resolution, and peacekeeping. Conflict prevention in UNPREDEP's case certainly held promise as a case study in a novel form of peacekeeping, and we encouraged him to pursue his research and writing with his original question in mind: Can UNPREDEP serve as a model for future preventive deployments? Does UNPREDEP serve as a new paradigm of peacekeeping—one that, as the author says, "promoted the conditions of a peace to keep"? Sokalski's research also certainly fit into the Institute's work on postconflict reconstruction and reconciliation in southeastern Europe through its Balkans Initiative, which has produced or sponsored many Special Reports on Macedonia, Kosovo, and the Dayton peace process, and he adds to the special book-length studies published over the years by the Institute's Press on new paradigms of statecraft and diplomacy in managing and resolving conflict, including Michael Lund's pioneering *Preventing Violent Conflicts: A Strategy for Preventive Diplomacy* and the comprehensive collections edited by Chester A. Crocker, Fen Osler Hampson, and Pamela Aall, *Turbulent Peace: The Challenges of Managing International Conflict* and *Managing Global Chaos: Sources of and Responses to International Conflict.*

An *Ounce of Prevention* is a fascinating work—part diplomatic memoir, part scholarly investigation, part peacekeeping desideratum, part cautionary tale—and the caution lies only insofar as a preventive mission's vulnerability to an untimely demise, as happened to UNPREDEP in a somewhat shortsighted (and yet, not unexpected in the world of great-power diplomacy) veto in the UN Security Council. Indeed, Henryk Sokalski has provided us with an interesting compendium of the theories and practical tasks surrounding preventive action by the international community. Most of the narrative in the pages that follow chronicles unfamiliar success in a world of statecraft and diplomacy that remains more than a bit skeptical about the UN's mandate for preventive missions.

As the author of this book will readily tell you, any peacekeeping mission is an extremely tough operation; prevention, though, has its own distinct challenges. As any physician will tell you, it is hard to make people follow a preventive regime of wellness: more often than not, they do not take action until symptoms appear. In the realm of nation-states, however, such symptoms have pernicious and deadly consequences.

RICHARD H. SOLOMON, PRESIDENT
UNITED STATES INSTITUTE OF PEACE

PREFACE

T HE LAST DECADE OF THE TWENTIETH CENTURY saw unprecedented interest in preventive diplomacy and early conflict prevention. The hopes that the two notions had kindled were perhaps farther ahead of their time than what, on more realistic reflection, could actually be achieved in this complex world of ours. Yet prevention has become an important political topic of the day. Firmly placed on the international agenda, the subject has preoccupied the minds and talents of many political leaders, academics, foreign policy analysts, peacekeeping practitioners, and international organizations (governmental and nongovernmental alike). Preventive action, particularly in its noncoercive dimension, has had its own appeal and potential. It has lost nothing of its importance in the period following September 11, 2001—even though, since that day, we have somehow felt as if we were waking up in a different world every morning.

The hideous terrorist attacks against New York and Washington, D.C. were also a blow to the novel approach and fresh ideas of conflict prevention. Sadly, we suddenly realized once again that noncoercive prevention alone may not suffice to make the world a happier and safer place to live. Ever since that terrible September day, a ghastly shadow—the shadow of international terrorism—was also cast upon conflict prevention. This new challenge to the fundamental precepts of international intercourse has left somewhat less room to classical preventive diplomacy. Pre-emptive action and coercive reaction have more forcefully entered the repertoire of preventive practices. Nevertheless, the 1990s left a theoretical and practical track record in early preventive action that is here to stay and, hopefully, to progress in its development as an important tool of conflict resolution.

This book is in tribute to the first and, thus far, only preventive deployment of United Nations peacekeepers and good offices to avert a conflict. It is a story of a small Balkan country, the Republic of Macedonia, and its independence and struggle for peaceful survival. The story is told against the backdrop of the heretofore untried UN early conflict prevention experience, set in the Balkan quagmire. The case of Macedonia has attracted numerous writers in the past ten years. So has the story of the United Nations Preventive Deployment Force (UNPREDEP), intrinsically linked as it is to Macedonia's most recent history—that taking place since the country's independence in 1991. Several important studies on both subjects have greatly facilitated my task; they relieved me from having to follow a strictly chronological discipline or engage in a detailed discussion of all the developments between late 1992 and early 1999.[1] In addition, I have relied on a great many other works to provide readers with a broader understanding of preventive diplomacy as well as Balkan politics and history, most all of which I detail in a bibliography at the end of this volume.

The U.S. Institute of Peace and its Balkans Initiative contributed their own fertile share to an analysis of Macedonia's present and future. All of these writings view UNPREDEP as one continuous operation, notwithstanding the mission's successive institutional phases. Although the mission began as part of the United Nations Protection Force in the Former Yugoslavia (UNPROFOR), and with a lower level of political representation in Skopje, UNPREDEP's successes and failures should be seen in their entirety, as a sum total of six years of efforts on the part of peacekeepers, their political leaders, and their military commanders. Each year of UNPREDEP's preventive presence in Macedonia offered specific and changing needs for practical action, especially as the host country advanced in its internal transformation and improved its international standing.

True enough, UNPREDEP has so far been a one-time operation; its experience has no parallel in diplomatic history. Yet the available literature on the subject reveals once again what a difficult task it often is to translate theoretical and empirical results into a policy context and from that produce workable implications for practice. Aware of what has been written before, I have chosen rather to concentrate on the spirit and methodology of our actions, and on what we managed to accomplish within the confines of the latest United Nations deliberations on the concept of early conflict prevention. Some of UNPREDEP's work was actually vindicated only after the mission's termination. In attempting this bird's-eye view of *what, why,* and *how* we were doing, I have tried to be faithful to that work which entitled me to follow up with a first-hand account as a practitioner and former head of mission.

The history of this region is long and complex, and in highlighting its more divisive periods, I may give readers the impression that interethnic discord arising from the emergence of an independent Macedonia—particularly between ethnic Macedonians and ethnic Albanians—is simply an additional manifestation of the "ancient hatreds" approach to explaining ethnic conflict. That is clearly not the case. For example, Macedonians and Albanians have spent long periods in mutual coexistence and have rarely threatened each other actively. The fact that they did so at the beginning of the twenty-first century is more the exception than the rule.

Similarly, I acknowledge at the outset that my historical survey of the region focuses primarily on the Macedonians. To do justice to the long and ancient history of the Albanians is beyond the scope of this book and would involve a lengthy discussion of Kosovo and Albania as well as Macedonia. Obviously, my historical perspective in this work is necessarily shaped by the principal subject matter at hand; hence, I examine interethnic relations in Macedonia within the framework of international organizations, precarious nation-states, and social institutions and civil society. My purpose here is to focus on what the United Nations could do in terms of traditional peacekeeping twinned with social development programs to stave off nascent interethnic conflict, not to trace the historical preconditions, if any, of such conflict.

Whereas, throughout the book, I use names rather sparingly, I wish at the very outset to salute most cordially the six eminent officers who, at different points in time, commanded the military component of the operation and offered their exemplary service to the cause of preventive peacekeeping. Brigadier-Generals Finn Saermark-Thomsen (Denmark), Tryggve Tellefsen (Norway), Juha Engström (Finland), Bo Wranker (Sweden), Bent Sohn Sohnemann (Denmark), and Ove Strømberg (Norway) have contributed their outstanding share to the mission's success and proved to be delightful colleagues and friends. Working with the three of them whose service coincided with my own was a fascinating professional experience and a personal pleasure. Macedonia and the international community owe much to them, as well as to the thousands of peacekeepers and civilian personnel who served the mission with pride and distinction. I pay a well-deserved and heartfelt tribute to all of them, especially those who worked with me during my tour of duty.

ACKNOWLEDGMENTS

PRIVILEGED AS I WAS to have served as one of many United Nations peacekeepers in Macedonia, I dedicate this book to all my friends in that brave land, regardless of their ethnicity. I would have not written it unless Professor Dennis Sandole of George Mason University had not convinced me that I should do so and if the United States Institute of Peace had not offered me its most helpful and, indeed, prestigious senior fellowship to pursue the project. To the Institute and its entire staff under the executive leadership of Richard Solomon and Harriet Hentges, I owe a special debt of gratitude. Their standards of professionalism and support served as shining examples for me to emulate.

I am particularly indebted to my dear colleagues at the Institute's Jennings Randolph Fellowship Program, including its remarkable director, Joe Klaits, and my program officer, John Crist. Their inspiration and encouragement proved to be priceless commodities in the process of writing. I remain equally grateful to a unique person, the editor of this book, Peter Pavilionis, who showed patience and perseverance in introducing me to the brave new world of the *Chicago Manual of Style*. Finally, my successive research assistants, Ramzi Nemo, Naren Kumarakulasingam, and Yohann De Silva deserve their own share of praise, which I extend to them wholeheartedly.

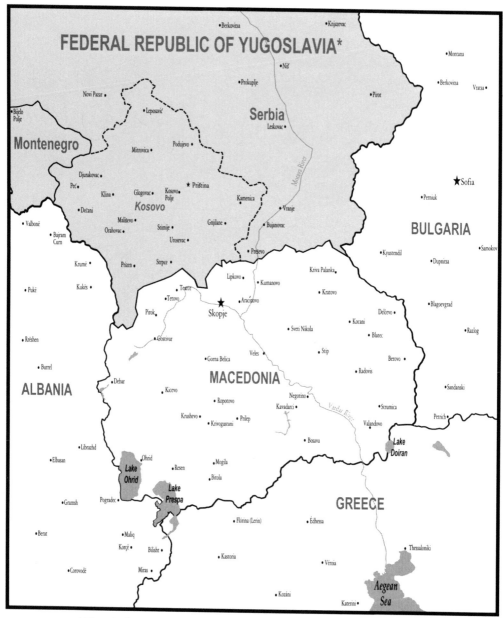

* The Federal Republic of Yugoslavia was succeeded by the union of Serbia and Montenegro, which was voted into existence by the Yugoslav parliament in February 2003.

PROLOGUE

DECEMBER 11, 1992 will go down in the history of international relations as the day that gave birth to the first and, thus far, the only United Nations operation in preventive diplomacy and troop deployment. On that day, the United Nations Security Council passed Resolution 795 (1992), authorizing the secretary general to establish a presence of the United Nations Protection Force in the Former Yugoslavia (UNPROFOR) in the Republic of Macedonia. This mission, subsequently known as the United Nations Preventive Deployment Force (UNPREDEP), was to be hosted by a young country, which had just emerged from the Yugoslav Federation—unlike the destructive examples of several other Yugoslav republics declaring independence—without a single shot being fired.

A call from New York

On a Thursday in early May of 1995, I was on a brief home leave in Warsaw following the preparations for and observances of the International Year of the Family, which I had coordinated worldwide on behalf of the United Nations. The message in the phone call from New York was loud and clear: "The secretary-general would like you to come to New York without delay. We do not know the reason." I cannot say I was not worried. Boutros-Ghali had been known for his tough treatment of staff. Yet for the life of me, I couldn't think of what I'd done to deserve a personal dressing down at headquarters—by the secretary-general himself, no less.

Having stopped for a day at my duty station in Vienna, on Monday morning I reported to my boss in New York, Undersecretary-General for Economic and Social Affairs Nitin Desai. He was either really unaware of the purpose of my visit to headquarters or thought that it might be better if the news be broken to me by the secretary-general himself or by others in his senior staff. Desai immediately informed the Office of the Secretary-General of my arrival. We were instructed to wait, and wait we did until the following day, when I was received by Boutros-Ghali's chef de cabinet and informed that I was under consideration for the post of chief of mission for UNPREDEP in Macedonia, at the level of assistant secretary-general. If I agreed to accept the post, I was told, I should contact Undersecretary-General for Peacekeeping Operations Kofi Annan for further details.

It was not until I saw Kofi Annan that I understood what a unique professional chance I was being offered. The unprecedented nature of a UN presence in Macedonia opened up opportunities that, if properly seized, might also set a model for, and pace of, conflict prevention elsewhere in the world. I decided to head up this rather novel experiment in UN peace-keeping—except, in this case, the mission's mandate was to make sure there would be a peace to keep.

In mid-June, just prior to my introductory visit to Macedonia, I had learned that a Macedonian government minister was in Vienna, attending the session of one of the functional commissions of the United Nations Economic and Social Council. I invited him to lunch, ready to listen attentively to what he would have to say on my forthcoming mission in his country. Right from the start, however, even before I had time to introduce myself properly, my interlocutor started bombarding me with questions regarding the Balkans. His basic query was whether I had ever been to that part of Europe. I had, I said, mostly on a few short business and private visits to former Yugoslavia; but, no, I had never served in the region. A severe expression of doubt appeared on the minister's face, and it did not seem to help much when I mentioned my thirty-five years in the foreign service, in both Poland's diplomatic corps and on the UN's senior staff; the long specialization in UN affairs; and my own homework on the Balkans, as well as the excellent briefings I had been given by many experts before my forthcoming departure to Skopje. Ultimately, the minister decided not to press me any further but did have a warning to sound: "You always have to remember that there are two sides to reality in the Balkans—one over the table, the other under the table." I was grateful to the minister for the warning as on several occasions in the following thirty-nine months I would become acutely aware of its significance. With the passing time, I was to learn several more traits of the unique Balkan mentality.

First visits to Skopje

On June 19 and 20, I paid my introductory visit to Skopje. On the first day, as I was escorted to see President Kiro Gligorov, I entered his spacious office on the second floor of the parliament building. The president stepped forward to greet me. He extended his arms toward me and said: "Mister Sokalski, from friendly Poland!" I later thought that I should have perhaps added, ". . . and from the friendly United Nations!" Upon reflection, however, I understood his words addressed to me as his recognition of the fact that the secretary-general of the United Nations was sending on this important mission someone from another country in transition, a country with a rich tradition of contacts with the former Yugoslavia, including Macedonia. This national "bonding" proved particularly helpful to me in the months to come, especially among Macedonia's ethnic communities, while the first meeting with President Gligorov had established the practice of my frequent discussions with him on a variety of issues regarding the United Nations presence and role in Macedonia.

On July 5, 1995, I arrived in Skopje again, this time to assume my permanent duties as head of mission. My arrival coincided with the visit to UNPREDEP of one of our senior colleagues from UN headquarters who was interested in meeting some leaders of Macedonia's major political parties. He was short on time, so it was suggested that he meet the party representatives together in one group. The party leaders flatly refused. They neither wished to be seen together nor create an impression that they shared common views that might be misunderstood by both their own publics and representatives of the international community. Consequently, each party leader spent no more than twenty minutes with our guest from New York and, in principle, discussed the very same topics subsequently taken up by others during their separate meetings with him. This unwillingness to enter into a shared dialogue was the characteristic feature of Macedonia's political elites until the mid-1990s.

"Because we are in the Balkans!"

From my first day as head of UNPREDEP in Macedonia, I would pose many different questions to my local interlocutors. Many times, I would

ponder a particular aspect of the country's social and political life and ask
them, "Why so?" Their customary response would be, "Because we are in
the Balkans!" I had consistently tried to fight this strange kind of Balkan
fatalism, although toward the end of my stay there my earlier persistence
seemed to have waned somewhat. History has its own inexplicable
dynamics. For Churchill, the problem was the region's excess of history
compared to its relatively small geography. My problem, however, was the
region's future—specifically, its high potential for unpredictable
post–Cold War events. Indeed, who could have ever predicted the disintegration of Yugoslavia? Who could have anticipated the inexcusable and
devastating wars in a region that, in many respects, was the least expected
not to be able to cope with such a crisis?

The quest for answers seemed to be unending.

1

A NEW MEANING FOR AN OLD AXIOM

THE SCIENCE OF MEDICINE was the first to discover that "An ounce of prevention is worth a pound of cure."[1] Progress in medicine in the past few decades has saved the lives of millions and infused the notion of longevity with a dimension of its own. Conversely, failures in timely prevention on the political and diplomatic front over the past decade have allowed some one hundred conflicts to erupt, resulting in a death toll of several million people. In both medicine and politics, prevention has a critical role to play. In the political realm, however, its full potential has yet to be realized.[2]

From time immemorial, various methods and instruments of diplomacy have been resorted to for the purpose of preventing what is now called armed, violent, or deadly conflict. In that sense, the art of prevention may have even predated its recorded history and the emergence of the nation-state. Throughout centuries, and not without success, emissaries and envoys traveled to faraway lands and between countries, with the goal of negotiating a settlement of conflicts, averting their recurrence, or preventing an outbreak of hostilities. Modern diplomacy has instilled a new spirit into the notion of conflict prevention. A great number of tools of diplomatic action have been developed for the purpose of the pacific settlement of disputes and the prevention of conflicts. These tools include negotiation, enquiry, mediation, conciliation, arbitration, judicial settlement, and "good offices." Diplomacy has gradually become recognized as *the established method of international discourse or the art of managing international relations, chiefly by negotiation.*[3] As such, at different points in history, diplomacy has served both constructive and destructive ends. It was certainly neither constructive nor effective diplomacy that, under the false expectations of preventing a major war, produced the Münich Agreement of 1938.[4] The same dubious ends were served by the Ribbentrop-Molotov Pact of 1939, which divided Central and Eastern Europe into German and Soviet spheres of influence.[5] Ultimately, any form of diplomacy practiced at the expense of other nations turns out to be destructive.

The emergence of multilateral relations among states, as well as the creation of a system of international organizations, broke new ground for the practice of diplomacy to expand its multifaceted tools of action, including conflict prevention. Conflict prevention, however, should not imply that traditional, bilateral diplomacy among states would in any way prove inferior to its multilateral counterpart in the efforts to resolve conflict. In fact, both great powers and smaller countries, determined to play an active role in world affairs, must possess a strong noncoercive preventive component applicable to their own relations with different countries, or meant for brokering solutions among other international actors. When the Clinton administration was profoundly concerned over the growing likelihood of North Korea's developing its own missile and nuclear potential, which posed a serious threat to international peace and security, U.S. secretary of state Madeleine Albright traveled to North Korea in October 2000, and her visit provided a clear example of preventive diplomacy by a major power. When, on the initiative of Norway in September 1993, the so-called Oslo Process culminated in the signing of the Declaration of Principles on Interim Self-Government Arrangements Between Israel and the Palestine Liberation Organization, the initiative was another manifestation of a successful effort in preventive diplomacy, in both pre- and post-conflict dimensions, by a smaller country and a consistent author and supporter of initiatives in conflict prevention. Preventive diplomacy can thus operate both bilaterally and multilaterally.

Modern prevention as a tool of diplomacy, backed by the newly created multilateral forms of international relations, has taken hold only at the turn of each of the past two centuries. The League of Nations, notwithstanding its well-known weaknesses, did serve to mitigate a few disputes, until the involvement of several totalitarian regimes in world affairs of the 1930s prevented the League from developing a more effective capacity for prevention. The bitter experiences of the Second World War taught the world community the lesson of extinguishing fires before they burn out of control. Soon afterward, the Charter of the United Nations became the world's major pledge toward prevention, enshrined in the Charter's very opening words: "We, the peoples of the United Nations, determined to save succeeding generations from the scourge of war. . . ."[6] Ever since, with varying degrees of success, the world organization has been trying to make this commitment a reality. Referring to the organization's New York headquarters, former UN secretary-general Javier Perez de Cuellar put it this way: "No one will ever know how many conflicts have been prevented or limited through contacts which have taken place in the famous glass mansion, which can become fairly opaque when necessary."[7] Indeed, with conflict prevention as its major preoccupation, the United Nations and its system of organizations and agencies have become the strongest generators of preventive action in all possible avenues of human endeavor under its global agenda.

A MULTIFACETED NOTION

The concept of conflict prevention is indeed multifaceted. Its simplest division consists in pre- (proactive) and postconflict (reactive) prevention. Notwithstanding their similarities, each has its own characteristics, which nevertheless have not been fully reflected in the numerous scholarly analyses of the subject to date. According to some authors, preventive measures "require greater diplomatic skills and more flexible negotiating techniques than the other more traditional reactive measures."[8] While postconflict prevention is normally a child of bitter lessons learned from an armed confrontation, preconflict prevention efforts generally emerge out of a different experience and call for an application of highly diversified techniques. Preconflict prevention could at times be an even more complex challenge because the parties to a potential conflict might not know the tragic costs of armed strife and, therefore, might be less inclined toward pursuing a path of dialogue and conciliation.

At the same time, the material requirements for successful preconflict prevention will doubtless cost less than those in a conflict or postconflict international preventive intervention—particularly so if the latter proceeds under Chapter VII of the UN Charter. At stake here is an objective perception of what really distinguishes genuine and timely conflict prevention from the prevention of conflict recidivism. While some techniques in both cases might be identical or similar, the contexts in which they are applied do set them apart quite distinctively.[9] An effective preconflict strategy means removing or at least mitigating the immediate causes of a conflict before they generate destructive effects. Such a preconflict strategy involves a timely precrisis intervention—before disputes escalate to become more complex and intractable—and an early resort to preventive action through the application of a concerted range of measures, with a view to averting a potential conflict.

The specific term *preventive diplomacy* has been relatively new to the repertoire of preconflict preventive practice. Both researchers and practitioners of the craft trace it back to the innovative thinking of the second secretary-general of the United Nations (1953–1960), the late Dag Hammarskjold.[10] He believed that the United Nations' efforts had to concentrate on keeping newly arising conflicts out of the sphere of superpower differences. In using the term preventive diplomacy, Hammarskjold largely applied it to cases where the original conflict might be said to be the result of, or to imply risks for, the creation of a power vacuum between the main blocs.[11] This framework definition, however, lost much of its legitimacy with the end of the Cold War and the waning of crises between the superpowers or their proxies.

SETTING THE STANDARDS

Cold War divisions, which took up nearly fifty years of the past century, failed to generate a climate propitious enough for resorting in good faith to preventive mechanisms based on the purposes and principles of the UN Charter, thus far the most complete source of conflict prevention. The end of bloc rivalries at the turn of the 1980s and 1990s had raised much hope for a "peace dividend." The UN Security Council, meeting at the level of heads of state or government on January 31, 1992, joined the spirit of the day by welcoming the "momentous change" and underscoring that "the ending of the Cold War has raised hopes for a safer, more equitable, and more humane world."[12] Moreover, there was the worldwide hope that, consequently, enormous resources could be released from burgeoning arms programs and turned into developmental ventures. In the meantime, although between 1990 and 1998 aggregate national military expenditures declined by some 30 percent and nuclear arsenals declined by half from 1982 levels, no such reallocation of resources occurred. The number of wars worldwide had not diminished. Their emphasis shifted from inter- to intrastate conflicts, and the military budgets of some countries have soared rather than dropped.[13] The end of the Cold War also produced a troubling qualitative change: nonmilitary sources and nonstate actors of instability intensified considerably.

The world seems to have thus lost an opportunity to perfect a significant tool of getting to the root causes of conflicts. A long-awaited unanimity of great powers, particularly in the Security Council, still leaves much to be desired. Only too often, warnings of imminent conflicts remain unaddressed by delayed action. Yet, in some regions of the world, impressive progress has been made toward democracy, responsive forms of government, and confidence-building measures among historically mutually suspicious states. A more forthcoming approach in the international community toward peacemaking and peacekeeping operations, particularly in their preventive dimension, has also exemplified these progressive trends. Still, the short-lived consensus following the Cold War has proved somewhat inadequate for the new kinds of mostly intrastate conflicts.

Following up on the earlier "United Nations Declaration on the Prevention and Removal of Disputes and Situations Which May Threaten International Peace and Security and on the Role of the United Nations in this Field" and the "Declaration on Fact-finding by the United Nations in the Field of the Maintenance of International Peace and Security,"[14] the Security Council, at its January 31, 1992 summit meeting, invited the secretary-general to prepare for circulation to the members of the United Nations by July 1 his analysis and recommendations on ways of strengthening and making more efficient within the framework and provisions of the Charter the capacity of the United Nations for *preventive diplomacy,* for peacemaking, and for peacekeeping.[15] Although the statement by the council's president had not directly referred to the declarations, they proved particularly relevant to the progress of conceptual work on the notion of preventive diplomacy and preventive action.

First, in the 1988 declaration, the General Assembly recognized the important role that the United Nations and its organs can play in the prevention and removal of international disputes and situations that may lead to international friction or give rise to an international dispute. Second, the declaration spelled out a number of principles for action by states, with a view to preventing in these states' relations the emergence or aggravation of disputes or situations, in particular by fulfilling in good faith their obligations under international law. Third, in rather uncommon language, the declaration urged the secretary-general to resort more frequently to his prerogatives under Article 99 of the Charter and become involved in preventive action.

The "Declaration on Fact-finding by the United Nations in the Field of the Maintenance of International Peace and Security" has also vested the secretary-general with new and stronger powers in the field of investigation and assessment. Among other things, it authorized him to pay special attention to using UN fact-finding capabilities at an early stage in order to contribute to the prevention of disputes and situations. It urged him to consider, on his own initiative or at the request of the states concerned, undertaking a fact-finding mission when a dispute or a situation exists.

The improved international climate, along with the novel provisions of the declarations and specific guidance by the Security Council, paved the way for the secretary-general's response to the council's January 31, 1992 invitation to submit his analyses of and recommendations on conflict prevention in general and *preventive diplomacy* in particular. Interestingly, at no stage had the Council offered a definition of what *preventive diplomacy* really meant. The publication of Boutros-Ghali's *An Agenda for Peace* in June 1992 marked the revival of this concept and its application toward broadly conceived early preventive action.[16] Yet, what seemed new in the framing of the notion lay in a timely resort to such action through the application of a concerted range of measures, including confidence building, early warning based on information gathering and formal and informal fact-finding, preventive troop deployment, preventive disarmament, and, in some situations, demilitarized zones. In other words, the traditional tools of active prevention as provided in Article 33 of the Charter have found enrichment in supplementary techniques to meet the new political challenges and to cope with the world's complex exigencies.[17]

An Agenda for Peace had generated an important international debate among both practitioners and academics. Two principal organs of the United Nations, the General Assembly and the Security Council, devoted considerable time and attention to the secretary-general's report, discussing different aspects of the document and proposals contained in it or sending them to the Special Committee on Peacekeeping Operations for further consideration. More immediate General Assembly reaction came with resolution 47/120A of December 18, 1992, titled "An Agenda for Peace: Preventive Diplomacy and Related Matters." This resolution welcomed the timely presentation of the study and offered comments on the peaceful settlement of disputes; early warning; the collection and analysis of information; fact-finding; confidence-building measures; humanitarian assistance; resources and logistical aspects of preventive diplomacy; and the role of the General Assembly in preventive diplomacy.

A few months later, the General Assembly followed with resolution 47/120B of September 20, 1993, titled "An Agenda for Peace," which addressed Boutros-Ghali's other proposals—namely, the role of the General Assembly; preventive deployment and demilitarized zones; use of the International Court of Justice in the peaceful settlement of disputes; addressing special economic problems arising from the implementation of preventive or enforcement measures; postconflict peacebuilding; cooperation with regional arrangements and organizations; and safety of personnel. During its forty-eighth session, the General Assembly passed resolution 48/42 of December 10, 1993, tackling a number of major political and housekeeping questions, including issues arising from *An Agenda for Peace,* with special emphasis on future cooperation between the United Nations and regional organizations.

Also, the Security Council took up the secretary-general's proposals concerning the council or addressed to it. For this purpose, the council decided to hold, beginning in October 1992, a meeting at least once a month devoted to the *Agenda.* The Security Council has consistently done so for many months and still continues its periodic sessions, especially under agenda items referencing "the responsibility of the Security Council in the maintenance of international peace and security"; "improving the capacity of the United Nations for peacekeeping"; "the situation in Africa";

"the role of the Security Council in the prevention of armed conflicts"; and "the maintenance of peace and security and postconflict peacebuilding." Successive meetings of this kind have led to either statements by the council's president or relevant resolutions.[18]

FINE-TUNING THE TERMINOLOGY

In *An Agenda for Peace,* Boutros-Ghali had not only revived the idea of preventive diplomacy in the changing context of a global transition but had also offered a definition of his own, integrally linking preventive diplomacy with peacemaking and peacekeeping. Accordingly, "preventive diplomacy is action to prevent disputes from arising between parties, to prevent existing disputes from escalating into conflicts and to limit the spread of the latter when they occur."

This revival of preventive diplomacy coincided with an unprecedented expansion of UN peacekeeping activities. Between January 1988 and December 1994, these missions grew in strength from five to seventeen full-fledged operations, from 9,570 to 73,393 military personnel deployed, with a total budget increasing from $230 million to close to $4 billion.[19] The two and a half years following the publication of *An Agenda for Peace* allowed the United Nations to accumulate more experience to fine-tune the conceptual framework for the new instruments of prevention. Encouraged by the response to *An Agenda for Peace* and the potential that the idea of prevention had offered, the secretary-general decided to publish in January 1995 a "Supplement to An Agenda for Peace: Position Paper on the Occasion of the Fiftieth Anniversary of the United Nations."[20] Its purpose was to highlight the quantitative and qualitative changes of approach up to that time. Again, preventive diplomacy and peacemaking constituted the gist of the paper.

The Security Council welcomed the position paper and its wide range of conclusions and recommendations with regard to instruments for resolving conflict.[21] In particular, the council approved the priority given by the secretary-general to action aimed at preventing conflict, and it encouraged all member states to make the fullest possible use of instruments of preventive action, including the secretary-general's "good offices"; the dispatch of special envoys; the development of small field missions for preventive diplomacy; and peacemaking. Council members also endorsed the view of the crucial importance of economic and social development as a secure basis for lasting peace. For the first time in fifty years, the council stated in unequivocal terms that social and economic development can be as valuable in preventing conflicts as in healing the wounds after conflicts have occurred.[22] As expected, such an innovative approach initially attracted its share of skepticism from some analysts, who questioned the wisdom of "equating preventive diplomacy with the job of correcting often pervasive and deeply rooted social ills."[23]

Six years later, in early February 2001, an unprecedented discussion on peacebuilding took place in the Security Council. Council President Said Ben Mustapha of Tunisia initiated a debate, also open to states that were not members of the council, on the topic "Peacebuilding: Toward A Comprehensive Approach." The debate preceded the Fourth United Nations/Regional Organizations High-level Meeting, which Secretary-General Kofi Annan had planned for February 6–7, 2001. Ben Mustapha had also circulated a working paper on the topic of peacebuilding and its organic links with conflict prevention.[24]

Opening the debate in the Security Council on February 5, 2001, the secretary-general stressed that whether it is started before, after, or during the eruption of conflict, peacebuilding must be seen as a long-term exercise. Peacebuilding done well is a powerful deterrent to violent conflict; it is a sum of many initiatives, projects, activities, and sensibilities. Peacebuilding is not the dramatic imposition of a grand plan, but the process of constructing the pillars of peace from the ground up, bit by bit. Finally, Secretary-General Kofi Annan affirmed that peacebuilding must not be seen as an add-on or afterthought, something to save for later when conditions or resources or politics permit; rather, it is a central tool of proven worth.[25] The Security Council offered unqualified support to all international efforts on behalf of peacebuilding aimed at preventing the outbreak, the recurrence, or the continuation of armed conflict.[26]

The idea of preventive diplomacy, although only partially defined, has continued to attract the interest of governments, policymakers, scholars, and practitioners. Yet, as was the case with the Security Council's conceptual linkage of development and conflict, some skeptics eagerly latched onto the rather new and seemingly complex concept of preventive diplomacy. A notable controversy on the concept's merits took place in the pages of *Foreign Affairs* between two American scholars, Stephen John Stedman and Michael S. Lund, in mid-1995.[27] Stedman essentially dismissed preventive diplomacy—a "common slogan" used by policymakers

—as grossly overrated and argued that real preventive diplomacy required prescience, prescription, and "mobilization"; "endemic" conflicts in the post–Cold War era posed "intractable problems" in terms of those three requirements. In his view, "to prevent the Bosnias of tomorrow demands major resources in situations where risks are high and success is in doubt." In response to Stedman's piece, Lund defended the utility of the concept and strongly disagreed with his colleague's charges that "proponents of preventive diplomacy oversell its potential and naïve policymakers are taking the bait."

Edward N. Luttwak promoted a unique approach to peacemaking and, indeed, prevention in another *Foreign Affairs* article, entitled "Give War a Chance."[28] Proceeding from the assumption that war also has "a great virtue: it can resolve political conflicts and lead to peace," Luttwak explains that "[t]his can happen when all belligerents become exhausted or when one wins decisively. Either way the key is that the fighting must continue until resolution is reached."[29] This Malthusian theory of prevention also holds that "if the United Nations helped the strong defeat the weak faster and more decisively, it would actually enhance the peacemaking potential of war."[30]

Most other debates on preventive diplomacy, however, do not question its effectiveness in situations warranting early prevention, no matter how semantically narrow they perceive the term "diplomacy." On the one hand, the very word connotes noncoercive actions taken at an early stage of a preconflict situation; on the other hand, the notion of diplomacy may not adequately reflect the major components of preventive diplomacy and peacemaking, particularly that of preventive deployment, as stipulated in *An Agenda for Peace* and its supplement. In fact, Boutros-Ghali himself would soon become aware of the term's inadequacy by suggesting a corresponding change of terminology: from "preventive diplomacy" to "preventive action." He concluded that, as much as diplomacy is a well-tried means of preventing conflict, there are other tools of effective prevention that can and should have an even more comprehensive and novel effect.[31]

IN SEARCH OF A DEFINITION

Several attempts to agree on an accepted definition of preventive diplomacy have thus far produced little result. Some authors equate preventive diplomacy with preventive action in general. Such an equation has been complicated by nuanced contrasts between *soft* prevention versus *hard* prevention; *low* versus *high* prevention; *pre-* versus *post*conflict preventive action; *light* versus *deep* prevention; and conflict management or coercive prevention versus power-based methods of influence, including military and economic sanctions.[32] Boutros-Ghali's proposed definition in *An Agenda for Peace* has been "noted" rather than "approved" or "adopted" by the General Assembly, which has encouraged different authors, and indeed the secretary-general himself, to propose new, more or less elaborate proposals.[33]

According to Lund, the term *preventive diplomacy* describes "actions or institutions that are used to keep the political disputes that arise between or within nations from escalating into armed conflict."[34] Stedman, notwithstanding his doubts regarding the very idea, sees it as "concerted action designed to resolve, manage, or contain disputes before they become violent."[35] Boutros-Ghali eventually amended his original definition to hold that "preventive diplomacy is the use of diplomatic techniques to prevent disputes arising, prevent them from escalating into armed conflict if they do arise and, if it fails, to prevent the armed conflict from spreading."[36] A year after publishing his definition in *Foreign Affairs,* Lund suggested that preventive diplomacy is "action taken in vulnerable places and times to avoid the threat or use of armed force and related forms of coercion by states or groups to settle the political disputes that can arise from the destabilizing effects of economic, social, political and international change."[37]

On a later occasion, Lund offered a more elaborate description: "conflict prevention may include any structural or interactive means to keep intrastate or interstate tensions and disputes from escalating into significant violence, to strengthen the capabilities to resolve such disputes peacefully, and to alleviate the underlying problems that produce them. Thus, it includes not only avoiding violence but peacebuilding."[38] Boutros-Ghali had highlighted the significance of that latter component earlier in his *Agenda for Development:* "Only sustained efforts to resolve underlying socioeconomic, cultural, and humanitarian problems can place an achieved peace on a durable foundation."[39] He termed such efforts "preventive development."

Bruce Jentleson cogently lists a number of core ideas of preventive diplomacy: "Act early to stop disputes from escalating or problems from worsening. Reduce tensions that if intensified could lead to war. Deal with today's conflicts before they become tomorrow's crises."[40] In a 1994 publication,

Sweden's Minister for Foreign Affairs proposed to treat the phrase in a wide sense. Consequently, she refers to the use of diplomacy "to prevent disputes from arising between parties, to prevent disputes from developing into conflicts, to eliminate conflicts when they occur, and to contain and limit the spread of those conflicts not amenable to swift elimination."[41]

A number of "institutionalized" or "group" attempts to define preventive diplomacy have also emerged of late. One, under the auspices of the Japan Forum on International Relations, holds that "preventive diplomacy is those activities to prevent an armed clash or like conflict or to head such off in the early stages and assumes that preventive diplomacy is synonymous with conflict prevention activities."[42] The authors of this definition assume that the various activities collectively referred to as preventive diplomacy would tend to emphasize nonmilitary over military measures and conflict prevention through collective—or cooperative—security arrangements based on the right of collective self-defense over conflict prevention. They point to widespread apprehension, especially in Asia and Latin America, regarding foreign intervention in the domestic affairs of other countries as one of the major constraints on preventive diplomacy.[43] The Japanese project also quotes a definition offered by the country's National Institute for Research Advancement, outlining preventive diplomacy as "[a]ll noncoercive activities by all parties to keep all disputes between whatever parties from turning violent, escalating, and spreading, and to keep all armed conflicts from endangering international peace and order."[44] The Swedish government has taken yet a broader view by equating conflict prevention mostly with either measures taken before an outbreak of violence or measures preventing violence from erupting once a cease-fire or a peace agreement has been signed.[45]

In a transatlantic cooperative effort, the Carnegie Commission in the United States and the United Kingdom's Ditchley Foundation have described preventive diplomacy as the "use of proactive, nonviolent measures to prevent political conflicts from erupting into violence and to promote peaceful dispute resolution."[46] The historic "Final Report of the Carnegie Commission on Preventing Deadly Conflict," which fostered the publication of close to a hundred major books and papers, clearly distinguishes between *operational prevention,* consisting of strategies in the face of crisis, and *structural prevention,* implementing strategies to address the root causes of deadly conflict.[47] The authors of the report agree that any successful regime of conflict prevention must be multifaceted and designed for the long term. Indeed, the enumeration of preventive measures they propose offers a holistic plan of action for both pre- and postconflict situations. Preventive diplomacy, in their view, falls under the rubric of operational prevention. However, in certain cases, tools of operational and structural prevention may interrelate or apply interchangeably; one such area is development assistance, especially under some form of "positive conditionality."[48]

A remarkable shift of emphasis highlighting both the merits of preventive action and an active search for strategy took place with Kofi Annan's assuming the office of UN secretary-general. Early in his tenure, he assured the Council on Foreign Relations that

> one lesson that we learned from these experiences is that *prevention is better than cure.* Peacekeeping is expensive. It is fraught with dangers, difficulties and uncertainties. Averting conflict saves far more lives and requires far fewer resources than stopping a conflict which has already erupted. That is why I am placing a great deal of emphasis on preventive diplomacy. I urge that the international community also give priority to the essential work of peacemaking and mediation. Look to any postconflict situation and you will realize the cost of diplomatic opportunities not seized and preventive initiatives not carried out.[49]

In most of his public pronouncements and reports—as well as in his active dialogue with the General Assembly and the Security Council on international peace and security, and with specific regard to peacekeeping in different regions of the world—Annan made strong pleas on behalf of preventive action. His message was loud and clear: "prevention of conflict begins and ends with the protection of human life and the promotion of human development."[50]

A New Impetus for Action

The central theme of the secretary-general's annual *Reports on the Work of the Organization* published in September 1997 and August 1999 involved cases for better and more effective prevention strategies, as well as for building a "culture of prevention."[51] These reports provided a new impetus for efforts aimed at implementing early preventive measures and preventive diplomacy. Proceeding from the assumption that the United Nations has no higher goal, no deeper commitment, and no greater ambition than preventing armed conflict, the reports reconfirmed that what

had become known as "postconflict peacebuilding" is a major and relatively recent innovation in preventive strategies based on human security,
good governance, equitable development, and respect for human rights—
all mutually reinforcing and interdependent. Moreover, the reports demonstrate how the prevention philosophy rests on the assumption of good
faith, on the belief that governments will seek to place the welfare of the
people as a whole over narrow sectional interests.

In March 2000, Secretary-General Annan convened a high-level panel
to undertake a thorough review of the UN's peace and security activities
and to present a clear set of specific, concrete, and practical recommendations to assist the United Nations in better conducting such activities. Before
the review's completion, Annan emphasized to Security Council members
that conflict prevention must become the "cornerstone of collective security
in the twenty-first century."[52] Other speakers in the debate on the same
occasion urged a new culture of prevention and peace combined with
healthy and balanced economic and social development. A major break-
through in UN peacekeeping seemed to be taking place.

A few weeks later, the international community received a momentous
report from the secretary-general entitled "We the Peoples: The Role of
the United Nations in the Twenty-First Century."[53] As one of its underlying precepts, the report contended that "it all begins with prevention."
Prepared for the UN's Millennium Assembly, the document suggested a
number of important political prerequisites for effective prevention:

◆ Strategies of prevention must address the root causes of conflicts, not
simply their violent symptoms.

◆ Policymakers must have clear understanding of these causes.

◆ Every step taken toward reducing poverty and achieving broad-based
economic growth also marks a step toward conflict prevention, especially in many poor countries, where poverty is often coupled with
sharp ethnic and religious cleavages.[54]

The General Assembly responded with an encouraging pledge. In its
Millennium Declaration, adopted by heads of state and government gathered in New York, September 6–8, 2000, the Assembly confirmed the
resolve of member states "to make the United Nations more effective in
maintaining peace and security by giving it the resources it needs for con-

flict prevention, peaceful resolution of disputes, peacekeeping, postconflict peacebuilding and reconstruction."⁵⁵ The day before at the Millennium Summit, the Security Council had adopted a declaration on ensuring an effective role for the council in the maintenance of international peace and security, particularly in Africa. In the declaration, the Council pledged to enhance the effectiveness of the United Nations in addressing conflict at all stages, from prevention, to settlement, to postconflict peacebuilding.⁵⁶

The summer of 2000 witnessed the publication of another unprecedented report—this one (hereinafter refered to as the "Brahimi Report") from the High-Level Panel on United Nations Peace Operations, chaired by the former Algerian foreign affairs minister Lakhdar Brahimi.⁵⁷ Pointing out that in the 1990s, such operations addressed no more than one-third of the world's conflict situations, the report urged member states to establish a more effective system for long-term conflict prevention. In the opinion of the panel, long-term humanitarian and developmental activities possess their greatest value when viewed through a "conflict prevention lens." At the same time, the panel identified two key impediments for short-term prevention. First, states harbored an understandable and legitimate concern about sovereignty—especially the small and weak among them. Second, there was a discernable gap between verbal postures and financial and political support for prevention.

Regarding the first aspect of the argument, the panel believed that "such concerns are all the greater in the face of initiatives taken by another member state, especially by a stronger neighbor, or by a regional organization that is dominated by one of its members."⁵⁸ A strong point had been made earlier by the secretary-general regarding the second impediment: "Building a culture of prevention is not easy. . . . While the costs of prevention have to be paid in the present, its benefits lie in the distant future. Moreover, the benefits are not tangible; they are the wars and disasters that do not happen. So we should not be surprised that preventive policies receive support that is more rhetorical than substantive."⁵⁹

The report of the independent panel found a willing audience among concerned professionals and academics. In transmitting the report to the General Assembly and the Security Council for consideration and action, the secretary-general assessed the panel's analysis as "frank yet fair; its recommendations are far-reaching, yet sensible and practical."⁶⁰ During the Millennium Assembly, the heads of state and government took note of the panel's report and requested the General Assembly to consider its recommendations expeditiously. Similarly, the Security Council welcomed the report and decided to consider quickly the recommendations that fell within its area of responsibility.[61] Subsequently, the secretary-general followed up this important document with his own reports on the implementation of the Brahimi Report's recommendations.[62]

The secretary-general's reports offered supplementary information to United Nations organs to facilitate consideration of the Brahimi Report's proposals. Convinced that the biggest deterrent to violent conflict lies in the promotion of sustainable human development and a healthy democratic society based on strong rule of law and civic institutions, including adherence to all human rights—economic, social, political, and cultural—Annan submitted to the General Assembly and Security Council on June 7, 2001, a new comprehensive report on prevention of armed conflict.[63] The document proved to be an outstanding contribution to discussions on prevention conceived as a sum total of the efforts by United Nations organs and other actors in conflict management and prevention. The Security Council reacted promptly to the report by adopting Resolution 1366 of August 30, 2001, which mapped out a program for further efforts toward developing a comprehensive strategy on the prevention of armed conflict, with a view toward developing a systemwide coordinated and supportive approach to conflict prevention.

LINKAGES AND EXPEDIENCIES

Despite their differences, the various attempts to define conflict prevention have generated a few common threads worth noting. First and foremost, they imply that action should be taken early enough to prevent an outbreak of hostilities. Lund has perhaps heavily influenced the debate by characterizing the value of prevention at three stages: "very early on, when preventive diplomacy focuses on the basic sources of disputes; later, when it tries to prevent disputes from becoming violent; and much later, when it seeks to contain an expansion of escalated violence."[64] Efforts at putting preventive diplomacy into context show that neither disputes nor their incipient circumstances are static. This taxonomy explains why Boutros-Ghali concluded that the focus of the term "preventive diplomacy" was too narrow for the concept it entailed and should, rather, be renamed "preventive action."

However, Boutros-Ghali's semantic reformulation does not fully reflect the sense of preconflict urgency, entailing the immediate deployment of peacekeeping troops and the dispatch of a fact-finding mission to a country where conflict seems to be brewing. Perhaps these ideas, therefore, find better expression interchangeably as *early preventive action,* incorporating *preventive diplomacy* as the major component. The foregoing analyses of preventive diplomacy confirm the existence of strong linkages and complementarity between democratic practices, good governance, civil society, and the achievement of peace, on the one hand, and the search for peace and cooperative security and development on the other. Whether labeled as preventive diplomacy, early preventive action, or timely conflict prevention, this concept seemingly operates in constant evolution, determined as it is by the consistency of political will among countries that form "coalitions of the willing" (in current diplomatic parlance) to undertake such interventions.

On the basis of adequate information, early warning will indeed constitute a basic ingredient for any successful preventive action. Such reporting and analysis, of course, must embody as rigorous as possible an assessment of the threats to peace and stability. Early warning will also require properly motivated policymakers with the political will and determination to generate not only the necessary consent among the affected parties but also the consensus of the concerned portions of the international community at large. Similarly, preventive efforts pursued as part of the mechanisms of quiet diplomacy and good offices, based on first-hand information by fact-finding missions, hold much promise for success at preventing conflict. For such efforts, the availability of sufficient resources and continuous monitoring and review stand out as indispensable attributes of such a process.

Political will and sound judgment supply basic foundations for successful preventive action. Apparently, international policymakers had not realized this early enough in one of the most flagrant cases of missed opportunities for early preventive action—namely, in the former Yugoslavia. To be sure, the wars of the early nineties there were not inevitable; in the long run, local and regional leaders probably could have averted the Yugoslav federation's disintegration. However, secession could have occurred somewhat later—and by peaceful means—if not for certain states' hasty recognition of some new republics and the refusal to offer Yugoslavia substantial economic aid. Boutros-Ghali recalls his predecessor's attempt, following the fruitless efforts by several negotiators, to stop the war between Belgrade and Zagreb. Perez de Cuellar urged Germany in the strongest terms possible to withhold diplomatic recognition of Croatia because he realized that such a recognition might be a beginning of a regional tragedy. His appeals went unheeded.[65]

A concerted preventive effort, both operational and structural, could have helped avert a sudden outbreak of hostilities. Yugoslavia posed a unique case in the Cold War period. Especially during the Tito era, the Socialist Federal Republic of Yugoslavia thrived on an active policy of nonalignment and equidistance between the two opposing superpower blocs. In a certain sense, it was being "spoiled" by both, which could not but rather negatively affect the public mind. Post-Tito difficulties, the ineffectiveness of the collective presidency, and the deteriorating economic situation came as a shock to citizens. By the early 1990s, political persuasion from the outside would no longer suffice, and Yugoslavia urgently needed external assistance. As one report noted, "the most fateful event was the brush-off delivered in 1989/90 by Brussels to the Yugoslav federal government, which under the reformist prime minister of the time, Ante Markovic, sought to buttress a bold reform program with Western aid and, especially, EU Associate status."[66] In the end, aid did not come, and the omission took its toll. Markovic had asked for a few billion U.S. dollars at the conflict's outset; a few years later, the cost of the armed conflict in the 1990s to outside powers and in Bosnia alone amounted to $53.7 billion.[67]

In the same manner, in December 1991, a few months before the outbreak of war in Bosnia-Herzegovina and six months prior to the publication of *An Agenda for Peace,* Bosnian president Alija Izetbegovic asked for a preventive deployment of peacekeeping troops. The UN ignored the request, citing a procedure banning the dispatch of peacekeepers before an outbreak of hostilities.[68]

THE PLACE OF TIMELY PREVENTION IN THE PHASES OF CONFLICT

Both international practice and analyses in the field of conflict prevention embody varying degrees of optimism for the preventive prospects of action at different stages of conflicts. In what has now become a classic point of reference, Lund offers a descriptive diagram of a conflict's lifespan, consisting of durable peace, stable peace, unstable peace, crisis, and war.[69] Naturally, not every conflict will pass through all of these stages. However, the more successful an early preventive action, the lower the level of the respective conflict's intensity on the diagram's scale. Before and after Lund's model reaches its apogee of war and descends gradually toward its late stage of possible conflict resolution, through each phase the model assigns specific roles to different tools of diplomacy or conflict management. Under this categorization, the stage of durable peace would not call for any preventive action—that is, it would constitute, to use Johan Galtung's terminology, "positive peace."[70] This stage's "negative" counterpart does not come into play until the third phase, that of unstable peace. The need for early or timely prevention combined with crisis management appears greatest during the stages of unstable peace and crisis. In Lund's view, the imperative for action would typically become pronounced when tensions in the relationships between parties risk shifting from stable to unstable peace or worse.

Japanese experts have arrived at another, though similar, classification of a conflict's emergence. In their view, conflicts start from an early incubation stage, go through a dangerous phase before erupting as an armed confrontation, and then wind down to closure.[71] Four stages underlie their development: one exhibiting no immediate threat of armed conflict, where the situation requires only "general conflict prevention"; a stage of immediate threat of armed clashes, which calls for preventive diplomacy; a stage when armed conflict has already begun; and finally a point when conflict has reached the highest level and has formally ended. This last stage actually marks the start of postconflict, reactive prevention.

The practicality of such categorizations was echoed in the Security Council during the November 1999 debate on the Council's role in the prevention of armed conflicts. Speaking on behalf of the European Union (EU), the representative of Finland declared that "a 'ladder of prevention' would facilitate identifying suitable preventive measures to be taken at each stage of an evolving conflict. The idea of a 'ladder of prevention' is partly, but not exclusively, based on the principle of proportionality; i.e. preventive measures should be taken in proportion to the level of conflict."[72]

Therefore, constant awareness that preventive action does not provide a universal remedy—a cure-all device for any crisis or conflict—remains crucial to understanding its prophylactic powers. Every single dispute has its own peculiarities. What might potentially help in one case or one country will not necessarily do so in another. In prevention, as in diplomacy at large, no "one size fits all" formulas exist.

SOURCES, MECHANISMS, AND ACTORS

Assuming that preventive action should serve positive objectives, and in the absence of agreement as to an ultimate definition of preventive action, the following three sources of prevention merit additional comment: direct prevention, indirect prevention, and prevention by enforcement. Depending on the circumstances, these three categories inter-link and complement one another.

The clearest global manifestation of direct prevention lies in the United Nations Charter and a number of other international instruments, based upon the principles of international law and the promotion of friendly relations and cooperation among states. Indeed, one might characterize this form of action as constant preconflict prevention; Article 33 of the Charter marks only one case in point. Indirect prevention can apply to pre- and postconflict situations in both inter- and intrastate crises. Such efforts comprise the entire sphere of the rule of law, human rights, and other international mechanisms to promote democracy and civil society and relate directly to the fundamental, social causes of conflict, such as exclusion, high population density, unemployment, unequal distribution of resources, and environmental degradation. Prevention by enforcement may not always prove popular when terminating a conflict or managing a crisis. Despite some notable exceptions, general perceptions view early preventive action as noncoercive. Any punitive action, including military measures, should occur as a last resort under Chapter VII of the Charter. Whenever possible, policymakers should also accord primacy to local and regional mechanisms of good offices, mediation, and conciliation.

In other words, initiatives within the confines of preventive diplomacy ought to function not as outright impositions from the outside or interference in the internal affairs of the parties concerned. Antagonizing or prejudicing one of them may diminish chances for settlement and aggravate the nature of the conflict. Cooperative approaches, such as persuasion, inducement, psychological strategies, and assistance in problem-solving, will likely work better at an early preventive stage than coercive, power-based methods of influence. Early, soft moves toward mediation may empower the parties themselves by enhancing their capacity to talk. Coercive diplomacy, on the other hand, may risk perverse effects by grossly restricting flexibility and maneuverability of one or more parties to the conflict. Thus, proactive preventive diplomacy must have impartiality as its middle name.

In the past few decades, the international community has developed a number of global, regional, bilateral, and even national mechanisms for conflict prevention and conflict resolution. In the area of direct prevention, the principal organs of the United Nations, notably the General Assembly, the Security Council, the Office of the Secretary-General, and the International Court of Justice, provide the major global mechanisms for conflict prevention.[73] The International Criminal Tribunals, established during the 1990s, as well as the International Criminal Court, can also play an important preventive role. They all operate on the principle of justice in the international community, a principle that in itself represents an important factor of prevention. However, because of the nature of its membership, the United Nations seems better equipped to deal with interstate rather than intrastate conflicts.

The second set of global preventive mechanisms derives from a host of international instruments, duly ratified by members of the United Nations. Such instruments provide for their mandatory implementation and include monitoring clauses or special organs to consider national reports; these instruments include the two International Covenants on Human Rights and a number of international conventions signed and brought into force under the aegis of the United Nations. Regrettably, effective global governance in keeping with these instruments' important provisions has not yet become fully consolidated.

The third set of such mechanisms stemming from the United Nations includes the recommendations and follow-up decisions of global conferences of the 1990s in particular: the World Conference on Human Rights, the World Summit for Social Development, the Rio Conference on Environment and Development, the Cairo Conference on Population and Development, and the Beijing Conference on Women. All of these summit recommendations, if consistently followed and implemented, may have a major preventive impact upon a gradual elimination of the root causes of conflict.

One focus of preventive action whose role has been growing steadily lies in the Office of the Secretary-General. For more than four decades following the Second World War, successive incumbents labored in the shadow of superpower rivalries, and the secretary-general's role under Article 99 of the Charter suffered drastically under the realities of those times. The activist trend initiated by the 1998 Declaration on the United Nation's Peace and Security Role has continued, especially in the past few years.[74] One demonstration of this trend came in Kofi Annan's swift and successful February 1998 visit to Baghdad and, consequently, Iraq's commitment to abide by United Nations resolutions calling for international inspectors' full access to Iraqi military sites. Annan's visit almost certainly averted new air strikes against Iraq.[75] Although the circumstances have drastically changed since then, that particular diplomatic act revealed at least the possibility of non-coercive measures to bring Iraq into compliance with relevant Security Council resolutions. Finally, there are several less formal, yet effective, examples of global preventive mechanisms, such as the Group of Eight; the Balkan Contact Group; and the "Friends of the Secretary-General," along with his special envoys, special representatives, or high commissioners of regional organizations.[76]

The end of the Cold War has also spurred active thinking and several ventures in early prevention by regional organizations, including the Organization for Security and Cooperation in Europe (OSCE), the Organization of African Unity (now the African Union), and the Organization of American States—often working in conjunction with UN operations. Similarly, the North Atlantic Treaty Organization (NATO), the European Union[77] and the Council of Europe, as well as the Organization for Economic Cooperation and Development, have substantially contributed to successful preventive efforts. It should be remembered that in fact all members of the aforementioned regional organizations, bodies, and groups are at the same time members of the United Nations and participate in its comprehensive conflict prevention programs.

REQUISITES, IMPEDIMENTS, AND INCENTIVES TO TIMELY CONFLICT PREVENTION

Embarking upon a multilateral venture in early prevention requires the satisfaction of several conditions. In his study, Jentleson distinguishes four such prerequisites, including early warning, diplomatic strategies, support of major international actors, and credible preventive military force.[78] Many similar tenets have appeared in the successive reports from the secretaries-general who have taken as their paramount focus the question of consensus among the international community, notably in the Security Council, and the consent of the party or parties directly concerned. Although preconflict prevention may begin upon the request or consent of one party alone, it goes without saying that consensual environments will more likely lend themselves to timely and successful preventive action. The issues that underlie the new perception of timely prevention also include a clear identification of the root causes and more immediate sources of a potential conflict; initiating intervention early enough to retain its preventive nature; ensuring respect for the sovereignty and independence of the country or countries subject to a preventive operation; maintaining constant awareness of a worst-case scenario; securing competent staff; and ensuring resources, often the most difficult to obtain.

The fact, though, is that regardless of how many analyses that elaborate on the conditions for and various components of preventive diplomacy, the incidence of armed conflicts has increased considerably. Most of these conflicts occur internally rather than externally, frequently with ethnic underpinnings. Consequently, along with terrorism, civil and internal conflicts continue to represent major problems in international security. These crises' multidimensional nature calls for multidimensional implements of action: when poverty or ethnopolitical rivalries underlie a conflict, traditional diplomacy and troop deployments alone may no longer suffice. Similarly, preventive deployment without accompanying political action will most likely not prove to be a fully effective instrument of prevention.

Notwithstanding the obvious merits of preventive action (its considerable cost-effectiveness included), many governments resist calls to intervene unless and until a discernable crisis has escalated into a full-fledged conflict. Policymakers still assign too low a priority to prevention and the resources for it. Governments often take the initiative to finance the reconstruction of war-torn countries, when a significantly smaller sum could have been devoted to early-prevention measures before those states' devastation. Then again, a fragile government of a failing state—or even parties in an intrastate dispute—may tend to view involvement by the international community as interference in their domestic affairs. Upon his departure from the region in early March 1996, the UN secretary-general's special envoy for the former Yugoslavia, Kofi Annan, noted his concern that, by its very nature, it was difficult to determine precisely when a preventive mission should be deployed, and it was equally difficult to set objective criteria for its termination with the risk that such a mission would be a never-ending story. Last but not least, there is the fact that an effective structure of preventive mechanisms for deployment at short notice still remains underdeveloped.

Domestic political concerns also account for global and regional inaction on preventive strategies. Decision makers fear that international preventive action will lack public support and that international operations will cost too much. Politicians are wary of the political costs of casualties incurred during peace operations and cite the difficulty of making open-ended commitments in far-off lands. The harm that mission failure will do to their public image is also a significant domestic political concern.[79]

In the gradation among types of preventive action, including preconflict prevention, there may occur a phase of transition from "soft" to "hard" measures of action—from pure diplomacy to stronger forms of enforcement. The selective use of incentives and disincentives, often described as "carrot-and-stick strategies," figure prominently among the latter, more robust tools of prevention. If used skillfully, without undue publicity—which could potentially embarrass one or more parties to a dispute—such strategies can form part of genuine early preventive action. In more extreme cases, intervening parties may employ incentive approaches more vigorously. While this intensified policy may enforce the international community's will on a particular party, such techniques also possess a high likelihood of public disclosure. Paradoxically, then, employing these firmer policies may have a reduced probability of success in the short run, given their apparent coerciveness. Such methods include restriction or denial of development aid; conditional recognition of statehood or delaying a party's acceptance into some regional and international organizations; and a temporary restriction of some forms of bilateral relations.[80]

Lund explains these sorts of actions as political conditionality, in which a donor makes aid or trade contingent upon a recipient's record with respect to human rights, democratization, or objectives of "good governance."[81] The Norwegian Institute of International Affairs offers an even stronger view on the subject. It points out that because development aid cannot be apolitical, the question is how aid flows can be used to provide extra political value to the prevention of armed conflicts.[82]

Partnerships

As part of the United Nations' primary task of preventing violent conflicts, the world organization has consistently sought the active cooperation of regional and subregional actors in this effort, pursuant to Chapter VIII of the Charter. For years, such cooperation had proceeded rather modestly and sporadically, mainly because of both shifting political exigencies and long-standing Cold War prejudices. Numerous statements and resolutions adopted by the Security Council in the past decade have underlined the increasingly important role of regional organizations and arrangements in the peace and security field.[83] Close to twenty regional, subregional, and interregional organizations or arrangements cooperate with the United Nations in peacekeeping and peace-related activities.[84] These collective efforts have become indispensable to any successful timely conflict prevention because the United Nations may lack the capacity, resources, or expertise to address the problems that may arise in particular conflict environments across the globe. In some cases, parties to a conflict may seek UN involvement, while others would prefer that of a regional organization. Regional actors may have more intimate knowledge than the United Nations about the root causes of a dispute or conflict in their part of the world, including the circumstances that led up to it. The United Nations Mission in Kosovo (UNMIK), for example, has been responsible for public security and civil administration, OSCE handles institution building, and the EU has been vested with reconstruction tasks.

For the past several years, the UN secretary-general has been convening High-Level Meetings on Cooperation between the United Nations and Regional Organizations. The fourth such meeting convened on February 6–7, 2001 in New York and addressed mainly the topic of improving cooperation between the United Nations and regional organizations in peacebuilding, again highlighting the importance of peacebuilding as an inseparable part of conflict prevention and identifying a number of basic principles that should guide the peacebuilding dimension of prevention.[85] The secretary-general also pointed out a fundamental paradox inherent in peacebuilding: one the one hand, effective peacebuilding requires the long-term engagement of the international community. On the other hand, there is always the danger of making the society permanently dependent on development assistance. "That is why," Kofi Annan summarized, "so many of us stressed that peacebuilding needs to be a homegrown process, supported by the international community, but aimed ultimately at promoting national self-reliance."[86]

Although the main responsibility for preventive action rests with states and governments, as well as with their regional and international organizations, other actors also devote themselves to averting crises and resolving conflicts. To date, the international community has underestimated the potential contributions of transnational corporations and businesspeople, particularly in early-stage conflict prevention. International businesses often suffer from political and social upheavals in various parts of the world; hence, they realize the tremendous benefits of risk analysis and conflict prevention efforts in countries encompassing their foreign operations. The larger of these international firms can afford the financial resources necessary to fund conflict-prevention projects, and they exercise discrete leverage on political leaders in host countries that appear to be descending into some type of civil or interstate war.[87] Indeed, structural efforts at early conflict preventive action would seem to serve the best interests of the private sector. An important example of involvement in structural prevention is Cable News Network founder Ted Turner, who in 1997 announced his donation of $1 billion to benefit UN agencies for special programs under their auspices. One year later, the establishment of the United Nations Fund for International Partnerships confirmed the importance of such UN–private sector collaboration.[88]

Finally, early prevention calls for the participation of different elements of civil society, notably nongovernmental organizations (NGOs), often the most genuine and committed allies in eliminating the harmful root causes of conflicts. Lately, a renaissance has occurred among NGOs actively involved in many aspects of conflict prevention, and the international community's confidence in NGOs, both national and international, has become greatly enhanced. More than one thousand NGOs have become affiliated with the Economic and Social Council of the United Nations or the Department of Public Information of the Organization's Secretariat.[89] With new strides in the construction of civil societies, the role of citizens' groups will only continue to grow.

THE SHIFT TO HUMAN SECURITY
THROUGH SOCIAL PEACE

As part of the search for the best means of attaining durable peace, the international community's focus has broadened significantly in the past few decades to include the level of individuals as the most salient stratum of international action, and this evolution has spanned a considerable breadth—from the concept of basic *needs,* through *equitable and sustainable human development,* to the most recent ideas of *human security* and *the responsibility to protect.* While the nomenclature has obviously undergone successive phases of refinement, none of these elements has lost any of its present-day validity—quite the contrary: modern wars tend to take more civilian lives than those of belligerents, thus the paradigm of security has seemingly shifted from a focus on territory to a focus on the protection of the person.[90]

Human security represents a new focus on the human costs of conflict, on human needs, and on human rights. An ever-wider recognition has emerged throughout the world that preventing violent conflict constitutes a *sine qua non* for the effective promotion and achievement of the goal of human security. As such, human security implies active, if not deliberate, avoidance of conflict. George MacLean has proposed nine major issues embodied in the human security concept: personal security of the individual from violence or harm; access to the basic essentials of life; protection of the individual from crime and terrorism, pandemic diseases, political corruption, and mass migration; provision of human rights; freedom from personal violation based on gender; rights of political and cultural communities; political, economic, and democratic development; preventing the misuse and overuse of natural resources; and environmental sustainability and efforts to curtail pollution.[91] Indeed, the foregoing components lie at the heart of most conflicts; successful efforts at eliminating these problems are tantamount to pure early preventive action, in the meaning of both pre- and postconflict prevention.

How can we improve the existing system of preventive action, particularly in its phase of timely preconflict prevention? Naturally, enhanced political will and better administration of existing mechanisms can help a lot, but it will not suffice. A fresh impetus to start with the root causes must occur, which obviously will require a special long-term effort at all levels of international relations. Particularly effective prophylaxis can

follow from a coordinated team effort of the United Nations, its specialized agencies, regional governmental and nongovernmental entities, individual states, and the business community.

Because poor governance and despotic rule often prove to be the prime
causes of tension, stimulating good governance and strengthening democratic transformations can supply one of the most effective means of mini-
mizing outbreaks of conflicts. Quite frequently, people will tolerate some
social stresses and strains as long as political institutions appear legitimate
and evenhanded; democracies do better than autocracies in containing conflicts. Above all, to achieve its full potential, preventive action has to become
an institutionalized instrument of human relations. In short, the world
should move "from a culture of reaction to a culture of prevention,"[92]
though the slogan is admittedly utopian in its appeal; as a pragmatic first
step, such outlooks should find their way into school curricula on a permanent basis. Education for prevention must become interchangeable with
education for peace.[93] Naturally, any supportive preventive practices must be
tailored to particular sociopolitical contexts, demonstrating sensitivity to the
requirements of specific policies and conditions. In some cases, these kinds
of practices may not be possible at all. As Allan James has noted, "prevention
is indeed better than cure. But where the political auguries for it are poor, it
might be prudent for the activity not to be attempted."[94]

THE FIRST AND ONLY

Paradoxically as it may sound in light of the extensive United Nations
record on behalf of preventive diplomacy and preconflict prevention, it is
only with the publication of *An Agenda for Peace* that the term "preventive
deployment" gained new currency. Soon after, the concept of early prevention would undergo its practical test, leading to the establishment of
the first—and thus far the only—United Nations operation in preventive
troop deployment and preventive diplomacy, at the request of a party
directly concerned. In November 1992, responding to a plea by President
Kiro Gligorov and the government of the Republic of Macedonia,
Secretary-General Boutros-Ghali informed the Security Council that he
would "envisage such a deployment, undertaken at the request of the competent authorities of Macedonia, as being a preventive deployment of the
kind discussed in paragraphs 28 to 32 of *An Agenda for Peace*."[95] At the

heart of his plan was paragraph 28, which outlined the concept of pre-ventive deployment as a new tool of conflict prevention, unanimously approved by the Security Council.[96]

A few weeks later, Macedonia became the testing ground of a new international experience in search of peace.

2

THE
BALKAN
RECTANGLE

G. W. F. HEGEL USED TO REPROACH his contemporaries and ancestors that "peoples and governments never have learned from history or acted on principles deduced from it." Nations' histories
may have many cunning passages, yet the history of the Balkans seems to
exemplify best the great philosopher's concerns. The collective "Balkan character" or "Balkan mind" has long preoccupied both historians and political
scientists. Toward the end of the twentieth century, it also had to become the
concern of politicians and practitioners in peacemaking and peacekeeping.
History, not surprisingly, obsesses the Balkans. People tend to think more of
the past than of the future, but the Balkan peoples' enchantment with the
past has developed and consolidated over centuries. Comprehensive evidence of this enchantment extends long into the past, particularly to an
unusual document of more than eighty-five years ago, the first *Carnegie
Report to Inquire into the Causes and Conduct of the Balkan Wars,* which gives
an account of the developments and resolution of the two regional conflicts
of 1912–1913.[1]

Generalizations often mislead, but one cannot escape the impression
that centuries-long occupations and persecutions in the Balkans have

engendered a sense of constant assault among its peoples. While the exceptional circumstances there must not justify the crimes committed in the recent wars in the former Yugoslavia, they nevertheless add considerably to a proper understanding of the background of those crimes. Outside observers in the Balkans have consistently highlighted its peoples' exceptional sense of pride, stubbornness, craving for freedom, mistrust of outsiders, strong sense of nationalism, and quick resort to arms. The cruelest Balkan conflicts have had a profound psychological impact on different social groups, especially those who felt discriminated against, victimized, or traumatized.[2] In many cases, these experiences of adversity have served to cement a collective identity among societies in the region. Indeed, nationalism in the Balkans

> is seen as an activist ideological movement which aims to unite all members of a given people on the basis of a putative shared culture. As such, it claims to represent the whole collective, however defined, and is antagonistic to competing cultural claims on the totality or parts of this collective, which is deemed by the adherents to constitute an actual or potential nation.[3]

Other authors offer similar reflections. George F. Kennan has characterized the expression of collective identity even more starkly, observing that "aggressive nationalism" was a much stronger motivating factor than religion in the Balkan wars. He derives the bellicose traits of character from a distant tribal past, which explained deep distrust of outsiders and the perception of adversaries as sworn enemies. Recalling how the Carnegie Project's three principal investigators encountered the region decades ago, Kennan recounts that in fulfilling their mission, the commissioners were struck by the amount of distorted information they would receive from their local interlocutors. One of the investigators, Baron d'Estournelles de Constant, wrote in his report that it was "impossible to avoid the reproach of a party, if one does not take sides with it against the others, and conversely."[4]

Other traits have struck more recent negotiators in the Balkans, including Richard Holbrooke: many Western interlocutors with Balkan leaders have learned that "reneging on earlier offers was a basic style."[5] Once enraged, leaders from the region "needed outside supervision to stop themselves from self-destruction."[6] Some of those regional elites believe—and not without reason—that they have fallen victim to history. They would less readily admit that they, too, have victimized others.

Political sarcasm marks one of the principal features of the Balkan character, charged as it is with emotional language. It spares nobody and, on occasion, reveals the speakers' feelings of utter helplessness. In early 1999, for instance, President Vaclav Havel of the Czech Republic had publicly supported NATO air strikes against Yugoslavia because of the Milosevic regime's crimes against the Kosovo Albanians. Reacting to this statement, a prominent Serbian writer attacked the president (and acclaimed playwright) for his alleged impertinence and ingratitude, asserting that in the past, Yugoslav theatres staged Havel's plays regardless, as he put it, of their poor quality.

These observations encapsulate the political and social environment of the Balkans over the centuries, during which the Macedonians had been exposed to a long and checkered regional history. At one time or another, most other peoples on the peninsula had had their own well-established states, but the Macedonians had to wait until the end of the Second World War to receive their autonomy and until the end of the Cold War to become a fully independent state. Life under different occupiers could not but affect their mentality and national conscience, regardless of their ethnic origin. The family of a prominent medical doctor in the town of Kumanovo, in northern Macedonia, felt little surprise to find upon the doctor's death that throughout his professional life, he had to use three different name plaques on the door of his office: *Dr. Dusko S. Aleksov,* during the Bulgarian rule of Macedonia; *Dr. Dusan S. Aleksic,* during the Serbian rule over his country; and *Dr. Dusko S. Aleksjevski,* as a full-fledged Macedonian in his own republic. As exemplified in this story, the Macedonian saga has been long and arduous.

In the introduction to the Carnegie Commission's 1914 report, Baron d'Estournelles reached the farsighted conclusion that "violence carries its own punishment with it and something very different from armed force will be needed to establish order and peace in the Balkans."[7] This judgment has not lost an iota of its validity today.

IN THE JAWS OF HISTORY

Writing on Balkan history, even for historians, has proven a herculean task. Misha Glenny believes that "it is impossible to engage in serious discussion about Macedonia without upsetting some or, more likely, all of the interested peoples or states in the southern Balkans."[8] Hugh Poulton, author of the excellent *Who Are the Macedonians?*, begins his second edition gingerly, noting that he was fully aware that the first edition of his book (1995) had upset a number of people, both inside and outside Macedonia. He admits that "history and questions of identity in the Balkans are literally explosive topics."[9] Nonetheless, no writer on what has become today an independent and sovereign Republic of Macedonia can escape from restating some basic facts of the past.

Historically, the geographic space assigned to Macedonia exceeded the territory of the present republic. Located in the very heart of the Balkans, the historic "Macedonia" covered some sixty-seven thousand square kilometers. The 1913 Treaty of Bucharest, following the Second Balkan War, provided for the region's partition among Greece ("Aegean" Macedonia—34,603 square kilometers), Yugoslavia ("Vardar" Macedonia—25,714 square kilometers), and Bulgaria ("Pirin" Macedonia—6,789 square kilometers). The former Yugoslav part constitutes the present-day Republic of Macedonia.

The modern Macedonians trace back their history to ancient, if not mythical, times. They consider Greeks and Romans to be brothers and the Macedonians of Philip's and Alexander the Great's eras as their cousins. Many historians agree that the first well-known rulers of Macedonia came from the Argead Dynasty, founded by King Perdiccas I in the seventh century B.C. Three centuries later, King Philip II had further strengthened Macedonia's role in the region and eventually controlled Greece. Following Philip's assassination in 336 B.C., his son, Alexander the Great, conquered new lands, including the Persian Empire, stretching his realm all the way to India. After Alexander's death, internal struggles for power led to the collapse of the Macedonian Empire, but Alexander's heirs still retained control over Macedonia and Greece. In the second century B.C. Macedonia fought wars with Rome, ultimately suffering a defeat in 168 B.C. In the following centuries, it became part of the Roman Empire and subsequently was incorporated into Byzantium. However, it must also be noted that Macedonian historical records underlying this narrative have met a firm challenge from Greek historiography.

Macedonians point out proudly that their ancestors had special qualities of dynamism, industriousness, and thirst for life. They were good dancers, they knew how to enjoy themselves, and they liked to indulge in alcohol. At the same time, they were humble and gentle, devoted to their families.[10]

In the sixth and seventh centuries A.D., the region was invaded and conquered by Slavs. These new neighbors brought with them their own political form, headed by Slavic tribal princes, and over a long period of time settled permanently in the area. They also impressed their own indelible mark upon prevailing Macedonian society. The process of their Christianization proved rather slow and complex. It also coincided with the activities of two brothers from Thessaloniki, Cyril and Methodius, who created the Cyrillic alphabet, translated Greek religious texts, and laid the foundations of Slavonic literature. To do so, the missionaries must have known the language spoken by the new Macedonian Slavs who had populated Thessaloniki and the areas around it. Clement and Naum of Ohrid, the founders of the Ohrid literary school (considered to be the first Slavic university), successfully continued the work of Cyril and Methodius. This part of history, in turn, generated a consistent objection from the Bulgarians, who consider the four scholars as their own and the Macedonian language as a dialect of Bulgarian.

In 864 A.D. Bulgaria invaded Macedonia. The Ottoman Empire officially recognized Macedonia as a Bulgarian province in 927. Several decades later, King Samuil repulsed the Bulgarians, establishing an independent Macedonian state with Ohrid as its capital. His empire extended from the Adriatic to Constantinople. Samuil also played an instrumental role in founding an independent Macedonian archbishopric in Ohrid. At the beginning of the eleventh century, Macedonia again came under the rule of the Byzantine Empire. In 1282, the Serbian King Milutin incorporated Macedonia into the Serbian Empire. Subsequently, as with most of the Balkans, Macedonia came under Turkish rule, remaining part of the Ottoman Empire for more than five hundred years (1392–1912). Several rebellions undertaken by the Macedonians against the Turks during this period did not succeed.

With the approaching disintegration of the Ottoman Empire, especially following Turkey's defeat in its war with Russia (1877–1878), the "Macedonian Question" frequently reappeared on the agendas of major European powers. By terms of the 1878 Treaty of San Stefano and with Russia's strong support, all of Macedonia was included in the newly established Bulgarian state. Three months later, at the Berlin Congress, in order to weaken Russia's main ally in the Balkans, the other great powers decided to return Macedonia to Turkey. Although never implemented with regard to Macedonia, the Treaty of Berlin did contain provisions offering Macedonia international recognition under an autonomous legal status, based on the Organic Law of 1868 for the Island of Crete.[11]

On October 23, 1893, a group of Macedonians in Thessaloniki founded the Internal Macedonian Revolutionary Organization (VMRO), led by Goce Delcev, Dame Gruev, Jane Sandanski, and Gjorce Petrov. Their main objective was a struggle for an independent Macedonia and its full territorial integrity. Some VMRO leaders, though, were more inclined to accept Macedonia's annexation by Bulgaria. Ten years later, when the organization started its intensive guerilla campaign and was close to launching a national uprising against the Turks, Goce Delcev—a national hero and mastermind of the insurgency—was shot dead. Still, the uprising broke out on St. Elijah's Day (August 2, 1903) and has been known as the Ilinden Uprising, cherished as one of the country's holiest national days. Contemporary Macedonians recite from memory the famous maxim of Goce Delcev: "I understand the world only as a field of cultural competition among nations."

Having liberated the town of Krushevo on August 3, 1903, the insurgents assembled some sixty representatives of all nationalities living there and formed a six-member government, consisting of representatives of the three most numerous nationalities in town. In the historic Manifesto of Krushevo, a proclamation to the Turkish people living in the Krushevo revolutionary region, the insurgents pledged: "We have not risen up to convert you to Christianity or to dishonour your mothers, sisters, wives, and daughters. You should know that your property, your lives, your religion, and your honour are as dear to us as our own."

The Ilinden Uprising and the consequent establishment of the short-lived Krushevo Republic, which the Turks cruelly suppressed after only ten days, symbolize the Macedonians' centuries-long craving for freedom and national independence. In many respects, both the struggle and this brief sovereignty mark a surge in Macedonian idealism. Many of its insurgents realized the long odds against them, yet they managed to transform their disadvantage into a symbol of a victory to come.[12] President Boris Trajkovski of Macedonia believes that "the Ilinden and the Krushevo Republic symbolize Macedonian people's eternal fight for freedom and independence. Macedonia's destiny would have been different without Ilinden."[13]

As a reaction to Ottoman repression and to serve their own national interests, Russian Tsar Nicholas II and Austrio-Hungarian Emperor Franz Joseph devised a 1903 program whereby Russian and Austrian civil agents would "assist" the Turkish governor of Macedonia. Responsibility for peacekeeping was apportioned among Austria, France, Italy, Russia, and the United Kingdom, which provided officers to command local gendarmes. The Young Turks, including many Macedonians, opposed the foreign officers. In 1906, they moved their headquarters to Thessaloniki and, two years later, seized southern Macedonia. They demanded restoration of the Ottoman Constitution of 1876, which diminished the sultan's autocratic powers and established the principle of democratic equality for all its subjects. As a result, the international commission was dissolved and the civil agents withdrew. A counterrevolution succeeded briefly in 1909, but the Ottoman Empire continued to disintegrate and anarchy reigned in Macedonia.[14]

The Balkan Wars of 1912–1913 represented the next phase of the struggle among Macedonia's neighbors for control over its territory. Shortly after Bulgaria, Greece, and Serbia had seized Macedonia from the Ottoman Empire in 1912, the Second Balkan War broke out, instigated but lost by Bulgaria, concerning the division of the spoils from the First Balkan War. Accordingly, the 1913 Treaty of Bucharest provided for yet another partition of Macedonia among Serbia, Greece, and Bulgaria. Six years later, the Treaty of Versailles sanctioned the partition, confirming that the Serbian portion of Macedonia would be transferred to the newly established Kingdom of the Serbs, Croats, and Slovenes. During the period between the two World Wars, all three of Macedonia's occupying powers forced Macedonians to assimilate into the occupiers' cultures. For instance, the Greek government's Decree No. 332 of November 1926 ordered that Greek names replace all Slavonic names of Macedonia's towns, villages, rivers, and mountains.[15] Similar practices followed, particularly with respect to the Macedonian language and culture, in the parts of Macedonia administered by Serbia and Bulgaria. The interwar period also saw intensified action on the part of VMRO, which actively promoted Macedonia's nationalist aspirations and tried to rally Macedonians in the three occupying powers under national liberation objectives.

During the Second World War, Bulgaria again occupied a considerable chunk of Macedonia. Having lost holdings in Macedonia after the two Balkan Wars and World War I, Bulgarian troops newly allied with the Axis Powers readily joined their Italian counterparts to occupy the Vardar region of Macedonia, called "South Serbia" by the Yugoslavs. Historical inevitability, however, had begun moving strongly in Macedonia by the early 1940s. Macedonian aspirations toward self-determination and independence coincided with some elements of the vision of postwar Yugoslavia drawn up by Josip Broz Tito, leader of that country's communist party and its future president. Assisted by the Yugoslavs and in the hope of advancing their national cause, the Macedonians started an active resistance movement against their occupiers. In 1944, the movement consisted of as many as sixty-six thousand partisans. Simultaneously, some five hundred national liberation regional councils throughout the occupied territory were established in preparation for what the Macedonians consider the second most important event in their modern history—the first session of the Anti-Fascist Assembly of the National Liberation of Macedonia (ASNOM). The assembly met at the Monastery of St. Prohor Pchinski on August 2, 1944 and decided to establish a Macedonian state, which would become part of the new federal Yugoslavia. Situated on the Serbian side of the border, the monastery is often referred to as "the Holy Shrine of the Macedonian state."

Ideological considerations aside, and notwithstanding some opinions to the contrary, an alliance with new political forces in Yugoslavia opened up the next historical chapter in the struggle for a free and sovereign Macedonia. After centuries of partition, violence, and repression, the postwar period witnessed the rebirth of a nation. The Republic of Macedonia received autonomous status of a constituent nation among the six confederated republics of Yugoslavia, with its own constitution that granted full recognition to Macedonia's distinct character and culture. The Macedonian language figured among the three official languages of Yugoslavia. Thus, today's pro-Western Macedonian leaders insist that "Macedonia and the Macedonian nation are not the creation of the Comintern, Stalin, and Tito, but a result of the long and hard struggle of Macedonian people for liberation."[16]

While social development gradually advanced in the Socialist Republic of Macedonia during Tito's rule, it generally had the poorest standard of living in postwar Socialist Federal Republic of Yugoslavia. Also, for all of Yugoslavia's openness to active relations with other countries, its domestic politics followed a rather hard ideological line and a one-party system, which did not spare the mentality of its diversified populations, including the Macedonians. Consequently, in the last decade of the twentieth century, societies in transition states such as Poland, Hungary, or the Czech Republic have had fewer problems adjusting to new sociopolitical circumstances than, for instance, Macedonians have had.

RELIGION AND POLITICS

Macedonia's nationhood has long been closely linked with its Orthodox Church, and the latter's patriotic aspirations have never been questioned. The church has been a repository of the national tradition and rich cultural record. Historically, it has shaped national consciousness and relations with both Macedonia's neighbors and its occupiers. Since the Balkan Wars, it functioned within the Serbian Orthodox Church. As of 1944, following Macedonia's proclamation as an autonomous republic within the Yugoslav federation, relations between the two churches have been less than cordial. In the mid-1950s, the Macedonian Orthodox Church took up efforts toward its full independence. The Serbs objected vehemently, fearing that an autocephalous status of their Macedonian counterpart might be the first step toward the republic's territorial secession. Ultimately, in 1967, the Macedonian Church declared its autocephaly, which has never been officially accepted by other Orthodox churches. The Greek Church, in particular, strongly objected to the self-styled status of Macedonian clergy because of the geopolitical implications of the adjective "Macedonian." As we shall see later in this chapter, Greece believes that it has exclusive rights over the name "Macedonia," which, it argues, can be used only for its province of the same name.

As of late, the Serbian Orthodox Church proposed that the Macedonian Church give up its autocephalous status and accept autonomy within the Serbian Church. The proposal divided Macedonian bishops and caused a public row. On May 17, 2002, in the Serb city of Nis, representatives of the two churches signed an agreement abolishing the Macedonian Church's autocephalous status and granting it autonomy within the Serbian Orthodox Church. Under public pressure, the three bishops who had negotiated the new formula were ultimately outvoted by Macedonia's Holy Synod—the agreement was rejected and the split continues. One of the three, Bishop Jovan, who had not agreed to disavow the Nis Agreement, was stripped of his clerical functions by the Holy Synod and ordered to withdraw to a monastery; he was subsequently expelled from the Macedonian Orthodox Church.

To Macedonians, the matter seems to be of utmost importance. Although there is formal separation between state and church affairs in Macedonia, its current president (and a Protestant), Boris Trajkovski, underscored in an interview for the June 7, 2002 edition of the weekly *Start* that the Nis Agreement was damaging to the state.

THE GIFT OF INDEPENDENCE

Secession by small and poor entities from larger and richer countries tends not to occur smoothly. When the richer republics of Slovenia and Croatia decided to secede from the Yugoslav federation, Macedonia's political leaders initially were not sure whether the country should follow suit. Similar apprehensions faced President Alija Izetbegovic with regard to the future of Bosnia and Herzegovina. In 1991, he and Macedonia's president Kiro Gligorov, elected earlier by parliament, tried to mediate between the Yugoslav collective presidency of the time and the two republics in the north. The Macedonians feared that insisting on secession might trigger action by thirty-six thousand well-armed Yugoslav National Army troops stationed in the republic, or further alienate the Serbian minority of forty-five thousand Macedonian citizens. They were extremely careful not to be even one step ahead of the other republics. The federation's final disintegration followed at least a half-dozen meetings of all six republics' presidents. The pressure of developments, however, left little time to lose. On September 8, 1991, the government put a cautiously worded question to a national referendum: *Do you agree to a sovereign or an independent State of Macedonia, with the right to join a future union of sovereign states of Yugoslavia?*

The popular response to the question was an overwhelming "Yes": an astounding 96 percent of those voting supported the idea of immediate independence. In its September 17, 1991 Declaration of Sovereignty, the National Assembly of Macedonia—elected in the first multiparty elections a year before—solemnly declared that

The Republic of Macedonia, as a sovereign and independent state, shall strive for persistent respect of the generally adopted principles of international relations, contained in the documents of the United Nations, the Final Document of CSCE from Helsinki, and the Paris Charter. The Republic of Macedonia shall base its international-legal subjectivity on respect of the international standards in relations among states and on full respect of the principles of territorial integrity and sovereignty, noninterference in the internal affairs [of states], strengthening of mutual respect and confidence, and development of overall cooperation with all countries and peoples of mutual interest.[17]

Yet at the same time, the 1991 referendum revealed the existence of basic problems on the part of some ethnic communities in Macedonia. Both ethnic Albanians and ethnic Serbs boycotted the vote; the former were dissatisfied with their status in the new republic, and the Macedonian Serbs preferred to live in a jurisdiction closely tied to their land of origin. According to Macedonia's 1994 census, the country's population comprised 66.5 percent ethnic Macedonians, 22.9 percent ethnic Albanians, and the remaining 10.6 percent Turks, Romas, Serbs, Vlachs, and others. When the Macedonian parliament approved the new constitution on November 17, 1991, ethnic Albanian MPs (members of parliament) abstained from the vote, charging that the new basic law relegated them to a status of an ethnic minority rather than grant their community a status equal to that of the ethnic Macedonians. On January 11, 1992, the two major ethnic Albanian parties of the time—the Party for Democratic Prosperity (PDP) and the People's Democratic Party (NDP)—organized their own referendum among ethnic Albanians regarding political and territorial autonomy. Reportedly, 99 percent voted for autonomy (the so-called Ilirida[18]). The Albanians presented the results of the referendum, though unrecognized by the authorities, to the International Conference on the Former Yugoslavia (ICFY) and the London Peace Conference. Since that time, ethnic Albanian grievances have profoundly shaped domestic politics in Macedonia.

For a variety of reasons, Macedonia's transition to independence has attracted close international scrutiny from the outset. First, independence came rather suddenly and proceeded under uniquely, if tenuously, peaceful circumstances. Given its particular provenance, Macedonian independence has aroused a great deal of skepticism among the new state's neighbors regarding the sustainability of the transition—indeed, could the shock of this snap independence smoothly accommodate the new exigencies of market economy, political pluralism, and freedom of speech? In addition, Macedonia has proven exceptional because of its formal request to deploy UN troops along its borders. Last but not least, because of Macedonia's stormy historical past as "an apple of discord" in the Balkans, regional observers feared a spillover of fighting from other regions of the former Yugoslavia which could turn into a larger Balkan war. To be sure, the new road for the young republic would prove to be a rough and uncharted trail. A peaceful separation from Yugoslavia counted as one of the poor, fledgling state's only assets. Otherwise, both externally and internally, the Macedonians faced grave concerns among some of their neighbors over the possible impact of fighting elsewhere in the former Yugoslavia and suspicions about their intentions regarding such conflict if it somehow spilled over into Macedonia itself. Such warfare was ripe for manipulation by various politicians, given the new sate's contentious and variegated ethnohistorical composition. Indeed, all four states neighboring Macedonia had long harbored their own grudges against it:

> Greece claims that there is no Macedonian majority in "The Republic of Skopje," so there can be no Macedonian minority in Greece. Bulgaria claims that there are no Macedonians in Macedonia since they are only Western Bulgarians, so there can be no Macedonian minority in Bulgaria. Albanian President Sali Berisha is not always sure what the ethnic identity of the minority living in Mala Prespa regions—Macedonians or Bulgarians—so sometimes he seems to think that Western Macedonia is really Eastern Albania. For the leaders of Serbian nationalism, Macedonia is only Old Serbia or Southern Serbia.[19]

The electoral landscape in the nascent Macedonian state provided no definitive clues as to the new government's policy direction, given the volatile nature of party politics soon after independence. The general elections in late 1990 gave 37 parliamentary seats to the newly established nationalist Internal Macedonian Revolutionary Organization–Democratic Party for Macedonian National Unity (VMRO-DPMNE). Because no party commanded the majority required to form a government, a "cabinet of experts" was formed in March 1991 under the premiership of Nikola Kljusev. Soon after, a coalition government followed, consisting of the Social Democratic Alliance of Macedonia (SDSM), the Liberal Party (LP), the Socialist Party (SP), and the main ethnic Albanian party, the PDP. The country's second parliamentary elections and the first election of a president by popular vote took place in October 1994. Notwithstanding the general opinion of international observers that the elections had, in principle, proceeded in a fair and orderly manner, the two main opposition parties, VMRO-DPMNE and the Democratic Party (DP), charged the authorities with fraud in the first round of elections and, therefore, decided to boycott the decisive second round. Thus the two parties excluded themselves from parliamentary representation for four years, while the ruling Alliance for Macedonia (SDSM, LP, and SP) secured 95 out of 120 seats in the unicameral National Assembly. The ethnic Albanian parties won a total of 19 seats. President Gligorov won re-election, defeating his opponent from VMRO-DPMNE, a well-known theatre producer, Ljubisha Georgievski.

After the elections, the two opposition parties chose not to recognize the new National Assembly or the new government under Prime Minister Branko Crvenkovski, repeating a common Balkan theme. In mid-1996, acting under the relevant provisions in the constitution, the two parties launched a nationwide campaign to collect one hundred and fifty thousand signatures in support of a referendum on early elections, securing two hundred thousand signatures in the end. However, the government and the courts failed to recognize the legitimacy of the initiative. A few months earlier, the Liberal Party left the ruling coalition and became the principal opposition force in the National Assembly. That same year saw an important manifestation of grassroots democracy through successful elections to local offices. All political forces in the country, including nonparliamentary opposition parties, participated in the elections, which international observers assessed as free and fair. In April 1997, the LP and DP merged to become the Liberal-Democratic Party (LDP).

In November 1998, Macedonia's third general elections concluded successfully in accordance with the new laws framed by authorities in consultation with all major political parties and experts from the United Nations, the Council of Europe, and international NGOs. The ruling coalition of Social Democrats suffered defeat in favor of a coalition of VMRO-DPMNE and a newly established party, the Democratic Alternative (DA), headed by Vasil Tupurkovski. In order not to divide the ethnic Albanian vote, the two major ethnic Albanian parties agreed to run a joint list of candidates in the majoritarian part of the elections. As a result, the two parties secured twenty-five seats in the new parliament. Ultimately, the new government of Ljubcio Georgievski included VMRO-DPMNE, DA, and the Democratic Party of Albanians (DPA), headed by Arben Xhaferi.[20] Since then, the DA has left the government and joined the parliamentary opposition. Also, a few MPs of VMRO-DPMNE and DA changed their party affiliations. In the fall of 1999, the citizens of Macedonia elected their new president, a young and dynamic politician from VMRO-DPMNE, Boris Trajkovski. Some 180,000 ethnic Albanians voted for an ethnic Macedonian candidate—a development of unique significance. Regrettably, in areas where ethnic Albanians held a majority, some irregularities and shootings took place, mainly to weaken the position of the rival ethnic Albanian PDP. International monitors took due note of those irregularities.

A TOWERING FIGURE

No discussion of the first years of Macedonia's independence can omit the name of President Kiro Gligorov, who has authored or creatively witnessed all of Macedonia's major transformations in this period. He proclaimed his country's independence following the 1991 referendum and contributed an outstanding share to the drafting of the republic's constitution. With the talent of a modern-day Pied Piper, he managed to lead the Yugoslav army out of Macedonia in the spring of 1992 and avoid seemingly inevitable bloodshed. In the most complex period of his country's history, Gligorov represented Macedonia abroad with dignity and perseverance, and his sterling efforts regarding Macedonia's international recognition have provided an example of leadership that future leaders should try to emulate.

Kiro Gligorov was born on May 3, 1917 in the city of Stip in Vardar Macedonia. In the nineteenth and early twentieth centuries, his family had actively participated in the national liberation movement. In 1938, he graduated from the law faculty at Belgrade University and returned to Skopje to practice law at a private bank. With the outbreak of the Second World War, he joined the resistance movement and soon became a member of ASNOM; in 1944–45, he took charge of ASNOM's finances.

After the war, Gligorov assumed increasing responsibility in Belgrade's network of federal institutions: between 1945 and 1960, he occupied the posts of assistant secretary-general of the federal government, assistant minister of finance, deputy director of the Federal Institute for Economic Planning, secretary of the Federal Executive Council for Economic Issues, federal secretary of finance, and vice president of the Federal Executive Council. A strong advocate of open economies, Gligorov held a number of positions on federal councils in charge of implementing market reforms in Yugoslavia. In the 1970s, he held a seat in the presidency of the Yugoslav federation and subsequently served as speaker of the federation's parliament. Soon after, he was sidelined from political life and spent more than a decade pursuing theoretical and applied research in economics and finance. In the late 1980s, Prime Minister Ante Markovic recruited Gligorov to his economic reform team. However, Gligorov rushed back to his native land when the call came to serve and make history. A few years later, he received a nomination for the 1996 Nobel Peace Prize.

Keith Brown, a scholar of Macedonian culture and society, has pertinently and accurately described the former chief executive: "Gligorov's documented willingness to play the role of mediator as president, insisting on the need to maintain coalitions across cleavages, rather than promote cleavages and then profit from them, marks a notable contrast with some of his peers."[21]

THE UPHILL STRUGGLE FOR RECOGNITION

Ironic as it may sound, few in the international community viewed Macedonia's peaceful transition to independence as sufficient reason to grant the new state prompt official recognition. On August 23, 1991, before the declaration of independence, Macedonia's Ministry of Foreign Relations published a paper entitled "The International Position of the Republic of Macedonia and Its Status in the Yugoslav Community." The paper stressed that Macedonia was preparing itself for full independence and, in pursuing this objective, it was ready to demonstrate its democratic orientation at home and constructive cooperation internationally as part of the European integration process.[22] The document was followed by a number of declarations by the government and National Assembly, asserting Macedonia's right to become a sovereign state.[23] In the meantime, Greece expressed serious reservations about Macedonia's recognition, effectively blocking that process in the entire European Community (EC, which became the European Union, or EU, in November 1993).

In response to the dissolution of the Socialist Federal Republic of Yugoslavia (SFRY), the EC convened the International Conference on the Former Yugoslavia, one of whose responsibilities involved assisting in the resolution of the seceding republics' political status. To advance this work, the conference created a commission to evaluate applications for international recognition, chaired by Robert Badinter, an eminent legal scholar from France. In January 1992, the Badinter Arbitration Commission concluded that Macedonia satisfied all of the EC's conditions:[24] constitutional changes making clear that the new state had no territorial claims beyond its existing borders; no use of hostile propaganda against its neighbours; and a pledge to fully respect the United Nations Charter, the Helsinki Final Act, and the Conference on Security and Cooperation in Europe's (CSCE) Paris Charter. The EU also conditioned recognition on Macedonia's guaranteeing the rights of ethnic minorities, respecting existing borders, adhering to all relevant commitments on disarmament, and supporting negotiated settlement of political disputes of state succession.

Upon the completion of the report, Greece claimed that the Badinter Commission had disregarded its concerns. One of the Greek government's most important objections to Macedonia's recognition stemmed from the belief that the very term "Macedonia" implied territorial claims, notwithstanding the commission's explicit statement in its opinion that "the use of the name Macedonia does not contain any territorial aspirations against any other state." Following the publication of the report, the European Community recognized Croatia and Slovenia in January 1992, and Bosnia-Herzegovina three months later. Croatia's recognition occurred despite the Badinter Commission's recommendations to the contrary. Undeservedly and unjustifiably, Macedonia remained ostracized.[25] Despite the EC's hesitations, Bulgaria, Croatia, Russia, Slovenia, and Turkey granted diplomatic recognition to the Republic of Macedonia without much delay. Some others, including China, followed suit.

Additional hurdles lay ahead in Macedonia's journey to full recognition. During an informal meeting at Guimaraes on May 1–2, 1992, EC foreign ministers declared that they were willing to recognize Macedonia "as a sovereign and independent state, within its existing borders, and under a name that can be accepted by all the parties concerned."[26] The EC's Lisbon Summit on June 27, 1992 marked yet another step backward. The conference's statement with respect to Macedonia made it clear that the

EC would recognize the country only under a name not including the term "Macedonia," a position reconfirmed by the European Council.[27] The council expressed its readiness to "recognize that republic within the existing borders according to their Declaration of 16 December 1991 under a name which does not include the term Macedonia."[28] On July 3, 1992, Macedonia's National Assembly, taking issue with the EC's approach, responded with its own declaration, rejecting as unacceptable any reference to the newly independent republic "under a name which does not include the term Macedonia."[29]

The participants at the December 1992 EC summit stated that the community "reexamined its policy on recognition of Macedonia in the context of the Lisbon decision."[30] In this way, EC governments that would have liked to finally resolve "the Macedonian Question" actually perpetuated it. In an unprecedented deadlock, a large and peaceful-minded international body had kept a small and weak country at bay for the sake of a cause that few could really understand. An inconsistent approach like this certainly did not serve the causes of peace and stability in southeastern Europe.[31] Consequently, at a very sensitive time in the region, the EC had created false impressions about Macedonia's uncertain future and unnecessarily preoccupied Macedonia's leaders, who instead could have used their energies to pursue many other pressing objectives of Macedonia's entry into the family of independent nations. It sounded hardly conceivable that EC diplomacy, known for its masterful handling of so many issues before and after the Macedonian case, could not have found a satisfactory way to facilitate Macedonia's early recognition. The EC's initial position also delayed action by the United States and by relevant international organizations. In 1993, members of the U.S. Congress were informed that Greece considered Macedonia's existence as a state as part of the legacy of Tito, who wanted the republic to be a hegemonic nucleus of a larger entity. Greece was dissatisfied with Macedonia's constitution and its alleged "expansionist" philosophy. It also questioned Macedonian maps as well, as the star marking the tomb of King Philip in the Greek town of Vergina was the emblem on the new country's national flag.[32]

Continuing Macedonia's diplomatic offensive, President Gligorov addressed a letter to the UN secretary-general on July 30, 1992, requesting Macedonia's admission to the membership of the world body. Along with the letter, Gligorov sent a declaration pledging that "the Republic of

Macedonia accepts the obligations contained in the Charter of the United Nations and solemnly undertakes to fulfill them."[33] Macedonia's president had already met Boutros-Ghali on February 3, 1992 in New York, during which he informed the secretary-general of Macedonia's struggle for recognition. Gligorov recalled that his country had adopted a constitution upholding all European standards of conduct and that the Badinter Commission had recommended Macedonia's international recognition, yet nothing had happened. Macedonia had fulfilled all the conditions for recognition, and did so in a peaceful manner; it had refused to participate in the war or to contribute either recruits or funds to the war effort. Macedonia's record not only upheld peace but also demonstrated the possibility of addressing ethnic tensions in a positive manner. Gligorov stressed that the only remaining objection to official recognition lay in the name "Macedonia." "[T]his was the name for centuries," Gligorov implored. "[I]t distinguishes us from other Slav nations"; the name of the country could in no way affect the interests of Greece. Moreover, from Gligorov's perspective, Macedonia had no intention of questioning the cultural heritage of Alexander the Great, or of pretending to belong to a civilization "to which we do not belong."[34]

What's in a name?

It took the United Nations more than eight months to consider the application and practically force Macedonia to accept a solution whereby the new member state would be "provisionally referred to for all purposes within the United Nations as 'the former Yugoslav Republic of Macedonia' pending settlement of the difference that has arisen over the name of the State."[35] Hugh Poulton notes that on the night of the admission, public reaction in Skopje was a mixture of satisfaction and anger. In parliament, only thirty MPs voted to accept the temporary name, while twenty-eight were against, with thirteen abstentions.[36] Ultimately, an early membership in the United Nations, even under a temporary compromise, proved to be a better solution than waiting for the final settlement of the name issue. Some authors believe—and rightly so—that, with admission to the United Nations, Macedonia was no longer a "limbo zone" on a political vacuum.[37]

Macedonia's presence in the United Nations over the past decade has allowed its representatives to present their country as a peace-loving nation, developing active positions on numerous international issues, including efforts to be elected to one of the nonpermanent seats on the Security Council for a two-year term in 1998–99.[38] Since 1992, some one hundred states have extended recognition to Macedonia, including eighty under the constitutional name. As Greek-Macedonian negotiations to resolve the problem continue, the term "Macedonia" has become a universally accepted name.

Before the crisis in Slovenia in the early summer of 1991, the United States had avoided active involvement in the former Yugoslavia. In fact, the U.S. administration initially had been against recognition of the newly independent Yugoslav republics. In the spring of 1992, the United States and the European Commission decided to coordinate their positions, making the recognition of Macedonia and Bosnia-Herzegovina "contingent on the resolution of the remaining EC questions relating to those two republics." In April, the United States granted its recognition to Slovenia, Croatia, and Bosnia-Herzegovina and left Macedonia's request pending. Greece's concerns over Macedonia's name issue were quoted as the reason for the decision.[39]

The United States recognized Macedonia under the provisional name in early 1994; full diplomatic relations at the ambassadorial level followed in September 1995. Earlier, in April 1995, the United States became an active diplomatic player in Macedonia with the establishment of the U.S. Liaison Office in Skopje. The mission functioned like a full embassy, with its own chief of mission and the same intensity and importance as any of the other missions or embassies in that country. The exchange of ambassadors occurred after Greece and Macedonia had concluded an Interim Accord on their mutual relations, negotiated with an active involvement of former U.S. secretary of state Cyrus Vance—working as special envoy of the UN secretary-general—and Matthew Nimetz, special emissary of the president of the United States.

While negotiations on Macedonia's official name continued, the Interim Accord—a masterpiece in evading the names of the contracting parties—opened up new avenues for Macedonia's accession to the OSCE and collaboration with the European Union.[40] The new country was also making an impressive start at inserting itself into the transatlantic security architecture. In line with pursuing EU integration, Macedonia joined NATO's Partnership for Peace program (PfP) and has actively sought membership in the alliance. Macedonia has also engaged with a number of other European entities, including the Council of Europe—considered the gatekeeper for full European political and economic integration.[41] In early May 1998, the government concluded a cooperation agreement with the EU and, in April 2001, added an agreement on association and stabilization (the latter of which came long overdue, as Macedonia had actually become eligible a few years before, at least at the same time that Bulgaria and Romania received their association status). In late 1998, Macedonia, Albania, Bulgaria, Greece, Italy, Romania, and Turkey agreed to establish a Multilateral Peacekeeping Force for Southeastern Europe, which reached operational status in 1999. Indeed, reconciling the intricate concerns over Macedonia's name required a lot of diplomatic ingenuity, but—pending a final agreement with Greece—most states genuinely wanted to accommodate the justified aspirations of the young state without offending Macedonia's Greek neighbors.[42]

LOVE THY NEIGHBOR AS THYSELF

History has shaped Macedonia's relations with each of its four neighbors in different ways. Each state has had to contend with a legacy of oppression; historical antecedents, therefore, have weighed heavily upon these states' present-day relations. Nation-states emerging from Ottoman domination used to compete for territories, to which each had laid historical and religious claims as part of the nation-building process; Macedonia numbered among these lands.[43] The past decade has witnessed a major Macedonian effort to establish mutual cooperation with immediate neighbors. For a number of years, that effort followed President's Gligorov's principle of "equidistance": to develop good and friendly relations with all, so that no neighboring state will have a privileged position in Macedonia.[44] With all the international controversy swirling around Macedonia's independence, this policy has stood the test of time. However, the new government formed after the 1998 elections placed a somewhat different emphasis in its policy pronouncements, highlighting in relations with neighbors what policymakers described as the principle of "positive energy": a process of rapprochement based on openness, transparency, and a climate of mutual confidence.[45] On a wider foreign policy plane, the government has highlighted Macedonia's involvement in the implementation of the EU's Stability Pact for Southeastern Europe.[46] Given the country's political compass, foreign policy—regardless of its special emphasis and nuances—was obviously a precarious undertaking.

Serbia to the north

Macedonia's relations with its northern neighbour have been the most ambivalent. Many ethnic Macedonians find it hard to conceal their sympathies for the Serbs, yet they remain highly distrustful of them. Despite their dramatic history, strong links have long existed between the two nations. Much of Macedonia's intelligentsia graduated from leading Yugoslav universities. Their common Slavic background and religious tradition in the Orthodox Church, numerous intermarriages, and very close ties in all walks of life throughout the federation's existence have left a lasting imprint of their own. A prominent Macedonian politician once told me that "the feelings of our shared life with the Serbs remain alive. Family links continue to be strong. The wars in the rest of Yugoslavia, especially the air strikes of 1999, were followed with great emotions. The bombings divided the public opinion in Macedonia."[47]

In reflecting on Macedonian-Serbian relations, one may distinguish four phases: up to 1944, the most traumatic period of history; the Tito era; the post-Tito years, particularly including Milosevic's rule; and the post-Milosevic's period. Despite its obvious limitations, we might consider the second phase as the most politically beneficial for Macedonians: after centuries of foreign domination, they regained their statehood and national identity. To the present day, the memory of Tito remains considerably widespread and revered among Macedonians; his portraits appear at various public venues, as well as in private homes.

Since gaining their independence, Macedonians have tried to retain a fair amount of loyalty to the Serbs, yet independent statehood and loyalty to the federation's primus inter pares have not always been compatible. They naturally disapproved of Belgrade's policies, and have always borne in mind the likelihood of unfriendly action originating there. Nevertheless, Macedonians have generally engaged in only subdued public criticism of the Belgrade regime. On several occasions, the country's leaders reiterated that Macedonian territory may not be used for military operations against a neighboring country, meaning Serbia first and foremost. At the same time, a country like Macedonia—strongly aspiring toward NATO membership

—could hardly afford denying freedom of operation and air space to an alliance with which the Macedonian government has consistently sought close ties. Foreign Minister Handziski once had to assure his nation that the military exercise taking place in Macedonia's air space was within the legal terms of the country's NATO/PfP membership and the Status of Forces Agreement with the United States. The president and cabinet (still led by the SDSM) had found themselves in a dilemma between NATO aspirations and PfP obligations, on the one hand, and the sentiments of many Macedonians, on the other. In both the 1998 and 1999 polls, large numbers of Macedonians viewed NATO flights over and presence in Macedonia as inimical to the existence of the Federal Republic of Yugoslavia.[48]

Reactions of major political parties to the air exercise also revealed the deep ethnic chasm within the country. In general, while the two ethnic Albanian parties, DPA and PDP, wholeheartedly supported the air maneuvers, the ethnic Macedonian parties were more circumspect in their support because of their old loyalties, similar ethnic and religious affinities and the reality of geopolitical considerations with the Federal Republic of Yugoslavia (FRY). According to the then opposition party, VMRO-DPMNE, by permitting the use of Macedonia's airspace, the government had taken sides in the Kosovo conflict. The LDP had called for an urgent parliamentary session to discuss a draft resolution prohibiting the use of Macedonia's territory for military action against any neighboring states. The government was caught between its conflicting desires of being a step closer in its integration with NATO through full cooperation with the Alliance and its intention to maintain good-neighborly relations with the FRY. Needless to say, Serbia's leaders must have viewed Macedonia's opening its air space to NATO and the decision to authorize the deployment of NATO's Kosovo Extraction Force on its territory as unfriendly acts and further straining relations between Skopje and Belgrade.

Between the proclamation of Macedonia's independence and the end of the decade, President Gligorov met Slobodan Milosevic on several occasions. Initially, their discussions concentrated on the withdrawal of the Yugoslav army from Macedonia, which happily surprised many observers. The success of negotiations on the subject stemmed from several additional factors.

First, the FRY government had hoped that, sooner or later, Macedonia would rejoin the federation or whatever remained of it. After all, the question in the national referendum on independence had clearly envisioned such a possibility. The FRY's hopes for reintegration of Macedonia also stemmed from a belief that Macedonians could not sustain themselves economically. Such hopes revived with the imposition of the Greek embargo against Macedonia in February 1994. Belgrade, too, expected Macedonia's destabilization as a result of its interethnic problems. Reportedly, during one of President Gligorov's meetings with Milosevic, the Serbian leader offered the FRY's "fraternal assistance" in case of uncontrolled unrest among the ethnic Albanians in Macedonia.

Second, developments in other parts of the federation, notably in the Krajina and Croatia, had kept Serbia occupied, as had mounting problems in Bosnia and Herzegovina, requiring deployment of troops on those other fronts. Third, the Macedonians had offered the Yugoslav army ample lead time to withdraw from their territory. Finally, Macedonia had no history of major ethnic clashes.

Macedonia's relations with Serbia during the Milosevic regime's ostracism illustrate some of the subtleties of the ties between the two states. While Macedonians had suffered greatly from mandatory sanctions against the former Yugoslavia, they had at the same time tacitly tolerated supply channels to Serbia. Following the European Union's suspension of sanctions against the FRY in December 1995, trade exchanges and commercial traffic between the two countries increased considerably. Between 1995 and 1999, the total volume of goods exchanged between Macedonia and the FRY had grown almost fourfold—from $150 million to $550 million—then dropped sharply with the onset of NATO air strikes in March 1999. New prospects for cooperation had emerged with the signing of an Agreement on the Regulation of Relations and Promotion of Cooperation between the Republic of Macedonia and the Federal Republic of Yugoslavia on April 8, 1996.[49] The date also marked the establishment of full diplomatic relations between the two countries.

Despite Macedonia's respect for the "tradition of shared life" with the Serbs, the fact remained that Milosevic and members of his regime did not deal honestly in their relations with their neighbor to the south. First and foremost, the threat of FRY aggression loomed constantly over Macedonia throughout the 1990s. Occasionally, reliable sources would confirm that Belgrade had plans for an invasion of the new republic, and one never knew whether or when the Damoclean sword might drop. Several immediate bones of contention lent credence to such a threat, including the final border demarcation between the two countries and the FRY's claim of succession to all the rights of the former Yugoslavia. Access to the Monastery of St. Prohor Pchinski had also become controversial, irking many politicians and war veterans on both sides.

The case of border demarcation poses a useful example of the FRY's tactics of evasiveness and delay in relations with Macedonia. While Macedonian authorities had official Yugoslav maps of a regular state border, the authorities in Belgrade treated the existing line as an administrative demarcation. In 1994, FRY officials directly or indirectly challenged the position of as much as half of the 240-kilometer border, from 100 meters to 3 kilometers deep into Macedonian territory. The signing of the April 1996 agreement also marked the establishment of a joint "diplomatic-expert commission that will prepare a draft international agreement with a textual description of the extension of the common state border."[50] The commission held many meetings, in both Belgrade and Skopje, but, except for enigmatic communiqués on its successive sessions, the results of its work proved rather disappointing. While FRY officials tried to minimize the differences, the two delegations stood poles apart. Not surprisingly, the international community treated the settlement of the border demarcation as a litmus test of the FRY's intentions toward Macedonia. As the FRY side claimed a number of strategically or economically important points on Macedonia's side, the process advanced very slowly. President Gligorov recalled:

> During my talk with Slobodan Milosevic on Crete, we discussed the issue. I presented my view that the border was a reality which had existed for fifty years, a reality which could not be reversed. Accordingly, I believe that the border should be demarcated only technically, which is the only possible solution. . . . We agreed that the border should be demarcated as it was, and each party committed itself to instruct its part on the joint border commission accordingly. However, although we had so agreed, the FRY side of the commission never moved from its position.[51]

The unfounded nature of Belgrade's claims came to light in the fall of 2000, with the accession to power of Vojislav Kostunica and his team: A comprehensive and final agreement on border issues followed in just a few weeks. Both parties agreed to accept the existing border line as their permanent frontier. The Monastery of St. Prohor Pchinski now has the status as a Macedonian cultural monument on Yugoslav territory, with free access to interested Macedonians. Reciprocally, Serbian graveyards in Macedonia became cultural monuments on Macedonian soil but under Belgrade's jurisdiction. Presidents Trajkovski and Kostunica concluded the final agreement on border demarcation during the summit of participating and observer countries to the Southeast European Cooperation Process, held in Skopje on February 22–23, 2001. Macedonia's parliament ratified the agreement a few days later, on March 1. Regrettably, the country's major opposition ethnic Albanian party, the PDP, chose to abstain in the ratification vote.[52] Objections regarding the validity of the agreement also came from Kosovo, whose leaders believed that equity required Kosovo-Albanian participation in the determination of the Kosovo-Macedonia segment of the border; they claimed that the agreement deprived Kosovo of some 2,500 hectares of its territory.

Bulgaria to the east

Against the backdrop of a long and painful history, Bulgaria was the first (on January 15, 1992) to recognize the Republic of Macedonia under its constitutional name. Yet, paradoxically, the most articulate complaints and criticisms from Macedonia's neighbors have come from political and academic quarters in Bulgaria. Bulgaria may have recognized the state, but they find it difficult to confer similar official recognition to Macedonia's language, which they consider a dialect of Bulgarian. Beneath the official expressions, though, Bulgarians simply refuse to accept the existence of a Macedonian *nation,* asserting that Macedonians are in fact Bulgarians.[53]

Bulgaria's early recognition of Macedonia marked a moment of historical boldness in its relations with a neighboring state. The disclaimers attached to this gesture, however, have profoundly concerned the Macedonians: during his fall 1991 visit to Washington, Bulgarian president Zhelu Zhelev explained that his country had recognized the right of the South Slavic state's existence as an independent Macedonian *state,* but that he could not accept the existence of the Macedonian nation, as Bulgaria always had "historical reasons" to disagree with claims regarding the existence of such a nation.[54]

The tension between Bulgaria's political recognition and cultural denial of Macedonia reflected itself in a number of substantive issues between the two countries. Another long-standing irritant in Macedonian-Bulgarian relations concerns the rights of Bulgaria's Macedonian national minority, inhabiting the Pirin area in the western part of the country. According to the first census after the Second World War (December 1946), close to three hundred thousand citizens of Bulgaria declared themselves Macedonians. Soon after, Macedonian schools, bookstores, and a theatre opened in the Pirin region. The local newspaper printed one page in Macedonian. Ten years later, the government deleted the national category of Macedonian origin from census forms; the only rubric left was "nationality." Consequently, 187,789 persons declared themselves Macedonians, which represented some 63 percent of Pirin's population at the time. In the third census, conducted in 1965, Macedonians disappeared altogether from the country's demographic map, while in 1992 they could identify themselves only under the category of "others."[55] Throughout the 1990s, police forces in the Pirin region prevented Macedonians from paying homage to one of the heroes of the Ilinden Uprising, Jane Sandanski, at his gravesite at the Rozen Monastery on Mt. Pirin. Bulgarian authorities also restrained the Pirin region's ethnic Macedonian organizations. According to the 2001 Bulgarian census, only 5,071 persons declared themselves Macedonians.[56]

Some authors on Bulgarian-Macedonian relations recall a little-explained episode of history relating to the lot of 7,000 Macedonian Jews during the Second World War.[57] Hugh Poulton recalls that, as early as October 1940, Nazi Germany had pressured the Bulgarian government to impose legal restrictions upon its Jewish population. Following Bulgaria's alliance with Germany, more repressive regulations followed, including a requirement that Jews identify themselves by wearing the Star of David on their garments. In August 1942, a Commissariat for Jewish Affairs opened in Sofia, headed by Aleksandar Belev, which oversaw the transfer of Jews to Nazi death camps on Polish territory. Massive opposition from different Bulgarian quarters, including the Bulgarian king, delayed action considerably. Ultimately, such resistance saved the Bulgarian Jews from deportation, and led to their segregation into labor concentration camps in the countryside. Poulton continues:

> While this defense of the Jews by Bulgarian society in the face of Nazi pressure was admirable, the treatment of Jews in Macedonia in areas under Bulgarian control was less so. Here responsibility for their transfer to Nazi authority and inevitable mass murder rested with [the Commissariat for Jewish Affairs], and it appears that despite Bulgarian claims to the contrary,

or claims that these transfers were all the work of the Nazis and that the Bulgarian authorities had no hand in the matter, the Jews of Macedonia and Thrace were knowingly transferred to their deaths by the Bulgarians—possibly sacrificed for the sake of the Jews in Bulgaria proper. The investigator into Nazi crimes, Simon Wiesenthal, confirmed on Skopje television in February 1986 that Alaksandar Belev and Bulgarian ministers who signed documents on the liquidation of the Macedonian Jews in February and March 1943 were included in his list of war criminals.[58]

Until late 1998, relations between Bulgaria and Macedonia had been shaped by Bulgaria's "big brother" attitude, with both positive and negative ramifications. During the operation of sanctions against the former Yugoslavia and the Greek embargo against Macedonia, Bulgaria behaved quite helpfully and cooperatively. At the same time, highly provocative statements and publications in Sofia's media outlets cast Macedonia on the verge of "disappearance" because of the "unnatural border" between the two countries. In addition, the frequent rhetorical acrimony provoked by similar statements on the language dispute had delayed the signing of more than twenty bilateral agreements for more than three years.

Greece to the south

Few sovereign and unconquered nations in world history have had to change their constitutions for the sake of their neighbors. Yet Macedonia is included in this group for the sake of good-neighborly relations with Greece. The two states' shared histories had engendered much mutual distrust, if not prejudice. The very appearance of a new state, independent of Belgrade and situated between Greece and Yugoslavia, caused serious concern for the Greeks. That new state, with close ties to Turkey, seemed to separate Greece from its traditional partner, Serbia.[59] Greece's apprehension has both historical and more contemporary roots. Some misgivings resurfaced with Macedonia's request for official recognition by the European Community and the work of the Badinter Commission. Other concerns, such as the issue of Macedonia's name, remained pending after the signing of the Interim Accord in 1995.

The debate over Macedonia's official name hinges on a conflict over history. Prevailing Greek opinion holds that the people living in Macedonia during Philip's time had Greek cultural identity and spoke the Greek language. By extension, this view considers modern Macedonia, or any reference to it by name, as an exclusively Greek preserve. On the other hand, Macedonians perceive themselves as a separate ethnic group with a distinct 2,500-year history: the Macedonians of Philip's time, as well as the contemporaries of Aristotle (also considered a "Macedonian"), trace a direct line to today's inhabitants of the former Socialist Republic of Macedonia.[60] This explains why the question of post-Yugoslav Macedonia's first flag, featuring the ancient sixteen-ray sun of Vergina, had become such a hotly debated issue. (Macedonia changed its flag in late 1995.)

The major problem, however, does not stem from suspicion of Macedonia's attempts at cultural hegemony. More important, and closer to the present, Greek policymakers and citizens alike have feared the possibility of expansionist Macedonian designs on Greek territory, particularly with respect to the region known to the Greeks as the Aegean Macedonia. Through a policy of forced assimilation and population resettlement, this part of Greece has undergone a long and dramatic process to eliminate all traces of Macedonian language, culture, and tradition. During the Greek Civil War in the late 1940s, some eighty thousand people from Agean Macedonia—including twenty-eight thousand children—had to seek refuge outside the country. Some fifty thousand of them settled in what was Yugoslavia's Macedonian Republic. For a long time, Greek authorities had prevented these refugees from visiting their families or maintaining property left behind. Numerous official Greek statements used to reject the existence of a Macedonian minority in Greece. However, in the mid-1990s, a group of ethnic Macedonians in northern Greece decided to establish an association they called "The House of the Macedonian Civilization." Greek authorities refused to register the group, whose members then lodged a complaint against the Greek government in the European Court of Human Rights at Strasbourg. The Court upheld the rights of the association to have legal status and for members to conduct their activities. In 2002, the Greek authorities approved plans for the construction of a House of Macedonian Culture in the town of Lerin.

In order to meet Greek concerns, the Macedonians went out of their way to accommodate their neighbor on a number of issues. The country's legislature adopted important constitutional amendments as early as January 6, 1992, supplementing original legislation that otherwise met all of the EC's requirements for constitutional safeguards. The amendments read as follows:

- The Republic of Macedonia has no territorial claims against neighboring states.

- The borders of the Republic of Macedonia can be changed only in accordance with the constitution and based on the principle of voluntariness and generally accepted international norms.

- The Republic shall not interfere in the sovereign rights of other states and their internal affairs.[61]

Several important Macedonian concessions did not convince Greece that a small, unarmed, and peaceful country like Macedonia would not use its name to stake historical claims on either Greek territory or the country's cultural foundation. Under different governments, relations with Macedonia became hostage to the complexities of domestic politics in the Hellenic Republic. On February 16, 1994, Athens initiated a unilateral embargo against Macedonia, closing Greece's border, the consulate in Skopje, and Macedonian access to the port of Thessaloniki, to counter the "unyielding stance of Skopje." Unilateral embargoes seldom prove to have international legal justification; nevertheless, if Greece meant to penalize Macedonia and weaken its economy, the embargo certainly served its purpose, costing Macedonia at least U.S. $40 million a month. Greece was not without its voices of reason, however. In his comprehensive book on Greek-Macedonian relations, John Shea quotes an article from the July 29, 1994 edition of the Greek newspaper *To Vima,* listing a number of weighty points in support of a more flexible, pragmatic policy approach toward Macedonia.[62]

Prior to the embargo, and immediately following Macedonia's admission to the United Nations, Macedonian-Greek talks began, aiming to resolve conflicts about differences over Macedonia's name and its national flag. Cyrus Vance and Ambassador Herbert Okun shuttled between the two delegations on behalf of Secretary-General Boutros-Ghali, trying to iron out a mutually acceptable settlement. Subsequently, the talks recessed for Greece's October 1993 elections; the new government brought to power at the polls would not resume talks until November. However, when the United States recognized Macedonia under its provisional name in February 1994, Prime Minister Andreas Papandreou decided to stop the negotiations and acted promptly on the embargo. Appeals from the EU for Greece to lift the sanctions fell on deaf ears.

Albania to the west

The state of relations between Macedonia and Albania during the past decade has depended principally on Albania's domestic situation and the conditions facing the Albanian minority in Macedonia. Among ethnic groups in the Balkans, Albanians awakened last to their national consciousness. The first Albanian state in modern history emerged in 1912. Armed resistance by the Albanians against the Ottoman Empire had not begun until the end of the nineteenth century. Great-power machinations in the Balkans contributed significantly to the development of strong Albanian nationalism. As R. L. Wolff notes, because of an early alliance with Mussolini's Italy, "World War Two allowed for a short-lived formation of a Great Albania under Italian and Nazi tutelage which included Kosovo and parts of Macedonia, adding some 700,000 new citizens to Albania, at the expense of Yugoslavia."[63] While Macedonians and Albanians have to date fought no armed struggle against each other, the two states have suffered their share of political tensions. This situation has resulted mainly from Macedonia's interethnic relations, dominated by some 450,000 ethnic Albanians inhabiting a considerable portion of western Macedonia. In addition, a small Macedonian community lives in Albania proper.[64]

In the fall of 1998, the Albanian Academy of Sciences published a position paper titled *Platform for the Solution of the National Albanian Question,* which contained the following disquieting statement: "Every Albanian, whether on this or that side of the border, within or outside the ethnic lands, aspires to a quick unification of their lands into one unique Albanian state, as the Great Albanian Renaissance men of the last century put down in their programs."[65] This statement typifies the sources of Macedonians' concerns with their neighbors, and the trend is not new. However, in the light of history and the current storminess of developments in the region, such aspirations justifiably upset Macedonians. President Gligorov once remarked that "all our neighbors still live in their dreams of some 'greater states' to say the least. They all dream of their ideas of Greater Bulgaria, Greater Serbia, Greater Albania or Greater Croatia."[66] Despite occasional assurances to the contrary, Macedonians pay particular attention to such sentiments expressed by the cream of Albania's intelligentsia.

During Sali Berisha's term as president of Albania, the international community perceived him as builder of a democratic Albania. While the international community invested hope and resources in his potential role, relations between Macedonia and Albania proceeded rather haltingly, aggravated mostly by the tactics of the ethnic Albanian leaders in Macedonia at the time. In early 1997, political crisis followed the collapse of the pyramid savings scheme in Albania. The crisis generated much anxiety in Macedonia, because Albania's state structures had disintegrated and the country had no public security institutions to handle the rapidly deteriorating situation—armed gangs were looting military depots all across the country.

For several months, the Albanian side of the Macedonian-Albanian border remained unprotected, and the Macedonian army remained on a heightened state of alert. On March 13, following an incident between Macedonian border guards and several Albanian soldiers trying to cross over, the government closed all border crossings with Albania. In the meantime, gunfire pierced the border from the Albanian side, and the mountainous terrain along the 182-kilometer common frontier facilitated many illegal crossings. Although historical migration patterns indicated that most Albanians would prefer to go to the more prosperous Greece (which has had its own Albanian minority) or Italy, Macedonian authorities worried about an influx of refugees. Also, smugglers regularly flouted border controls, usually trading weapons, cigarettes, and narcotics.[67] In addition, the illicit border trade included several illegal channels in human trafficking. A few incidents resulted in armed skirmishes: between the outbreak of the crisis in Albania and the end of August 1997, 117 border incidents occurred, 65 involving the use of weapons.[68]

The Kosovo cauldron

In 1998, the tragedy of Kosovo unfolded during the hottest summer for decades in the Balkans. Before the world's eyes, Yugoslav authorities killed hundreds of innocent people, and more than 200,000 became homeless in the wake of a fierce scorched-earth policy, a new and cruel manifestation of ethnic cleansing. Indeed, the humanitarian tragedies of the past decade in different parts of the world have jaded the global community, rendering many apathetic in the face of actions fueled by hatred and intolerance. But as long as the riddle of Kosovo remains unsolved, the specter of instability will continue to haunt Macedonia. The natural geographic location of one and the same ethnic community in three neighboring countries offers irrepressible temptations for all kinds of extremism. Historically, "the ethnic Albanians in Macedonia and those in Kosovo have always been bonded in blood and politics. . . . During the war in Kosovo, ethnic Albanians from Macedonia . . . gave millions of dollars to the Kosovo Liberation Army."[69]

The crisis in Kosovo seriously affected the nature and pattern of Macedonia's political and ethnic mosaic; certainly, it alarmed Macedonia's establishment and raised fears of a wider regional conflict. In early February 1998, the long-standing conflict entered a new phase, aggravated by the Milosevic regime's continued intransigence on the one hand, and the further radicalization among local Albanian forces, on the other. But at that early stage, observers asked: Why should the imminent unrest occur at that very point in time? Did Albanian Kosovars have the organization and equipment to start a full-scale military confrontation? Could the Kosovo Liberation Army (KLA) make a real difference on the scene? What kind of forces had the FRY built up there? How might Belgrade react to a possible uprising?

Observers saw the situation as the sum total of several brewing problems, including the Kosovars' frustration with the international community's inaction to ease or eliminate Belgrade's repression; pressure on Milosevic prior to the Yugoslav "elections" announced for March 1998; a message of dissatisfaction from the international community to the Albanian government (which, compared to President Berisha's comments, had toned down its support for Kosovo); and an attempt by the Kosovo Albanians to establish a favorable negotiating position should talks on the province's political status ensue as a result of trying to quell a mass uprising. Later that spring, increasing numbers of young men began to arrive at the Skopje airport from the West on their way to Kosovo. These young Kosovars, carrying valid FRY passports, lived and worked in Western European countries but stood ready to join the ranks of the KLA.[70] One could also note growing civic mobilization among the Kosovo Albanians—both at home and abroad, notably in Western Europe, where fundraising among them had considerably intensified.

At that early stage, the KLA had remained something of an enigma. Many analysts doubted its existence; others believed in the existence of a detailed military plan by the Kosovo Albanians to start a guerrilla war, at least to provoke an "internationalization" of the conflict. Still others anticipated that the Kosovars would rather launch their own form of *intifada* than unleash a full-scale uprising so as not to provoke a Serbian blitzkrieg in response. Most observers agreed on the difficulty of estimating the Kosovars' strength. For decades, if not centuries, almost every Albanian household traditionally had a gun among its possessions.

Ethnic Macedonians from all walks of life engaged in anxious and ominous speculation about what might happen if Kosovo exploded. Many felt confused and viewed developments in light of the region's tragic history; in their mind, the prospect of an influx of several hundred thousand ethnic Albanian refugees would threaten the very existence of a Macedonian nation-state. Rightly or wrongly, many in Macedonia believed that such a massive wave of refugees could spark Macedonia's eventual disintegration. Some estimates put the number at 200,000 and 400,000 ethnic Albanians from Kosovo descending upon Macedonia. Few countries could sustainably absorb such a movement; without doubt, neither Albania nor Macedonia was among them. President Gligorov had developed the idea of a "corridor" through which prospective refugees could enter Macedonia from the north, at the Blato border crossing; they would continue past Skopje, through to Tetovo, Gostivar, and the Radika Valley, proceed to the border crossing at Debar, and ultimately conclude their journey at Peskopeia, Albania. The "corridor" idea did not prove very popular among international officials: it fulfilled neither international standards regarding refugees nor the obligations of a receiving state. Other forms of contingency planning proved equally insufficient. In classic fatalistic Balkan fashion, Macedonians eschewed early preparations for a flow of refugees, believing that action in the anticipation of such a negative event might ultimately make it happen.

The ax eventually fell hard, of course. During the Kosovo crisis in early 1999, not only did some 350,000 refugees pour into Macedonia over a few weeks, but also markets and transit routes to the north for Macedonian products became abruptly clogged. The magnitude of the problem seemed to take everyone by surprise. International assistance came slowly or not at all. Macedonia's deputy minister for foreign affairs—the future president, Boris Trajkovski—criticized the international community for "losing its sense of responsibility in dealing with the problem of Kosovo refugees."[71] Prime Minister Georgievski was even harsher in his assessment, describing Macedonia "as the only innocent victim in this war" and accusing the international community of "leaving us alone with the problem of the Kosovo refugees. . . . [T]he gentlemen from Brussels started the war and then left for Easter vacation."[72] That same day, Georgievski convened a meeting of donors and international organizations at which he vented his frustration and deep disappointment over the international community's failure to provide any financial assistance in the context of the refugee crisis. He pointed out that the government had earmarked resources that could take care of only 20,000 refugees. At the beginning of May, some 242,000 registered Kosovar refugees had arrived in Macedonia. The prime minister said that he had heard many promises but that, forty-five days into the crisis, his government directly or indirectly had supported the refugees unaided.

3

FROM AUTOCRACY TO DEMOCRACY

A S THE WAR RAGED in the former Yugoslavia, many observers had hoped that in the Europe of the 1990s, an independent Macedonia might provide the key to peace in the region. This fact alone determined the new country's importance, not to mention the growing interest of the international community in having a presence in Macedonia. While originally encouraging three priorities for Mace-—donia—peace, stability, and democracy—the international community appeared to put more emphasis on the first two. While Macedonia's international friends and partners literally interpreted the notion of peace and stability in a common house, conflicting political and ethnic factions within Macedonia read this formula mainly as a pretext for establishing an order in service to their agendas. Consequently, at the beginning of the young country's road to civil society, the overall scene appeared more a manifestation of dissension than democracy.

Popular and elite inhibitions that carried over from the previous system exerted an important psychological effect on developmental progress.

International actors seeking to assist Macedonians and others in the former Yugoslavia could not fully comprehend their local partners' apparently haughty reactions. In the eyes of international officials, political actors too often perceived criticism or small concessions as humiliating defeats. The Macedonia of the early 1990s faced five central problems in the long term, each requiring a good solution to ensure its future as a full-fledged member of the Euro-Atlantic community. The central problems were the need for a more united stand among Macedonia's political and intellectual elites, the tense state of interethnic relations, the slow pace of democratic transformations, the deteriorating socioeconomic situation, and—as already discussed in the preceding chapter—the not-so-cordial bilateral relations between Macedonia and neighboring states.

SHAPING UP THE NEW ESTABLISHMENT

From the very day of independence to the present, observers of Macedonia's political scene have consistently pointed out ethnic lines of division among the political parties; practically every ethnic group operates a corresponding political party. Few or no ethnic Albanians, Turks, Roma (Gypsies), or Serbs have joined ethnic Macedonian parties, and vice versa. In their efforts to gain public support, most Macedonian political parties have given priority to ethnic interests, contributing to the growing nationalism of all ethnic groups in the country.[1] As a result, during the great change of 1991, nationalist factors seemingly played a much larger role than any other.

Analysts admit that the changes in Macedonia's leadership had not been as sudden as they had in other postsocialist countries. Kiro Gligorov, former member of the State Presidency of Yugoslavia, was elected president of Macedonia; Stojan Andov, former deputy prime minister and Macedonia's member of the Yugoslav parliament, became speaker of the republic's parliament. The League of Macedonian Communists split into three political parties: the Social Democratic Union, the Liberal Party, and the Socialist Party; in Macedonia's 1994 elections, they formed a coalition—the Alliance for Macedonia—and won more than three-fourths of the seats in parliament.[2]

One political analyst recalls that after the SFRY's demise, three main political camps formed in Macedonia: the "postcommunists," ethnic Albanian nationalists, and ethnic Macedonian nationalists (VMRO-DPMNE); a pseudo-political line ran between "anti-" and "postcommunists." In short, a new political establishment was taking shape in the new country, and every step was being taken, particularly by President Gligorov, to keep escalating divisions under control. Initially, this supervision included the formation of a nonparty government, followed by a coalition cabinet of the three "post-communist" parties and one ethnic Albanian party. There were few purges in state administration.[3] At the same time, a new group of young administrators emerged from the ranks of the Social Democratic Union. Most of them, born in the 1940s or 1950s, were professors or lecturers at the Skopje University, selected mainly for merit and organizational skills. They included Branko Crvenkovski, the future prime minister; Ljubomir Frckovski, the would-be minister for foreign affairs and internal affairs; Jane Miliovski, minister of finance and deputy prime minister; Vlado Popovski, minister of defense and justice; and Blagoj Handziski, minister of defense and foreign affairs. Each of them contributed his or her own important share to running the affairs of the young republic.[4]

A school of hard knocks

For many young politicians, both immediately following independence and under the recent VMRO-DPMNE coalition (1998–2002), actual governing provided on-the-job training. A generation of younger policymakers have had successes as well as failures, both during Branko Crvenkovski's and Ljubcio Georgievski's premierships. With passing time, their degree of cooperation with two successive presidents—Kiro Gligorov and Boris Trajkovski—would leave much to be desired.[5] In addition, fragmenting political parties did not help to build a stable political landscape. In the initial phases of the United Nations operation in Macedonia, sixty-five different political parties registered and operated, but only twelve won seats in the parliament. In 1998, the corresponding number of registered political parties declined to thirty-eight. Constant rivalries have added to profound political polarization, most of all between ethnic Macedonian parties and the other ethnic groupings, notably those run by ethnic Albanians. An inexperienced electorate also complicated efforts toward democratic deliberation—in polls, the group of so-called do-not-know voters ranged between 40 and 50 percent of the electorate.

In these first years of independence, the complete absence of dialogue among the country's political forces concerned many observers; partisan wrangling dominated Macedonian politics. Political leaders and their parties failed to understand that a country in dire need of all-around progress and more foreign support could ill afford a political scene in which they took positions mainly for the sake of contradicting or embarrassing their opponents. This trend began to wane as the international presence in the country and its bilateral relations expanded, notably with member states of the European Union and NATO. However, partisan impasses have continued to recur.

In just a few years, Macedonia developed an unusually active foreign policy and a high volume of travel to and from Skopje, signifying a new opening in Macedonians' quest for peace and stability in the region. Hardly a day would go by without important foreign visitors arriving in Skopje. These visits have had a clear objective: paving Macedonia's way into Euro-Atlantic and European security and economic structures. Such efforts have proceeded in earnest, based on the conviction that because of Macedonia's unique circumstances and position in the heart of the Balkans, the international community owed a debt to and had a decided interest in the new country. Indeed, dialogue with leading European and U.S. politicians raised many expectations. However, in view of this process of intensive consultation, many of these exchanges' positive effects went unacknowledged on both sides of the table: most of the Macedonians' interlocutors had apparently promised more than they could actually deliver.[6] Also, because of Macedonia's strained interethnic relations, international visitors praised the government's accomplishments uncritically, even though observers knew that sooner or later—certainly before Macedonia entered the European Union—the country's officials would one day have to make definitive decisions on controversial issues.

Notwithstanding these difficulties, all coalition governments in Macedonia have made significant headway along the path of building a pluralist state based on democratic principles of civil society. Yet the pace of the transformation has been agonizingly slow—slower certainly than in similar changeovers in East-Central Europe. Macedonian authorities argue that shortcomings in their democratic transformation result from the complexities of shifting from a society shaped for decades by the concept of collective rights to a society that respects above all the rights of individuals. Officials insist, too, that Macedonia's collectivist legacy also inhibits individuals from opposing some actions by the state through courts or other agencies established for this purpose. As much as such arguments have meant, recovery should and could have occurred more quickly.

One of the principal obstacles to greater progress in building Macedonia's civil society lies in a discrepancy between the pace of national and international standard setting and the ability to implement such standards. Although the country can boast of a more representative mass media, in many respects, levels of public awareness and official experience—particularly among lower-level officials, members of the judiciary, and the police—did not keep pace with citizens' newly obtained rights and duties in a democratizing society. Improvements were also pending at the top level. Article 78 of the constitution, for instance, provided for the establishment of a Council for Interethnic Relations, consisting of the speaker of the National Assembly as its president "and two members each from the ranks of Macedonians, Albanians, Turks, Vlachs, and Romanies, as well as two members from the ranks of other nationalities in Macedonia." The mandate of the council was to consider issues of interethnic relations in the republic and make "appraisals and proposals for their solution." The National Assembly was "obliged to take into consideration the appraisals and proposals of the council and to make decisions regarding them." Regrettably, the results of the council's work in the first decade of independence have proved to be negligible or nonexistent.

Macedonia has acceded to all major international human rights instruments, including those of the United Nations, the OSCE, and the Council of Europe. Domestically, the National Assembly has built a comprehensive legislative network to comply with the provisions of the International Covenants on Human Rights and other binding international standards. By virtue of the constitution, international agreements duly ratified—including human rights instruments—have permanently become incorporated into the domestic legal order, immune from acts of the parliament. The parliamentary establishment of an ombudsman's office has marked an important step toward an effective system of institutional protection for individuals and their rights.

Macedonia's Law on the Election of Members of Parliament of May 19, 1998 offered an impressive example of positive action in this regard: legislators adopted the law with only one dissenting vote, and the impressive majority in favor of the bill resulted from the government's incorporating most of the opposition parties' key recommendations. Also, legislators drafted the bill in consultation with experts from the United Nations, the OSCE, the Council of Europe, and the Washington-based National Democratic Institute. All of the consultants agreed that the final draft met democratic criteria. Along similar lines, the parliament adopted a Law on Higher Education in mid-2000.

Intensifying exposure to the outside world and the presence in Skopje of a number of active international representatives encouraged Macedonia's top leadership to launch initiatives aimed at integrating the political scene somewhat. In mid-March 1997, Macedonia's National Assembly held a special session on the situation regarding protests by ethnic Macedonians against the adoption of the Law on Languages at the Pedagogical Faculty of Skopje University and on "ways and means for the advancement of interethnic relations within the framework of the Constitution of the Republic of Macedonia and the institutions of the system."[7] Subsequently, the National Assembly passed a "Declaration on the Advancement of Inter-ethnic Relations in the Spirit of Tolerance, Dialogue, Mutual Respect and Trust."[8] Stressing the advancement of ethnic relations and tolerance as one of the fundamental tenets of Macedonia's constitutional order, the declaration emphasized in particular the importance of academic institutions in investigating reasons for, and consequences of, intolerant practices and in promoting action to overcome them.

Perhaps most important that same year, President Gligorov invited leaders of the main political parties to begin a dialogue aimed at reaching consensus on issues of vital national interest. Three sessions under Gligorov's chairmanship took place in October 1997, February 1998, and early April 1998. Eleven political parties attended the first session. Discussions centered on developing Macedonia's relationship with NATO and the EU, as well as on relations with neighboring states.

Following the first meeting, parties to the talks issued a joint statement, describing an interparty consensus on the three issues under discussion. The second session yielded fewer results, because leaders of two major political parties—VMRO-DPMNE and LDP—refused to participate. The agenda included bilateral relations among regional states, developments in Kosovo, and the possibility of post-UNPREDEP preventive efforts. Nevertheless, a joint statement issued by the president and nine other participating parties reiterated that they should continue to seek greater regional consensus through a dialogue fully respecting Macedonian identity, sovereignty, constitutional order, and territorial integrity. Conferees appealed to both FRY authorities and Kosovo Albanians to resolve their problems peacefully through dialogue. Implicitly referring to the possibility of refugee flows from Kosovo, the statement acknowledged Macedonia's obligations under international law but, at the same time, stressed the need to "guarantee the security of its citizens as well as the territorial integrity of the country."[9]

The third political summit under the auspices of President Gligorov took place on April 2–3, 1998, focusing on interethnic relations. The session provided an open forum for all political parties to state their positions on this contentious but crucial issue. Differences of opinion prevented the third session from producing a joint declaration; however, a statement released by the presidential cabinet noted that those attending had highlighted the harmonization of interethnic relations as crucial for Macedonia's stability, democratic prospects, and prosperity. In his subsequent address on the state of the nation before the parliament, President Gligorov warned the country of the dangers of nationalism and conclude that his dialogue with political parties had not demonstrated the opportunity to reach a consensus on Macedonia's internal problems.

Ethnicity versus the nation-state

National minorities make up one-third of Macedonia's population.[10] Acording to the European Commission against Racism and Intolerance (ECRI), Macedonia

> [h]olds together a very delicate ethnic balance, made up of a majority of ethnic Macedonians, a large Albanian minority, and other minority groups including inter alia Turks, Roma, Serbs and Vlachs. Despite this diversity, each of the main ethnic communities tends to live in a relatively homogenous world of its own. Even where members of different ethnic groups live and even work alongside each other, they often have limited contact in daily life.[11]

Ethnic Albanians amount to at least 24 percent of Macedonia's inhabitants.[12] In ethnic Macedonians' view, ethnic Albanians' numbers, their sharply demarcated national identity, and their vociferous political aspirations considerably outweigh the scope of rights conventionally accorded to national minorities. Extremists on both sides have, in their own ways, worked actively to excite emotions that could turn intergroup struggles into a major political problem. Different segments of the international community assessed the explosiveness of Macedonia's interethnic relations in different ways: most observers believed that the political system had gradually addressed the complaints of the Albanian community, despite recurring rough patches along a turbulent road; on the surface, this reading seems accurate. The situation, however, involved much complex sensitivity, full of disquieting undercurrents and promising but unpredictable consequences. The ECRI report continues:

> At present, interethnic relations are tense, with each group harboring negative stereotypes and fears about the others. Relations between the two largest ethnic groups, Macedonians and Albanians, are often complex. These relations are intertwined within the regional context of the Balkans, reflecting not only the internal reality within the country, but also the events in neighboring countries. Thus the Kosovo crisis increased mistrust and reduced tolerance between groups, exacerbated in some cases by media reporting.[13]

To be sure, a deep psychological rift exists between ethnic Albanians and ethnic Macedonians.[14] Rightly or wrongly, ethnic Albanians simply do not feel comfortable in Macedonia; given their sense of exclusion, they believe that Macedonian society treats them like "second class citizens," and that the corrective to this type of discrimination lies in much greater autonomy. Radical ethnic Albanian leaders have actively preached elaborate formulas of multiethnic federation, which would accord to Albanians equal participation in decision making with the ethnic Macedonian majority and give rise to ethnic Albanians' claims to self-determination, thereby satisfying the international legal precondition of identifying a people capable of forming a state. Such schemes have evolved through different stages, including ideas for the country's "cantonization," federalization, confederation, autonomy for areas inhabited predominantly by ethnic Albanians, or the establishment of a parliament for all ethnic Albanians residing in Balkan states.[15]

Ethnic Macedonians, in turn, do not trust their Albanian compatriots. In the 1990s, they believed that satisfying even some Albanian claims would trigger a chain reaction of new demands, threatening the country's territorial integrity and demographic unity. They feared that the suggestion of so-called consensual democracy would practically give ethnic Albanians a right to veto most decisions on state affairs.[16] Ethnic Albanians' reactions persistently evoke a strong sense of fear of secession and territorial losses, which would jeopardize Macedonia's very existence as a state. Historical parallels only intensified such feelings. Government authorities and ethnic Macedonian parties have tried to deny or belittle the tensions. In their view, ethnic minorities in Macedonia enjoy a degree of rights exceeding the expectations set by relevant international standards. Macedonians lay blame with ethnic Albanian extremists, many of whom had come from or had their roots in Kosovo. Throughout the 1990s, many observers in Skopje believed a lack of real dialogue and a wait-and-see attitude only postponed solutions and, at the same time, steadily increased the price that would come due one day. Also, the other ethnic minorities believe that Albanians' ferociously ethnocentric demands overshadow their own.[17] As much as the situation of the other ethnic minorities calls for constant attention, political stability in Macedonia has become contingent upon the satisfaction of Albanian grievances. Against this general backdrop, observers have concluded that "the persisting underlying problem is that Macedonian public life and policy debate are too imbued with ethnicity."[18]

Both of the Macedonia's major ethnic groups appeared to be at an impasse as the new independent country embarked on the path of democracy, but the ethnic Macedonian forces, overwhelmingly constituting the government, seemed to have an advantage: after all, this was a country in transition and, as such, would have as much leeway as its new sovereign powers allowed to chart its own course with respect to its human and civil rights policies. Yet in no state do modern standards of ethnic and human rights operate in a vacuum. They derive from rich international experience that has for centuries enabled countries to reach a satisfactory level of their implementation and respect. Our instant task as the UN's preventive mission in a region that seemed quite distant from international human rights laws and norms was to help articulate these standards to all concerned in the host country.

INTERLINKAGES OF ETHNIC AND HUMAN RIGHTS

As the postwar international system has sought and defined standards for individual human dignity, an organic link has formed between understandings of ethnic and human rights. Some authors have traced the progressive evolution of the current concept of human rights from the protection of minorities, recalling that the earliest document ensuring certain rights to members of a religious minority group was the 1648 Treaty of Westphalia, which recognized the rights of German Protestants. Only the Congress of Vienna, the Treaty of Berlin (1878), and the International Convention on Constantinople (1887) saw further expansion of the protection of minorities beyond a purely religious arena.[19]

Ever since, much work followed with regard to international protection of minorities, notably by the UN's Commission on Human Rights, the Subcommission on Prevention of Discrimination and Protection of Minorities, and the Subcommission's Working Group on Minorities. These three bodies have benefited from the wisdom of a prominent Macedonian diplomat and human rights expert, Ambassador Ivan Toshevski. His eminent colleague on the subcommission, Asbjorn Eide of Norway—director of the Norwegian Institute of Human Rights—has distinguished four categories of claims under the rubric of minority rights, including equality or nondiscriminatory treatment; conditions required to preserve minorities' identity, such as language, religion, and culture; autonomy or local self-government; and right to secede and have statehood.[20] Clearly, each of these claims could provoke plenty of controversy and, in irreconcilable cases, engender civil wars in states characterized by ethnic tensions.

A missing definition

Although scholars and policymakers have made many attempts to define and codify the definition of "minority," the international community has not yet developed a widely accepted formula. Even the drafters of the United Nations Declaration on the Rights of Persons Belonging to National or Ethnic, Religious, or Linguistic Minorities have not reached a consensus on such a definition.[21] In two instances, however, the drafters have come close to agreeing on interesting texts. A study prepared by Francesco Capotorti—rapporteur of the Subcommission on Prevention of Discrimination and Protection of Minorities—proceeds from Article 27 of the International Covenant on Civil and Political Rights and consultation with states, to offer the following provisional definition of a minority group:

> A group numerically inferior to the rest of the population of a state, in a nondominant position, whose members—being nationals of the state—possess ethnic, religious, or linguistic characteristics differing from those of the rest of

the population and [who] show, if only implicitly, a sense of solidarity, directing toward preserving their culture, traditions, religion, or language.[22]

Another example of a viable draft definition of minorities has emerged from the preparatory work for the European Convention for the Protection of Minorities.[23] Recognizing the political sensitivity of any proposed definitions and seeking to avoid any restrictive interpretations, none of the standard-setting bodies involved decided to retain these proposals in the instruments they finally adopted.

The principle of protecting minority rights has become a basic norm of international jurisprudence.[24] Further expansion of such protection followed from the general comments of the UN's Human Rights Committee, established by terms of the relevant provisions of the International Covenant on Civil and Political Rights.[25] The rich corpus of other standards on the subject applies equally to all members of the international community, particularly to multiethnic states such as those in the Balkans, including Macedonia.[26]

In the summer of 1998, the Human Rights Committee considered the initial report of the Macedonian government on the implementation of the international covenant.[27] The committee took note of the Macedonian delegation's statement that the principal difficulty in ensuring effective implementation of the covenant lies in the complex and difficult process of making the transition in political systems—specifically, from one that embraced collective centralism to one that attempted to promote individualist pluralism. While recounting relevant positive achievements in Macedonia, the committee addressed some troubling aspects of the country's interethnic relations.[28]

In fact, the Human Rights Committee expressed serious concern over ethnic clashes involving the police in Gostivar on July 7, 1997, in which three people were killed and hundreds more injured. The committee also noted that trials of local officials, in connection with the July 1997 events, failed to enforce fair trial guarantees under Macedonian law. The committee recommended a thorough independent investigation of these events, that those found responsible receive appropriate disciplinary sanctions, and that the government adopt all necessary measures to prevent recurrence of these violations anywhere. Committee members also voiced concern over the continued practice of forcing citizens to attend "informative talks" at police stations, in spite of a Constitutional Court decision and the enactment of the new Law on Criminal Procedures, both of which provide that police may not compel such attendance without a court order. Moreover, such "talks" violated Article 9 of the international covenant.

Finally, while noting an increase from 1990 in minority participation in political, administrative, cultural, and other institutions, the committee's report also recalled that the degree of minority integration still fell short of levels proportional to these groups' share of the population. The committee encouraged Macedonia's government to strengthen programs aimed at increasing the representation of the ethnic Albanian and other minorities in the country's public institutions, including the civil service, the army, and the police. Also, the UN committee called attention to the Roma population's situation. The committee's reply to the government report recommended that Macedonia continue to encourage minority participation in the design, organization, and operation of the educational system—particularly at the secondary and higher education levels—as well as to provide for the training of teachers of minority languages in public institutions.

The major interethnic front

One of the most characteristic features of Macedonia's interethnic scene stems from the ethnic Albanians' long-standing belief that they do not constitute a minority and that because of their numbers, they merit treatment as a community equal to their Macedonian counterparts. To a large extent, the problem originated with the 1991 referendum on independence and the adoption of the constitution by the Macedonian parliament. The nascent country's ethnic Albanians did not participate in the referendum, arguing that the question allowed for the unacceptable possibility that Macedonia might eventually become part of a reconstituted Yugoslav federation. Ethnic Albanian MPs did not vote for the new constitution primarily because of its preamble, which, among other things, stressed "the historical fact that Macedonia is established as a national state of the Macedonian people, in which full equality as citizens and permanent coexistence with the Macedonian people is provided for Albanians, Turks, Vlachs, Romanies, and other nationalities living in the Republic of Macedonia."[29] Addressing a public meeting on the constitutional situation at Debar in early 2001, Muhamed Halili, secretary-general of the opposition PDP, referred to the constitution as "the crisis generator."[30]

Ethnic Albanians objected to their characterization in the constitution as
an ethnic minority, claiming in their public pronouncements that they
actually represented as much as 40 percent of the country's population—
possibly much more, if one believes their allegations that the 1994 national census failed to demonstrate the true size of their plurality because of
alleged government manipulation.

Arben Xhaferi, leader of DPA—the ethnic Albanian party in the ruling
coalition after the 1998 elections—believed that the process of amending
the constitution began with his party's joining the government. The constitution, he notes, "describes Macedonia as the state of Macedonians—
where the official language is Macedonian, the official alphabet Cyrillic,
and the official religion Orthodox." Xhaferi added that "Albanians are very
angry about this kind of possessiveness, but we haven't gone to the source
of the crisis, the constitution itself."[31]

Of course, most ethnic Macedonians strongly disagreed with such interpretations. Some, however, admitted that the constitution might have
indeed offered too strong a preference for majority and collective rather
than individual rights; they did not oppose some adjustments, short of recognizing more radical ethnic Albanian claims.[32] The preamble, however,
remained a sensitive point, loaded with emotional ethnic overtones, even
though Macedonians on the whole interpret the preamble's significance in
historical, not legal-normative, terms. In the consitutional precis, ethnic
Macedonians saw a guarantee of their state's continuity, the legality of its
(and their) name, and a confirmation of the one place where they could
firmly retain and develop their ethnic identity.

The second characteristic feature of Macedonia's interethnic relations is
found in the role of the two major ethnic Albanian parties—the DPA and
the PDP.[33] Every Macedonian coalition government since independence
has included one of them, and this fact alone has always been viewed as a
sign of realism and strength. During the PDP's incumbency, DPA legislators served in opposition. When DPA joined the new government in
1998, PDP members crossed the aisle.[34] The new government of political
unity temporarily formed in the spring of 2001 comprised both major
ethnic Albanian parties. On many issues of local politics, the two parties
acted together; while on the national scene, they often remained political
rivals, even to the extent of denigrating members of the other party as
"traitors and collaborators." While in government, the PDP encouraged

change by means of "working within the system," and this ethos indeed may have provided a constructive basis to build accommodation between Macedonia's principal nationalities. Yet the opportunity went unused, as PDP leaders had proven incapable of presenting their constituents with any meaningful accomplishment on behalf of the ethnic Albanians as a result of their presence in government.[35]

The 1991 Constitution and other laws of the Republic of Macedonia contain important provisions guaranteeing equal rights to all citizens without exception, and a number of them directly address minorities and the protection of their ethnic, cultural, and religious identity.[36] Units of local government responsible for populations with a particular ethnicity exceeding 50 percent could use that group's language and alphabet along with Macedonian in official government transactions; the Law on Local Self-Government, drafted in accordance with the European Charter for Regional or Minority Languages, further enumerates such rights.[37] The Macedonian Constitution also guarantees ethnic minorities' rights to establish institutions for culture and art, as well as scholarly and other associations for the expression, fostering, and development of their identities. The same holds true for the minorities' right to instruction in their languages in primary and secondary education; the Law on Higher Education has extended this right to university education. The Law on Identity Cards provides that names of Macedonia's citizens belonging to ethnic minorities should appear on identifying documents in their language and alphabet. Other relevant legal acts guarantee participants in court proceedings the right to use their first language and to have free access to interpreters.

On a more practical plane, as of 2001, 25 out of 120 members of parliament identified themselves as ethnic Albanians; the government, comprising fifteen ministries, included five ministers and five deputy ministers of Albanian extraction. According to a government spokesman, the number of ethnic Albanians employed in state administration has grown steadily.[38] In 1993 ethnic Albanians made up just 3 percent of state employees; in the next eight years, that proportion grew to 10 percent. Of the country's 123 municipalities, ethnic Albanian mayors headed 26. Two ethnic Albanians served as Macedonian ambassadors to foreign countries. Two of the seven generals on the army's General Staff were of Albanian origin. Skeptics contend that such examples are superficial and meant primarily for international consumption while in actual fact the ethnic Macedonians have neither the will nor the determination to follow a path of genuine cohabitation.

What about school enrollment? Does the share of ethnic Albanians in Macedonian educational institutions indicate a more representative attitude on the part of governmental authorities? More than 30 percent of pupils in Macedonia's schools at the primary level are of Albanian descent, as are 17 percent of students at the high school level;[39] for both of these segments of the school population, instruction occurs mainly in Albanian. The government expected a considerable increase in the number of ethnic Albanian students at the universities of Skopje and Bitola, as part of the so-called affirmative action policy, whereby schools exercise preferential admissions policies toward students coming from ethnic-minority families. A special teachers' college prepares educators in the Albanian language. Since 1971, a department of Albanian language and literature has resided in the Faculty of Philosophy at Skopje University. Construction for the establishment of a private South-East Europe University in Tetovo has been completed, and a sizeable share of instruction is conducted in Albanian.[40]

Government officials point out the support they have offered to ethnic communities in cultivating their cultural traditions. A permanent theatre for ethnic drama, along with a separate Albanian drama unit, has long operated in Skopje. Considerable progress has occurred in expanding the range of Albanian media outlets: at least two daily papers, five weeklies, and ten monthly magazines reach Albanian readers in their own language. Several private Albanian-language radio and television stations have registered in Skopje and western Macedonia. The second channel of Macedonia's national television service offers six special programs a day in languages of the country's ethnic minority communities, including four hours of programming in Albanian. A new third national television station airs programs exclusively in the languages of local ethnic communities, primarily in Albanian.

Persisting grievances

The apparent progress in interethnic relations, however, did not satisfy ethnic Albanians in Macedonia. New details of their position surfaced in mid-February 2001. At the time, major ethnic Albanian political parties joined a dialogue on the future of the country initiated by President Boris

Trajkovski. In response to the president's initial agenda for dialogue, the DPA was the first to submit a "nonpaper" summarizing its position: Albanians and Macedonians find themselves in the midst of an interethnic contest of perceptions regarding the concept of the state and the representation of ethnic Albanians in state institutions.[41] DPA viewed the notion of the state in Macedonia's constitution as "ethnocentric" and "incompatible with the multiethnic reality." According to the "nonpaper," although the constitution has inherited some negative legacies of the previous system, the new constitutional framework failed to retain the earlier, more advantageous position of ethnic Albanians in Macedonia.[42] This was apparently true of Articles 177–183 of the Constitution of the Socialist Republic of Macedonia of 1974.[43]

The second issue that incited a crisis of confidence from DPA's perspective involved the marginalization of ethnic Albanians in the labor force and the need for proportional ethnic representation in state institutions. DPA highlighted as the third issue the lot of former political prisoners "and those who at the time of communism were treated as suspicious elements." The DPA estimated that some fifty thousand such people found themselves seriously dissatisfied and in dire need of social inclusion and other forms of assistance. These three areas of concern also included earlier grievances, such as the lack of education in the Albanian language at all levels; Albanian as the second official language; the use of Albanian national symbols in Macedonia, including the Albanian flag; and conducting the national census so as to include every ethnic Albanian.[44] Position papers were also submitted by the PDP and the NDP, and some of their demands sounded more radical than those of DPA.

Human rights: an inherent part of preventive action

At the outset of his first term of office, UN secretary-general Kofi Annan identified three cardinal linkages between human rights and successful prevention.

First, gross violations of human rights go hand-in-hand with situations that may threaten peace and security and are likely to degenerate into confrontation. The United Nations' work in the field of human rights in these situations should be seen as an inherent part of its work in the field of preventive diplomacy. Second, experience has shown that respect for human rights is crucial to peacebuilding and to the broader task of ensuring devel-

opment. Third, truly sustainable development is possible only when the
political, economic, and social rights of all the people are fully respected.
This fundamental triad of rights helps to create the social equilibrium that
is vital to a society's peaceful evolution.[45]

Such interrelationships must have underlay in part the strong interest of
the international community in human rights observance in Macedonia
from the very start of the UN's preventive deployment. Ever since, several
dozen reports on human rights in the young republic have been published
by prominent human rights organizations, including Amnesty International, Freedom House, the Helsinki Committee for Human Rights,
Human Rights Watch, the International Crisis Group, the International
Helsinki Federation for Human Rights, the World Audit Organization, and
the U.S. Department of State.

An analysis of the State Department's country reports on human rights
practices in Macedonia between 1992 and 2000 offers an interesting cross-
section of assessments by outside observers of the local scene.[46] The nine
annual reports follow a standard format, including an introductory section
followed by sections addressing the integrity of the person; respect for civil
liberties; respect for citizens' political rights, including their right to change
their government; the government's attitude regarding investigation by international organizations (IOs) and NGOs of alleged human rights violations;
patterns of discrimination; and workers' rights. All of these categories flow
directly from provisions in the 1948 Universal Declaration of Human Rights.

Introductory section. The 1992 report observes that "Macedonia is the
only former Yugoslav republic to have gained independence peacefully
and without bloodshed"; subsequent reports describe Macedonia as "a
parliamentary democracy." The State Department's analyses repeatedly
recount international monitors' endorsement of the 1990, 1994, and
1998 elections as "generally free and fair." While international monitors
generally sanctioned the first round of Macedonia's 1999 presidential elections in October, the final round in December produced disputed results,
violent clashes, and concern among monitors. In addition, the State
Department's 2000 report indicates that "[n]ationwide local elections held
in September drew OSCE and other international criticism due to poor
organization, sporadic violence, and voting irregularities."

The 1992–95 reports have consistently noted that "fundamental human rights are provided for in the constitution and are generally respected," or that (in the 1996–99 reports) "[t]he Government generally respected the human rights of its citizens." Reports for 1992–96 find, however, that "[m]inorities, including Albanians and Serbs, have raised various credible allegations of human rights infringements and discrimination." All of the studies place Macedonia's human rights situation in the context of the state's economic and sociocultural histories, noting that Macedonia has always lagged behind the other Yugoslav republics with respect to economic development. In addition, Macedonia has suffered from the effects of economic sanctions previously imposed by the West against Serbia, and by Greece against Macedonia itself. Likewise, Macedonia's cooperation with NATO during the Kosovo conflict in 1999 complicated important economic ties with Serbia.

Each report also notes the difficulties of advancing economic development against a backdrop of poverty and ethnic tension. Generally speaking, controversies concerning alleged human rights violations have stemmed directly from ethnic tensions, particularly with regard to Macedonia's ethnic Albanian and Roma minority groups.

Respect for integrity of the person. The State Department's reports note that while some ethnic Albanians have died in ethnic clashes, extrajudicial killings have not occurred with any notable frequency in Macedonia. Moreover, the reports regularly noted that the government did not practice a policy of forced exile or disappearance and generally respected citizens' privacy.

According to the reports, Macedonian authorities generally observed legal safeguards against arbitrary arrest and detention. However, all of the reports have noted that law enforcement agencies have had trouble complying with laws requiring that suspects face an arraignment hearing within twenty-four hours of their arrest and specifying that detention of suspects awaiting trial not exceed ninety days. In fact, the 1999 report indicated that the National Assembly has amended the relevant law to extend this period to one hundred and eighty days. Although the reports indicated that the Macedonian government did not mistreat prisoners or practice torture, they also consistently observed that "police occasionally used excessive force during and following the arrest of criminal suspects." Reports covering the 1997–99 period describe a police practice of compelling some citizens to appear at police stations for "informative talks" without a court order.

The State Department has noted the passage of legislation authorizing a human rights ombudsman, the establishment of that office, and some examples of its operations. However, the reports noted without exception that while "[t]he Constitutional Court has a mandate to protect the human rights of citizens, . . . [it] has not taken action in any case in this area." More broadly, the reports recounted the difficulty of establishing a professional, apolitical, and otherwise impartial judicial process in Macedonia.

Respect for civil liberties. All of the State Department reports observed that Macedonia's constitution protected freedoms of speech and press, and that the government has generally respected these rights in practice. However, they repeatedly reported that the Macedonian government operated most of the newspapers and magazines in the country, not to mention most newsstands and one of the few high-speed printing presses in the country, inevitably exercising some degree of media control. Several reports cite allegations by opposition groups that "government control and manipulation of the media prevent [the opposition] from getting their message across." The State Department's 2000 report mentioned the introduction of a bill in the parliament to revise communist-era information policies and encourage a freer media environment.

Early reports warned especially that it was difficult for the government to refute charges of media manipulation "in the absence of a transparent regulatory regime." Subsequent reports, however, indicated improvement: the State Department found that despite some complaints and conflicts, "[i]nternational monitors noted that the media provided generally unbiased coverage of the full spectrum of parties and candidates" in elections. Furthermore, after the establishment of a broadcast-licensing council in 1997, the 1998 report concluded: "Concerns [that] the . . . council's recommendations would be subject to political pressure proved unfounded."

The reports also noted that opposition parties and NGOs faced a legal requirement to register with the Interior Ministry. By and large, however, the government has neither barred parties from registration nor revoked many active groups' registrations. As with controversies over other administrative matters, incidents involving the registration of parties and NGOs generally stemmed from ethnic tensions. Along similar lines, the only allegations concerning denial of academic freedom in Macedonia involved the lack of government recognition for Albanian-language educational institutions. The most prominent of these cases involved the illegal "Tetovo University," where violence broke out in 1995.

The State Department found that the Macedonian government "generally does not interfere with the practice of religion." Reports after 1997 recount the adoption of a law requiring registration of religious communities. The 1998 report specified that the law prohibited religious activities by unregistered groups; limited registration to permanent residents or citizens of Macedonia; required the registration of foreigners entering Macedonia with the intent to perform religious work or rites; and stipulated that religious observance and instruction must occur in public spaces generally used for these purposes. All reports have noted the Serbian Orthodox Church's lack of recognition for the Macedonian Orthodox Church and the associated tensions that have resulted between the two states. The 2000 report noted consultations between representatives of the two churches during the past year. Several reports noted that the government had denied registration to Islamic and Protestant groups.

The U.S. reports consistently pointed out that Macedonia's "highly restrictive" citizenship law required fifteen years' demonstrated residence within Macedonia for people who had not received citizenship by the time that Macedonia had become independent. The reports also observed that this requirement tended to hinder the naturalization efforts of ethnic Albanians, and that the administration of the government's naturalization system suffered from anti-Albanian bias and corruption. Finally, the 1998 and 1999 reports indicate that, in keeping with the government's signature of the Council of Europe's Convention on Citizenship, the residency standard has changed to ten years, and that the government has cooperated with the UN High Commissioner for Refugees to "develop appropriate laws in this area."

Respect for citizens' political rights. As noted, the State Department has found that elections in Macedonia have proceeded along generally free and fair lines. The reports highlighted the existence of a broad array of parties representing different ethnic and ideological perspectives and assessed that changes of power have occurred relatively peacefully. While the reports affirmed that Macedonia's laws did not formally exclude women or ethnic minorities—that is, Albanians, Turks, Serbs, Roma, and others—they also expressed concern about the existence of electoral districts made up principally of minority voters, contributing to a proportional underrepresentation of women and ethnic minorities in the Macedonian parliament. Again, while political and electoral processes have received international endorsement, they have not proceeded without significant incidents of ethnic tension, including opposition boycotts in the 1994 elections.

Government attitudes toward human rights investigations. The State Department reports consistently found that representatives of Macedonian civil society "meet freely with foreign representatives without government interference." Both the 1994 and 1999 reports cited a lack of vitality in the human rights activities in Macedonia; the 1997 report noted some tension between the government and international human rights efforts pertaining to the former Yugoslavia. However, the 1999 report stated that in light of the Kosovo crisis, "many international NGOs . . . establish[ed] new offices in Macedonia," noting additionally that "[t]he government is generally responsive to the concerns of human rights groups."

The reports have also traced the evolution of Macedonia's national human rights ombudsman; the 1999 report, however, expressed concern that "[t]he office has yet to be called upon by the citizenry in any significant way," observing that "[m]ost complaints filed with this office do not relate to human rights."

Government responses to discrimination. A summation of ethnic tensions in Macedonia appeared in reports from 1994 onward: ethnic tensions and prejudices exist in Macedonian society. The government has made a commitment to pursuing a policy of peaceful integration of all ethnic groups into society but faced political resistance and the persistence of popular prejudices in the lower levels of administration. Moreover, the economic crisis made it difficult for the government to find resources to fulfill minority aspirations, such as more education in the minority languages. Popular prejudices could affect the relationship that ethnic minorities have with the government.

As discussed earlier, key points of tension concerning rights and representation for ethnic minorities—particularly ethnic Albanians—revolve around concerns about the objectivity of census-taking, underrepresentation of minorities in the military and law enforcement, and education in minority languages. The Macedonian government made additional efforts to count the size of the ethnic Albanian population objectively. As the 1996 report noted, even though a 1994 recount initiative met some threats of boycott, "the Council of Europe monitored the conduct of the census and was generally satisfied that it was carried out fairly and accurately and that virtually the entire ethnic Albanian community took part."

The government had taken a consistent tack with respect to both security forces and education: in the military and the police, the government had invested in efforts to recruit and retain ethnic-minority trainees. Though recognition of the university at Tetovo remained a sore point, the government allocated an increased number of places at the recognized universities in Skopje and Bitola to minority group members and has initiated teacher training in Albanian at Skopje. Among members of the ethnic Albanian community, only a small proportion of students received secondary education, particularly in rural areas.

The reports have repeatedly cited concerns about violence against women in Macedonian society.

Workers' rights. The State Department repeatedly acknowledged the formal existence and practical observance of workers' rights to organize, bargain collectively, and strike; the reports also suggested general adherence to laws concerning hours of work, a minimum wage, and conditions of work and indicated that the government effectively monitored the status of the young with respect to school and the workforce.

Significantly, reports from 1997 onward have noted the incidence and resolution of strikes across a variety of economic sectors. Furthermore, the 1999 report indicated that the frequency of strikes had diminished, and that "most strikes were well organized and passed without serious incident."

The 2000 report noted the emergence of serious problems concerning the traffic of local and foreign women for sex work, one of the many byproducts of organized crime in the region.

Against the backdrop of the human rights situation in many countries, as described in other U.S. State Department country reports, Macedonia's record has demonstrated gradual progress and commitment to international standards. The process may have begun slowly but certainly became more rapid and determined.[47] This has also been acknowledged by

Elizabeth Rehn, special rapporteur of the Commission on Human Rights, in her final report on the situation of human rights in the former Yugoslav Republic of Macedonia in 1997.[48] Accordingly, in the same report Rehn recommended to the commission that it remove Macedonia from her mandate.[49] The Council of Europe followed suit some three years later by terminating its special monitoring of the human rights situation in Macedonia.

THE SOCIOECONOMIC ROOTS OF MACEDONIAN CONFLICT

Events in Macedonia exemplify in classic fashion the way that social and economic conditions undergird potential conflict. While crises' military and political dimensions usually prove the most salient and attention-grabbing, their social and economic causes can have their own pernicious results. As the most economically disadvantaged of all the former Yugoslav republics, Macedonia has faced enormous problems in its democratic transition, involving the maldistribution of resources; stereotypically hostile psychological images; and new, complex—though not unfamiliar to the region—manifestations of crime. Regarding external causes, Macedonia has not yet fully recovered from the mandatory sanctions against the former Yugoslavia and the unilaterally imposed economic blockade by Greece.[50] But in assessing Macedonia's record of achievement in socioeconomic development, two distinct approaches have prevailed: a moderate one, noting accomplishments amid too many failures; and an optimistic one (adopted mainly by the Bretton Woods institutions) holding that, under the circumstances, the outcome could have hardly proven better. Above all, though, the international community still faces a situation embodying the well-established axiom that neglecting underlying socioeconomic problems inevitably exacerbates political tensions.

It goes without saying that successive Macedonian governments have done much to improve the competitive environment for business enterprises.[51] Central bankers have held the exchange rate relatively constant and have brought inflation under control, increasing foreign currency reserves, ensuring stable wages, and reducing government subsidies. International financial institutions have disbursed significant amounts of credit.[52] Yet some observers have worried about the management of incoming funds and the susceptibility of some institutions and politicians to corruptive practices.[53]

For several years now, analysts have called for improvements in three basic areas to lift Macedonia's free market economy effectively—reducing unemployment, accelerating privatization, and combating organized crime. These challenges, as well as the absence of an investment-friendly legal framework, have long discouraged foreign capital from maintaining critically needed investments in Macedonia to help generate sustained real growth.

According to International Monetary Fund (IMF) estimates, only 53 percent of Macedonia's working-age population actually participated in the labor force in 1999.[54] The official unemployment rate for that year ran as high as 32.4 percent, amounting to more than a quarter-million jobless citizens, with an additional 25 percent of employees on forced leave without pay. Most university graduates still cannot find suitable jobs. The same IMF report observes that Macedonia's problem of "nonemployment" even exceeds unemployment rates as conventionally measured. This issue acquires a certain urgency in the context of a disproportionately higher percentage of unemployed ethnic Albanians.

Privatization and foreign investment have gone through their painful stages, too. In addition to restructuring a relatively light command economy into a largely private one, Macedonian policymakers have also had to reorient their country's industrial structure. Former managers or employees of state-owned enterprises bought a number of such firms for negligible amounts of local currency. Many among these initial buyers lacked both long-term capital and experience in business management. In other cases, the state continued to play a leading role in the process by targeting particular enterprises and entrepreneurs for the privatization process. New businesses grew mostly in the area of small trade, consisting of one- or two-person enterprises, and thus offered little opportunity for job creation. Last but not least, foreign investors proved slow to acquire equity in Macedonia, withholding capital because of the unstable situation in the region. Ultimately, by the end of the year 2000, 95 percent of the enterprises that entered the process had become completely privatized. Consequently, a *Business Week* report concluded that privatization efforts "boosted foreign direct investment to $140 million in 2000, up from $30 million the year before. As a result, 2000 was the most successful year for the economy since independence, with GDP [gross domestic product] growth more than 5 percent, up from 2.7 percent the year before, and inflation controlled at less than 6 percent."[55]

In particular, two external factors have accounted for Macedonia's poor economic performance, aggravating social tensions. First, the international community failed to understand that a country like Macedonia, having made a unique contribution to peace and stability in the Balkans, deserved a special "peace dividend." Second, as mentioned earlier, the young republic had to suffer for too long from the effects of international sanctions against the former Yugoslavia and from Greece's unilateral embargo.

Considering the overall situation in the region—particularly given the tragic ramifications from atrocities and political manipulation in other parts of the former Yugoslavia—a small country like Macedonia could and should have become a showcase for Western support of nascent democracies. Because analysts viewed Macedonia as a linchpin for regional democracy and stability, and because of Balkan geopolitics, in many respects the significance of Macedonia's current security needs matches Western states' perceptions of the prerequisite security conditions for the existence of an independent Israel. In the early 1990s, a well-conceived, one-time "Marshall Plan" for Macedonia would have certainly done the job. Instead, politicians' deliberations concerning development aid for Macedonia have proceeded all too routinely—that is to say, most of them consider Macedonia "just another former Yugoslav republic." Moreover, in some respects, developmental assistance in the past few years to some other former republics of Yugoslavia has exceeded that provided to Macedonia, proportionally speaking.[56]

The Stability Pact for Southeastern Europe has certainly helped in this regard, but the accord came rather late, and the pace of its implementation thus far has matched neither the strength of the region's more pernicious socioeconomic legacies nor the urgency of the region's emerging needs.[57] Moreover, the size of this program will not allow the special treatment merited in the particular case of Macedonia, which definitely needs and deserves a program of its own.[58] More active international involvement in stabilizing Macedonia's economy would undoubtedly yield great benefits beyond the state's borders. A rapidly growing economy could alleviate a great deal of Macedonia's interethnic tensions: among many other advantages, more investment in educational opportunities and better standards of life—especially for the ethnic minorities—would help to offer women a dignified status as equal partners, rather than confining them exclusively to traditional domesticity.

The other external factor determining the condition of the Mace-donian economy today—that of mandatory sanctions—raises two basic questions: First, when do sanctions provide an effective instrument of coercive prevention? Second, if the Security Council adopts preventive enforcement measures against one state, what kind of duties does this entail for the international community with regard to economic problems arising in other states as a result?

SANCTIONS: COLLATERAL DAMAGE

In their informative book on UN sanctions in the last decade of the twen-tieth century, David Cortright and George Lopez recall that the Security Council had on three occasions imposed sanctions against the Federal Republic of Yugoslavia—an arms embargo in September 1991, compre-hensive economic sanctions in May 1992, and an arms embargo in March 1998.[59] On each occasion, Macedonia became an innocent victim of the negative ramifications of sanctions aimed at a neighboring state. To be sure, the sanctions cost the Macedonian economy between U.S. $3 and U.S. $4 billion.[60]

According to Article 50 of the UN Charter, if the Security Council takes preventive enforcement measures against any state, any other state that finds itself confronted with special economic problems arising from the application of such measures shall have the right to consult the Security Council with regard to the resolution of these unintended conse-quences.[61] In *An Agenda for Peace,* Boutros-Ghali stressed the importance of states unintentionally impacted by sanctions not only having the right to consult the Security Council about such problems but also having a realistic possibility of the council's addressing their difficulties.[62] The Security Council shared the secretary-general's observations and agreed that "appropriate consideration should be given" to the situation of coun-tries confronted with special economic problems as a result of sanctions instituted under Article 41 of the Charter.[63]

The secretary-general returned to the important subject of sanctions in his supplement to *An Agenda for Peace,* noting that the Security Council had greatly increased the use of sanctions, which had brought a number of difficulties to light.[64] These issues related especially to the objectives of sanctions, the monitoring of their application and impact, and their unintended effects. According to Boutros-Ghali, "sanctions are a measure taken collectively by the United Nations to maintain or restore international peace and security. The costs involved in their application should be borne equitably by all member states and not exclusively by the few who have the misfortune to be neighbors or major economic partners of the target country."[65] Conspicuously, the heads of the international financial institutions consulted by the secretary-general had acknowledged the collateral damage of sanctions but did not agree that special provisions should be made outside existing mandates for the support of third-party states facing negative external shocks and consequent balance-of-payments difficulties arising from sanctions. The Security Council agreed with Boutros-Ghali that the object of economic sanctions lay not in punishing but rather modifying the behavior of countries or parties representing a threat to international peace and security.[66] Several other of the secretary-general's arguments revealed numerous significant inconsistencies of existing sanctions regimes; to be sure, sanctions applied unilaterally in the 1990s seemed to have lost much of their initial utility.[67] Secretary-General Kofi Annan has taken an equally clear position, believing that "it is simply not enough to adopt sanctions as the first and easiest line of response and then hope for the best. Sanctions are not something that you can 'fire and forget.'"[68]

Regrettably, in the case of Macedonia, sanctions as part of the international reaction to the Milosevic regime were indeed "fired and forgotten." Though exposed to serious hardship as a result of the sanctions enacted against the FRY, Macedonia neither deserved punishment for anything nor merited any "behavior modification." Still, Macedonia has become a flagrant example of an innocent state having the misfortune of both propinquity and close economic ties to a target country. Between 1993 and 1996, the General Assembly and the Security Council adopted several resolutions appealing to member states and international development agencies to provide immediate technical, financial, and material assistance for the adverse impacts on the economy of states affected by compliance with the sanctions against the Federal Republic of Yugoslavia.[69] In addition, the secretary-general, specifically referring to Macedonia in his report to the Security Council, suggested that the council might wish to invoke

Article 50 to draw increased international support, which would play a key role in contributing to future peace and stability in the republic.[70] On another occasion, he pleaded: "Member states, donor countries, and international institutions should not lose sight of this important issue and support the efforts of the country to overcome the effects of the special economic problems arising from the implementation of measures adopted by the Security Council."[71] Sadly, the response to such appeals has proven rather insignificant.

Without substantial external assistance, Macedonia could not apply the sanctions regime against its northern neighbor. In the view of the government, certain trade transactions, including the sale of agricultural products and electricity, had to proceed as an indispensable component of Macedonia's survival. Combined with the pressures from Greece and in the absence of any compensation—specified under Article 50 of the Charter —the sanctions only perpetuated Macedonia's instability. After the imposition of the sanctions, up to 40 percent of Macedonia's foreign trade passed through the Greek port of Thessaloniki, but this route proved useless following Greece's unilateral embargo against Macedonia. Trade subsequently turned toward Bulgarian ports on the Black Sea and through illegal routes to the north.

In the initial phase of the sanctions, the number of illegal commercial crossings to and from Serbia amounted to some 60 percent of pre-sanctions trade levels between the two countries, and the rate of illegal crossings remained high throughout the 1990s. As a result of sanctions, smuggling, corruption, and other forms of organized crime began to proliferate.[72] Perpetuation of the arms embargo against Macedonia, as one of the former republics of Yugoslavia, marked yet another mistake of the international community in dealing with the Balkan crisis. Lifting the arms embargo at the proper time would have importantly and positively differentiated Macedonia—which, by all existing standards, the country fully deserved. Overextension of the arms embargo left Macedonia defenseless and unprepared for outside intervention. Last, the collateral damage of sanctions and embargoes could not have but negatively affected the well-being of Macedonia's population, thus violating the basic human right to dignity and slowing down the implementation of human rights standards, including the International Covenant on Economic, Social, and Cultural Rights.[73]

Up to this point, this study has examined the backdrop of imminent conflict in Macedonia in both its external and internal dimensions, which, more often than not, seemed to overlap and aggravate each other. What follows in the next two chapters is a survey of the UN preventive mission's methods of addressing these myriad sources and manifestations of conflict simultaneously.

4

UNPREDEP
AT WORK

O N NOVEMBER 23, 1992, Secretary-General Boutros-Ghali
addressed a letter to the president of the Security Council, informing the council that during the visit to the organization's headquarters two weeks earlier, Macedonian president Kiro Gligorov had
conveyed a request for the deployment of UN observers in his country in
view of his concern about the possible impact of fighting elsewhere in the
former Yugoslavia.

Four days earlier, the secretary-general had received a recommendation
from Cyrus Vance and Lord Owen, co-chairmen of the ICFY Steering
Committee, who themselves had conversations with President Gligorov.
Vance and Owen favored the very early deployment to Skopje of a small
group of United Nations Protection Force (UNPROFOR) military and
police observers with supporting political staff. The group's immediate
mandate would be to visit Macedonia's border areas with Albania and
Serbia and prepare a report detailing how a larger deployment of UN military police and personnel might help to strengthen security and confidence
in Macedonia.[1]

Gligorov needed somehow to address Macedonia's postindependence lack of defense preparedness, and in the weighty request for a United Nations presence in his country, he had good reason on several fronts: a possible spillover of the war from the north; the situation in Kosovo intensifying concerns over Macedonia's own interethnic relations; irredentist notions that had not lost currency among many politicians in the region; tense relations with Greece; and, last but not least, the debilitating effect of Macedonia's precarious economic situation on whatever ethnic stability the country enjoyed.

The semi-urgent appeals worked, and the Security Council reacted instantly. On November 25, the Security Council president informed Boutros-Ghali that he had brought the secretary-general's letter to the attention of the council, whose representatives agreed with Boutros-Ghali's proposal of sending a group of military, police, and civilian personnel as Vance and Owen recommended.[2] Significantly, at the time of the Security Council's decision, Macedonia had not yet become a member of the United Nations.

Two weeks later, Boutros-Ghali submitted a report to the Security Council on the possible deployment of elements from UNPROFOR in Macedonia.[3] The special mission dispatched by the secretary-general stayed from November 28 to December 3, 1992. Brigadier General Bo Pellnas headed the group, which met President Gligorov, Prime Minister Branko Crvenkovski, Minister for Foreign Affairs Denko Maleski, Minister of Defense Vlado Popovski, Minister of Internal Affairs Ljubomir Frckovski, and Chief of General Staff General Mitre Arsovski. Many other meetings took place at different levels, both in Skopje and in the field.

The mission first of all sought to gain a full understanding of the circumstances that moved President Gligorov to request a UN presence in Macedonia. Discussions highlighted concerns that if conflict erupted in Kosovo, fighting would spill over into Macedonia, and the meeting's participants believed that Albanians in Macedonia would also enter the conflict, the western part of Macedonia becoming a base for Albanian incursions into Kosovo. Macedonian officials feared that such developments could then set off a wider Balkan war but, more to the point, that such a nascent ethnic Albanian insurgency in Macedonia might then provide a rationale for the Yugoslav army to enter the country. The Milosevic regime's potential territorial ambitions in Macedonia were not lost on the young country's leaders, who emphasized Macedonia's particular vulnerability if regional hostilities broke out: when the Yugoslav army withdrew from Macedonia after independence, it removed all heavy weaponry, aircraft, and border-monitoring equipment, leaving Macedonia with very limited security and defense capabilities. Crvenkovski's cabinet understood that if conflict erupted in Kosovo, an exodus of refugees would stream into Macedonia, a nightmarish prospect for an already fragile society.

The mission also sought to determine the Macedonian authorities' objectives for a UN presence. It ultimately emerged that President Gligorov and his ministers wanted UN personnel to monitor the borders and report any developments that could threaten Macedonia's territory; a UN presence would also deter foreign aggression against Macedonia. In addition, a UN contingent could assist in maintaining separation between the country's potentially conflicting major ethnic groups, thus enhancing regional security.

Regarding that last objective, the mission's staff further inquired if the government would need UN assistance to calm ethnic tensions, particularly in border regions. Initially, President Gligorov and his team saw no need for such help, as the government had begun to address interethnic relations through dialogue and negotiations. Subsequently, however, the officials agreed with mission staff that placing UN civilian police monitors along the border could augment the government's efforts. Visiting Macedonia's borders with the Federal Republic of Yugoslavia and Albania, members of the mission discovered that ethnic tensions did indeed exist there: Albanians trying to enter Macedonia illegally had died in clashes with Macedonian troops, and more incidents like these might worsen concerns among the members of Macedonia's ethnic Albanian community living in these border areas. On the whole, leaders of ethnic Albanian political parties had their doubts about the advisability of a UN deployment along the Albanian border. In their view, the source of conflict would not come from the west, but from the north. In fact, Macedonian authorities had not expected the United Nations to defend their borders but, rather, to ease tensions by providing a respected international presence.

Based on these considerations, the mission's members believed that a UN force should deploy first in the northern and western border areas of Macedonia with the following objectives:

◆ To monitor the border areas and report to the UN secretary-general, through the force commander, any developments that could pose a threat to Macedonia.

◆ By its presence, to deter such threats from any source, as well as to help prevent clashes that could otherwise occur between external elements and Macedonian forces, thus helping to strengthen security and confidence in Macedonia.

According to the mission's members, achieving these objectives would require the constant presence of UN personnel to staff observation posts (OPs) on a twenty-four-hour basis. Because of road and weather conditions, each team would have to live close to its observation post. Military observers could do the job, of course, but would have to deploy in numbers as sizeable as a peacekeeping force, and no one wanted to trigger alarms by positioning such a large, armed contingent—especially if, in this case, mass conflict had not erupted. Thus, Pellnas and the rest of the mission recommended the deployment of a battalion-sized infantry force with up to seven hundred members from Debar on the western border, northward and eastward as far as the Bulgarian border; they also believed that thirty-five UN military observers (UNMOs) and twenty-six UN civilian policemen (UNCIVPOL) should support the operation. The policemen would essentially monitor the Macedonian police operations; on the western border, UNCIVPOL would respond to complaints alleging Macedonian police's abuse and harassment of ethnic Albanians, mainly in the context of illegal border crossings. Such UN monitoring would particularly serve to calm ethnic tensions.

Boutros-Ghali endorsed the mission's report, which expressed "the belief that a small United Nations deployment of this kind on the Macedonia side of the border would help Macedonia and the two neighboring countries concerned to make safe passage through a potentially turbulent and hazardous period."[4]

In accepting the mission's proposals, the Security Council authorized "the secretary-general to establish a presence of UNPROFOR in the former Yugoslav Republic of Macedonia, as recommended by him in his report (S/24923), and so to inform the authorities of Albania and those of the Federal Republic of Yugoslavia (Serbia and Montenegro)."[5] Council members also requested that Boutros-Ghali immediately dispatch the military, civil affairs, and administrative personnel recommended in his report and deploy the police monitors immediately after receiving the Macedonian government's consent to do so.

Pending the outcome of the secretary-general's consultations with prospective troop-contributing countries, the UN had made arrangements for the interim deployment of a Canadian contingent, which arrived in the area of operations shortly after New Year's Day and remained in Macedonia until February 18, 1993, when a battalion-sized regiment assembled by the Nordic governments took over the operation. Brigadier General Finn Saemark-Thomsen of Denmark, designated commander of UNPROFOR's Macedonian Command, assumed his duties on January 25, 1993.

The Nordic Battalion (NORDBAT) numbered 434 troops, organized into three rifle companies and operating eighteen permanently staffed observation posts—four along the border with Albania, and fourteen along the border with the Federal Republic of Yugoslavia. At the same time, the UNCIVPOL contingent numbered twenty-four (later, twenty-six) monitors, with ten based in Ohrid, monitoring Macedonia's western frontier, and the remaining fourteen located in Skopje, with responsibility for monitoring the northern border. Similarly, the first nineteen UNMOs assumed responsibility for patrolling the western border south of Debar and the northern area closer to headquarters in Skopje. Likewise, a small civil affairs staff and civilian administration staff operated from the Skopje headquarters.[6]

In June 1993, the U.S. ambassador to the United Nations, Madeleine Albright, addressed a letter to Boutros-Ghali, informing him that the United States had decided to offer a reinforced team of approximately three hundred troops to operate with UNPROFOR forces stationed in Macedonia; these forces would augment rather than replace the existing UNPROFOR units there. The U.S. government characterized the offer "as further evidence of its commitment to support multilateral efforts to prevent spillover and contribute to stability in the Balkan region."[7] The Security Council accepted the offer, and the U.S. force arrived in Macedonia in early July.[8] By deploying to the Macedonian side of the border with the FRY, the U.S. Battalion (USBAT) considerably relieved the Nordic peacekeepers, who could now concentrate on the Kosovo section of the border and along the border with Albania.

Thus the first UN mission in preventive deployment and early preventive action came into being. Summarizing UNPROFOR's experiences for the first six months of operation, Boutros-Ghali noted that the UN presence in Macedonia "made a valuable contribution to stability in the region and served as an additional source of support for the international community's efforts to promote a peaceful resolution of the overall situation in the former Yugoslavia."[9]

SETTING THE PACE

Retrospectively, the UN mandate in Macedonia can be divided into three major operational phases: The first, from December 1992 to March 1994; the second, from April 1994 to March 1995; and the third, from April 1995 to February 1999.[10] In the first phase, the mission operated as part of UNPROFOR, headquartered in Zagreb, Croatia. As a component of UNPROFOR, it bore the name "Macedonia Command," subsequently changed to "FYROM Command." The second phase started with the granting of a broadened political mandate—involving good offices—to the Special Representative of the Secretary-General (SRSG). The third phase began with Security Council Resolution 983 (1995), by terms of which UNPROFOR's FYROM Command was made a separate mission, renamed the United Nations Preventive Deployment Force—UNPREDEP. The Security Council thus approved Secretary-General Boutros-Ghali's proposal that UNPROFOR in the former Yugoslavia "be replaced by three separate but interlinked peacekeeping operations," each to be headed by a civilian chief of mission at the assistant secretary-general level.

According to the new arrangement, each operation would have its own military commander. Yet given the interlinked nature of the problems in the area, and the desire to avoid the expense of duplicating organizational and command structures, overall command and control of the three operations still fell to the SRSG and a theatre force commander (FC) working either from UNPROFOR or from United Nations Peace Forces (UNPF) headquarters in Zagreb.[11] From 1993 to early 1996, the Macedonia Command and, subsequently, UNPREDEP reported to successive SRSGs in Zagreb, first to Yasushi Akashi and later to Kofi Annan. Although the Balkan meltdown demanded the SRSGs' primary concentration on more pressing issues just beyond Macedonia's borders, their periodic visits to Skopje represented important milestones in developing relations with Macedonia's leaders and in guiding the work of a mission that was meant to stanch the spread of such regional carnage.

Following the initialing of the Dayton Accords on November 21, 1995 and the signing of the Peace Agreement in Paris on December 14, 1995, the Security Council authorized the establishment of the multinational Implementation Force (IFOR) to carry out the military aspects of the peace agreement.[12] The Council also established the United Nations Transitional Administration in Eastern Slavonia, Baranja, and Western Sirmium (UNTAES).[13] All of these actions had important practical consequences for UNPREDEP's functioning: the mission was separated from other missions in the former Yugoslavia and received operational independence.[14] Consequently, its head of mission gained the status of an SRSG; I was designated the SRSG for the Former Yugoslav Republic of Macedonia a few months after arriving in Skopje to head the preventive mission in July 1995. Boutros-Ghali also appointed an UNPREDEP force commander.

These changes proved particularly welcome on several fronts. First, they showed that the UN had begun to understand that Macedonia's case was different from those of Bosnia and Herzegovina, Croatia, or Serbia. Establishing and running the Macedonian operation as an integral component of UNPROFOR for the first two years had not proven the most effective arrangement because the bulk of UNPROFOR's responsibilities covered *postconflict* situations, which did little to address Macedonia's need for conflict *prevention*. Prudent decisions by the UN Security Council had, in fact, distinguished between the early preconflict, preventive activities in Macedonia from the postconflict prevention and corresponding peacebuilding work in other parts of former Yugoslavia. But by delinking the operation in Macedonia from missions in the rest of the former Yugoslavia, the Security Council offered the Macedonian government and its citizens a modest bonus that they had deserved for some time. Second, the new status of the mission was a step toward meeting Macedonia's desire to have an independent peacekeeping operation on its soil. And third, the operation received a new image within the host country, greatly facilitating contacts at the highest level and enabling the SRSG to contact UN headquarters directly with first-hand information from the mission area.

More than a complete mandate

Many complexities of Macedonia's internal and external situation caught the attention of the first-ever UN preventive deployment mission. Each issue had a direct relevance to the provisions of the organization's charter and, if left unattended, might have jeopardized the success of the opera-tion. A full year had passed before Boutros-Ghali decided to draw the Security Council's attention to his findings on the basis of direct reports from the mission's area of operation; he noted in his report to the council that, successful as it was, the operation had no mandate in relation to Macedonia's internal situation, which could be more detrimental to the stability of the country than any sort of external aggression.[15] The council reacted promptly: in its subsequent resolution, it encouraged the SRSG for the Former Yugoslavia, in cooperation with the authorities of the for-mer Yugoslav Republic of Macedonia, "to use his good offices as appro-priate to contribute to the maintenance of peace and stability in that Republic."[16]

According to long-standing international practice, "good offices" repre-sent an instrument of peaceful settlement of disputes between states or other parties, whereby a third party tries to bring the conflicting parties into an agreement. To be sure, the preventive deployment mandate received a major new political shot in the arm—namely, the provision of "good offices," which were to be used in cooperation with Macedonia's officials to contribute to the country's peace and stability. Consequently, the mandate of the UN force assumed a starkly new qualitative dimen-sion, permitting the operation to expand considerably the use of preven-tive techniques based on a three-pronged approach:

◆ To monitor, primarily in the northern and western border areas of the country, and to report to the secretary-general any developments that could pose a threat to the country.

◆ To deter, by the force's presence, such threats from any source, as well as to help prevent clashes that could otherwise occur between external elements and Macedonian forces, thus helping to strengthen security and confidence in the republic.

◆ To use good offices, as appropriate, in cooperation with the country's authorities, and to contribute to the maintenance of peace and stability in the republic.[17]

The terms of reference, composition, and operation of the force thus became set in place. Its three-pronged mandate remained unchanged until July 1998, when the Security Council extended it by six months, until February 1999, charging UNPREDEP also to continue "by its presence to deter threats and prevent clashes, to monitor the border areas, and to report to the secretary-general any developments which could pose a threat to the former Yugoslav Republic of Macedonia, including the tasks of monitoring and reporting on illicit arms flows and other activities that are prohibited under Resolution 1160 (1998)."[18]

Throughout their existence, UNPROFOR and UNPREDEP in Macedonia enjoyed considerable leeway in both conceptualizing and implementing day-to-day tasks of contributing to the maintenance of peace and stability in the new country. The missions' very mandates allowed them—particularly UNPREDEP—to adopt a flexible approach. Given the preventive deployment's somewhat experimental quality, guidance from UN headquarters tended to interpret the mission's mandate liberally and to give corresponding guidance that focused on the mission's overall political objective, which included the "good offices" component of the mission, offering enough space for a prudent and dynamic—rather than a prudent and restrictive—manner of implementation and adding a useful ingredient of quiet diplomacy to the tasks at hand. To those in the field, a precise understanding and proper interpretation of each and every element of the mandate—under the specific conditions in the host country and in those of its neighbors—were crucial for comprehending the role of the United Nations in Macedonia.

In their search for optimal methods for carrying out their mandate, UNPREDEP staff members faced two daunting but helpful challenges: How would they reconcile in practical terms the unique nature of the operation with the widely accepted principles, formulas, and tools of traditional peacekeeping?[19] And how would they convince Macedonia's officials that a UN preventive operation, with a mandate of "good offices," could not remain exclusively restricted to the narrow confines of border troop deployment, failing to monitor and report on the country's parlous internal ethnic situation? The latter point also required convincing those concerned in Macedonia that the mission acted out of genuine goodwill and that it had no hidden agenda in mind when it initiated specific actions or joint projects. Because of the Balkan mindset and Macedonia's tragic historical conditions, the task was often not an easy one.

In tackling the first challenge, UNPREDEP proceeded from two crucial precepts: We adopted a proactive approach to conflict prevention that we felt would be more effective than a reactive one. We also thought that dealing with the underlying causes of conflict was preferable to addressing their destructive postconflict outcomes. Many of the factors in Macedonia's crisis had very, very deep roots, and addressing them would call for perseverance, astute methods and strategies, financial support, and educational programs.

In the post–Cold War world, prevention no longer means watching for cross-border intrusion or aggression alone. It also means looking for signs of potential national crises; usurpation of established democratic institutions; and nonmilitary pressures, both external and internal. It comprises both institutional reform and social and economic development, including issues of social integration. Subject to its mandate, a mission in early prevention and good offices would demonstrate an active interest in nonmilitary aspects of the host country's situation, particularly true with respect for human rights, improved police and judicial systems, or other issues directly relevant to the structure and function of civil society. In Macedonia, we saw all our efforts as a singular preventive operation with a multitrack and multifunctional approach, in which national, regional, and international initiatives complemented one another. In conflict prevention, major issues and partnerships function interdependently and reciprocally. Our comprehensive approach clearly distinguished between the preconflict peacekeeping we were practicing and the UN's more conventional troop deployment, whether pre- or postconflict.

The search for mutual confidence

The challenge of gaining the confidence of Macedonia's officialdom often entailed dealing with incompatible concerns; the comprehensive and multi-dimensional application of UNPREDEP's mandate did not necessarily coincide with the host country's perceptions of the mission. To the Macedonian government, the sole purpose for a UN presence in the country was to deter invasion, so its officials tolerated but occasionally questioned the activities of the mission's civilian political personnel. UNPREDEP's mandate was to use good offices, as appropriate, in cooperation with the country's authorities; consequently we took particular care to show that the UN presence provided a stimulating asset—rather than a handicap—to Macedonia's efforts toward peace and stability. Following our mandate to seek these sorts of synergies with the host country, we tried in both word and deed to assure our local interlocutors that the intent of such a preventive mission inherently proscribed infringing on the prerogatives of democratically elected authorities. We pointed out that the United Nations did not deploy to Macedonia to solve the country's problems single-handedly but, rather, to create a climate conducive to self-reliance. In other words, we tried to convince Macedonia's political leaders that we came not to teach, but to share international experience, and that our purpose was to seek and identify points of convergence among parties to a potential conflict and bring them closer together. We treated our hosts as partners, not as supplicants. Impartiality was the name of our game, and it determined the degree of our credibility. Over time, all this helped in easing a discernable feeling of uneasiness or fatigue among some local quarters over the apparently domineering presence of an international operation; occasionally, Macedonians viewed the UN mission as a kind of national stigma or a form of undeserved penalization for some ineffable offense against the international community.[20]

In a letter to Boutros-Ghali, Macedonia's Minister for Foreign Affairs went the farthest his government ever had in publicly contesting the desirability of a full-spectrum preventive operation. Carefully weighing his words, the minister observed that

> [t]aking into consideration the qualitatively different situations of human, especially minority rights, in the countries of the region, the international community should develop a differentiated approach in monitoring the same, [and] identify and propose solutions for resolving the real problems aimed at providing permanent peace and stability in this traditionally turmoil(ed) region. In that direction, the Republic of Macedonia highly evaluates the role of UNPREDEP, which *although is not strictly in its mandate*, significantly influences the rationalization and easing of the debate on these issues.[21]

Governments hosting peacekeeping operations have generally expected a maximum of external help with a minimum of interference. In the case of our Macedonian partners—including major political and ethnic groups at all levels—UNPREDEP enjoyed exemplary mutual cooperation. After all, while the bulk of the force's mandate in the first two years concentrated on external security threats, no one could deny that the presence of UN troops contributed to internal stability and greater confidence within the republic. For a long time, the government had believed that Macedonia faced only external threats, and that no need existed for involving the international community in domestic developments. At the same time,

Macedonia's political leaders made no secret of the way the socioeconomic situation—aggravated by the sanctions regime and the Greek embargo— would likely lead to "social clashes, which may grow into new conflicts."[22]

The SRSG

The history of UN peacekeeping operations has also included a number of misunderstandings regarding the responsibilities of the Special Representative of the Secretary-General in countries hosting such missions. Our Macedonian hosts were not spared such misinterpretations. It took quite some time, especially following the adoption of the good offices mandate, to bring the message home that once there is an SRSG posted in a given country, he or she alone is responsible for the coordination of all United Nations activities and cooperation with other international organizations. In his March 1995 note to the Committee on Program and Coordination, Boutros-Ghali strongly recommended that "peacebuilding should be an integral part of a mission's strategy. The role of the Special Representative of the Secretary-General heading a multidimensional peacekeeping operation should include establishing overall policy to guide peacebuilding activities."[23] Similarly, Kofi Annan stressed in his mid-July 1997 report that "in the field, the Special Representative of the Secretary-General will have authority over all UN entities."[24] Along with their functions as heads of peacekeeping operations and the responsibility for implementing their mandates, SRSGs can and should play a very important role in ensuring an integrated approach to United Nations activities in the field, especially "where lack of cohesion or differences among the United Nations entities can be exploited by the parties."[25] Naturally, their authority ought to be exercised by taking into account the mandated responsibilities and financial accountability of individual UN entities operating in the mission area.

Accordingly, UN standard directives will require SRSGs to follow closely the evolution of the situation within the area of operations, particularly as it affects the discharge of the mission's mandate. They must maintain close contacts with the parties, including political and military officials, and take the initiative in solving problems that arise among the parties and in building confidence among them. In the same vein, SRSGs must maintain close contact with the governments of interested countries and regional and international organizations and NGOs, as appropriate. SRSGs must endeavor to ensure, through regular contacts, that the activities of non–United Nations entities such as NGOs and bilateral donors are in harmony with the aims of the mission.[26]

Heavy responsibilities rest upon SRSGs in terms of their relations with the organizations and agencies of the United Nations system. In exercising authority over all such entities in the field, SRSGs must ensure that the efforts of the different components of the system complement and reinforce one another. This requirement assumes greater importance in the context of the mission's end and its exit strategies, necessitating planning to ensure a smooth handover to conventional UN actors, who then assume responsibility for promoting the sustainability of the processes of peace and stability.

Public communications and media relations carry no lesser weight as SRSG tasks. Because the media play an instrumental role in support of peacekeeping missions, SRSGs should use the opportunities the media offers, while always keeping in mind what impact their statements may have on public opinion and on the parties to a dispute or conflict. SRSGs should move to devise a coherent media strategy for the operation in coordination with UN headquarters and agencies active in the mission area.

All of these directives were faithfully followed in the case of UNPREDEP, although, in the case of this preventive deployment, following the directives required a great deal of innovation.

BROADENING THE VISION: THE THREE PILLARS

Every preventive action must be formulated to respond to the specific situation it is intended to address. The overall mandate for the UN presence in Macedonia offered a new multidimensional identity to a peacekeeping operation. Its modalities evolved along with its mandate and political status.

After we set up our headquarters in Skopje, we soon discovered that preventive diplomacy, combined with troop deployment, in a country undergoing profound political, social, and economic transformations, could not be conceived abstractly. We realized that preventive practices must be tailored to particular social and political contexts and must be sensitive to the requirements for specific policies and conditions. Preventive troop deployment itself implied some forms of humanitarian assistance, yet UNPREDEP's mandate of good offices was broad enough to pursue proactive prevention and build confidence between the United Nations and the host country. The major task was to combine all the elements of the mandate into one coherent whole for the purpose of maintaining peace and stability in and around a newly independent country. Accordingly, the work of the mission evolved into three distinctive pillars of action: *troop deployment, good offices and political action,* and *the human dimension.*

Troop deployment was the backbone of the operation. It assumed and performed a preventive function by its very visibility, which determined the value of troops as a minimal deterrent in an unpredictable environment. The national composition—from Denmark, Finland, Indonesia, Norway, Sweden, and the United States—and professionalism of the troops enhanced the overall performance considerably. The use of force was limited to self-defense; it was crucial, therefore, to avoid misperceptions by the host authorities and the public at large that UNPREDEP would be able to protect the country in the event of an armed threat, and the Macedonian government was fully aware of our peace force's capabilities.[27] Still, the focus of attention on this particular pillar was further enhanced by the continued immediacy of a potential military threat.

Good offices and political action created a new qualitative dimension that allowed us to expand the range of traditional preventive techniques available to UNPREDEP. Dialogue, discretion, and quiet diplomacy were the basic tools of action. The mission developed and maintained active contacts with political forces and ethnic groups in the country as a means of promoting domestic stability. Constant efforts were made to reduce the level of mistrust among the country's political and ethnic actors and set in place a dialogue on questions regarding the rights of ethnic communities and national minorities. UNPREDEP was recognized as a significant instrument for facilitating dialogue, restraint, and practical compromise between the different segments of Macedonian society. UN troop patrols along the northern and western borders of the country effectively complemented such activities; this outreach had a calming and stabilizing effect throughout the area. The contingent of UN military observers and the team of civilian police monitors rendered equally invaluable services.

UNPREDEP's third pillar, the *human dimension* component, highlighted developmental and peacebuilding aspects of the operation. As such, it was quite a novel idea for a venture in preconflict prevention. Until it proved its practical utility, the third pillar would raise a few eyebrows initially, among both some UN member states and veterans of traditional peacekeeping.[28] Prior to the Security Council debates on peacebuilding in early 2001, some UN organs were unequivocal on the matter. In a June 1997 commentary on a report by the UN Joint Inspection Unit, titled *Strengthening of the United Nations System Capacity for Conflict Prevention,* the secretary-general and the Administrative Committee on Coordination stated that peacebuilding—economic and social development, respect for human rights, institution building, better governance, democratization, and the like—was of utmost importance to improving human wealth, health, and happiness.[29]

Poverty, intolerance, or a combination of the two are the most common root causes of conflict in the world today. More and more crises warranting preventive action invariably have sociopolitical ramifications, thus requiring a complementary and coherent balance between the tools used to resolve conflict-prone emergencies. As such, the human dimension had a positive spin-off effect in generating mutual trust when resorting to good offices and helping to forge solutions to sensitive political and interethnic problems. The emphasis on the human dimension was not an end in itself; it placed the UN presence in the forefront of the development process and advocated positive change. In other words, UNPREDEP was perhaps the first UN peacekeeping mission to foster the conditions of a peace to keep.

Based on seed contributions from extrabudgetary sources, UNPREDEP's human dimension component consisted of a set of catalytic activities meant "to show the way." It had been designed and executed to demonstrate to different institutions in the host country how to draw on duly approved international standards and experience gained in their implementation by countries on their way to civil society. Many of these endeavors promoted indirect peacebuilding through support for the revival and development of a network of civic, professional, and other nongovernmental organizations, all of which were committed to societal development and stability.

Our strength: impartiality

Refraining from taking sides in early preventive action will not always guarantee that all parties concerned will perceive it as impartial. After all, what is impartial for one side may be considered partial to the other. This universal tenet may turn into a greater challenge in peacekeeping operations that are mandated, as UNPREDEP was, to use good offices "in cooperation with the country's authorities." In such cases, next to consistent action in the field, one of the major instruments demonstrating UN impartiality is the quality of reporting to the Security Council. The secretary-general's periodic reports to the council included a range of topics directly relevant to implementing UNPREDEP's mandate. Unlike numerous public reports on the situation in Macedonia by other prominent international and regional organizations and NGOs that mainly covered various aspects of interethnic relations, the secretary-general's reports, with our inputs from the field, always addressed a broad spectrum of military, political, social, and operational issues, thus showing a more balanced and comprehensive picture of developments with respect to both external and internal circumstances affecting the host country. The reports were a litmus test of our impartiality; more important, though, they gave us some leverage to make the relevant disputing parties follow a line of action more consistent with international standards.

Summarizing Macedonia's military situation in mid-1994, Boutros-Ghali stated that it remained relatively calm and stable: few border violations by military or police patrols had been observed along the border with Albania. However, since April of that year, there had been a rise in the frequency of encounters between patrols from the FRY and Macedonia along their common border. Most of the encounters had been nonconfrontational, indicating that neither party was interested in provoking conflict. The FRY's continued nonrecognition of Macedonia's border worried the UN secretary-general, though. Because of the threat to stability arising from unresolved border issues, he urged the parties to establish an international border commission.[30] From 1996, the secretary-general consistently reminded the international community that peace and stability in Macedonia were intimately linked to the overall situation in the entire region. In late 1996, regional developments and the enhanced international standing of Macedonia had made the scenario of a spillover of conflict from the north more remote.[31] In early 1997, though, we found few positive signs. In most of the countries neighboring Macedonia, conflict and tensions were evident. In Bulgaria and the FRY, there was social unrest. In Albania, state institutions had collapsed and social structures suffered a meltdown. The situation in Kosovo remained tense. In Bosnia and Herzegovina, difficulties arose in implementing civilian aspects of the Dayton peace agreement. There had been no progress on the border demarcation between Macedonia and the FRY. As a result of the crisis in Albania, a large number of weapons circulated in the region, some of which had been interdicted in the border areas by Macedonian authorities. The passage of a year witnessed very troubling threats to regional stability, and such threats could not be ignored.[32]

Yet by mid-1997, we felt that Macedonia's relations with its neighbors continued to strengthen, as had its relations with other members of the world community. Its active participation in a wide range of international organizations and programs, including NATO's Partnership for Peace and the European Union's PHARE program, were further evidence of its enhanced international standing.[33] A few months later, the report for the Security Council again noted that there had been further gradual improvement of relations between Macedonia and some of its neighbors. However, its dispute with Greece over its name remained unresolved. Both countries continued negotiations under the auspices of the secretary-general's personal envoy, Cyrus Vance. The situation along the Albanian border had been plagued by a number of disturbing incidents, including the exchange of gunfire. Armed individuals along that border had exposed UN personnel to indiscriminate firing. Progress on the border demarcation with the FRY had been insignificant. At the same time, a continuing pattern of border patrols by Macedonia and the FRY had been observed on both sides. When encountering each other, the patrols of both armies appeared to honor their commitment to avoid hostile action. However, concern had emerged following the uncertain outcome of the presidential elections in Serbia, and increased violence in Kosovo had raised fears of a spillover effect on the ethnic Albanians in Macedonia. Several other factors kept underscoring the need for long-term commitment by the international community in Macedonia. Although none of them represented an immediate threat to peace and stability in the host country, they did highlight the unpredictability of developments outside the control of Macedonia's authorities.[34] The dramatic influx of refugees from Kosovo in the spring of 1999 and an armed invasion of northern Macedonia by groups of Albanian extremists in early 2001 have shown how justified those apprehensions had been.

As Macedonia's bilateral relations with its neighbors and more distant partners steadily improved, questions concerning the border dispute with the FRY remained unresolved. The protracted discussions of the Joint Border Commission had led to intensified patrolling by both parties in some of the disputed border areas. This placed an additional burden upon

UN peacekeepers who had established a presence in those areas to prevent accidents. We could not fail to note that the issue of the border demarcation had become hostage to extraneous political considerations and that finding a mutually agreeable solution would most likely be difficult. More alarming were our findings on the impact of developments in Kosovo. We were warning that the situation there highlighted the danger of renewed violence in the area and that the repercussions of such violence could have a serious impact upon the external and internal security of Macedonia.[35]

Growing domestic tensions

As much as Macedonian officials appreciated UNPREDEP's impartial manner of reporting on military and external issues affecting Macedonia, they contested some portions of the reports covering the domestic situation. This trend became particularly evident with the publication of the secretary-general's report that led to the adoption of the "good offices" mandate, and which suggested that "more likely sources of violence and instability are internal and thus beyond the mandate of the force."[36] A few months later, pursuant to Security Council Resolution 908 (1994), the council was informed that internal political tensions between Macedonians and ethnic Albanians had increased.[37] In March 1995, the mission was compelled to alert the council of heightened tensions between the government and elements in the ethnic Albanian population, as well as between the government and nationalist elements in the ethnic Macedonian majority. Upon the invitation of the National Assembly speaker, the mission monitored the October 1994 parliamentary and presidential elections (under the UN's good offices mandate), joining the then Conference on Security and Cooperation in Europe, the Council of Europe, and other international organizations. Boutros-Ghali reported that the elections had been conducted in a generally orderly manner; however, two important opposition parties—VMRO-DPMNE and the Democratic Party—had considered the first round to be fraudulent. They boycotted the second round, which allowed the parties already in power to secure an overwhelming majority of 95 out of 120 seats in the Macedonian parliament—a development that obviously was not conducive to constructive political dialogue.

The Security Council was informed in the same report that certain leaders of Macedonia's ethnic Albanian population had stepped up their demands for improvements in their community's overall social and legal status, including recognition of Albanian as the republic's second official language. In particular, there had been a confrontation over an attempt to establish an Albanian language university in Tetovo. The ethnic Albanian leaders involved in this effort had argued that the two existing state universities in Skopje and Bitola, where instruction was in Macedonian, as well as the Pedagogical Academy in Skopje, which had restored some instruction in the Albanian language, did not meet the Albanian community's needs. The government took the view that the project to establish such a university outside the state system was against the constitution and the laws of the republic, and it charged the project's supporters with using a purportedly educational issue to advance their political ambitions of "federalization," aimed eventually at creating a "Greater Albania." Police had intervened on several occasions to halt the project, culminating in an incident on February 17, 1995, in which an ethnic Albanian was shot dead and a number of policemen were injured. The Ministry of Internal Affairs filed criminal charges against five supporters of the project. Shortly after the incident, ethnic Albanian MPs, who held 19 seats in the parliament, boycotted parliamentary sessions in support of their demands for the use of Albanian as Macedonia's second official language. An impartial conclusion was obvious: the situation in Macedonia was marked by a complex network of external and internal factors that contributed to economic and political uncertainty and rising social tension.[38]

Some ups and downs

In our reporting, we were always careful to give proper weight to the positive developments in the country. Toward the end of 1995, we were able to report that Macedonia's growing international role had contributed considerably to maintaining its internal peace and security. Although opposition parties continued to challenge the outcome of the 1994 elections, the ruling coalition in the National Assembly had managed to pass several important laws on democratization, privatization, formation of political parties, local self-government, and education.

Internal threats to the country's stability had not ceased, however, and dissatisfaction continued to be strongest among the ethnic Albanians. The government believed that any focus on the country's interethnic relations unnecessarily "internationalized" domestic issues, and so throughout 1995 it had taken steps to meet some of the ethnic Albanian community's concerns. All persons serving prison terms related to an arms incident and the disturbances at Tetovo were released. A special four-year course for teachers in the Albanian language had been offered at the Skopje Peda-gogical Faculty. A 10 percent quota had been established, reserving places at institutions of higher learning for students representing ethnic minorities. The army for the first time had appointed an ethnic Albanian general. Also, ethnic Albanian MPs had ceased boycotting parliamentary sessions and resumed active participation in the work of the parliament.[39]

Nevertheless, the situation remained turbulent for months. Notwith-standing considerable progress in many areas of domestic life in Mace-donia, internal difficulties and threats to stability persisted. The political scene remained divided across ideological and ethnic lines. Fierce political partisanship continued, running deep between the nonparliamentary opposition parties and the ruling coalition headed by the SDSM, on the one hand, and between the ethnic Albanian community, the government coalition, and the ethnic Macedonian parties, on the other. The absence of an effective parliamentary opposition added to political controversy, as did the lack of a viable dialogue on the country's future among the various political forces. The claims and aspirations of smaller ethnic groups, including Romas, Serbs, Turks, and Vlachs, also constituted a source of concern. While taking gradual steps toward reconciliation, the govern-ment maintained that the main demands of the ethnic Albanian commu-nity—to be given the status of a constituent nation; that university-level education be conducted in Albanian and that a special university be estab-lished at Tetovo; that there be proportional representation in all insti-tutions of public life; and that Albanian be recognized as an official language—could not be met immediately because of constitutional rea-sons or the time needed to rectify the situation. Boutros-Ghali believed at the same time that admission of the republic to a number of regional inter-national organizations, including the Council of Europe and the OSCE, raised the hope that the concerned political forces would reach a mutual understanding with a view to establishing a stable pluralist society.[40]

As time passed, the secretary-general continued to see tension charac-terizing Macedonia's domestic political scene. The government main-tained that its "affirmative action policies" had produced positive results, particularly in the field of minority-language education. According to offi-cial statements, the existing quota system provided for the university enrollment of students of a given ethnic group in proportion to that group's representation in the country's total population. Information provided by the government also indicated that there was a steady increase in the number of staff from the various ethnic groups in state institutions. Naturally, ethnic Albanian political parties did not share the government's assessment of the situation. Through both political action and street demonstrations, they demanded that the government improve the political status of Albanians and officially recognize "Tetovo University" within the existing educational system. They also called for the release of all political prisoners, including the rector of "Tetovo University." After four years of a UN presence in Macedonia, it became increasingly evident that the primary threat to Macedonia's stability might come from internal political tensions rather than from external ones. Accordingly, UNPREDEP devoted considerable attention to strengthening dialogue between the political forces and assisted in monitoring human rights and interethnic relations.[41] Ethnic Macedonians reacted to our references to the threats inherent in their domestic situation with criticism and even sarcasm. For instance, following the publication of the UN secretary-general's periodic report on UNPREDEP of November 19, 1996, the independent daily *Dnevnik* charged that the secretary-general "announced a complete change in the world organization's policy toward Macedonia. He essentially recommends that the Blue Berets should remain in Macedonia and preventively defend us: not from others but from ourselves. From 'ethnic tensions'!?"[42]

Under the circumstances, we continued to follow the roller-coaster of Macedonia's domestic politics. On the positive side, the country's local elections, in which all political parties participated, had strengthened the pluralistic composition of the political scene and the exercise of grassroots democracy. As mentioned earlier, the parliament had established the Office of the Ombudsman and had adopted a law on instruction in the languages of the ethnic communities at the pedagogical faculties. It had also passed a declaration on promoting interethnic relations. The rector of "Tetovo University" had been released before the expiration of his prison term. The government dampened mounting social discontent over the collapse of a large private savings bank in Bitola and allegations that some public figures had been involved in the scheme responsible for the collapse by assuring that the matter would be investigated thoroughly.

At the same time, however, UNPREDEP witnessed a number of

worrisome events. The passage of the law on instruction in the languages of ethnic communities sparked daily protests, followed by a hunger strike, by ethnic Macedonian students. The slogans displayed by the demonstrators and the opposition by some segments of the academic community to any instruction in languages other than Macedonian reflected the degree of intolerance and xenophobia in the country. Ethnic Albanian political parties also criticized the law as insufficient. They continued to call for a comprehensive law on education that would also legalize "Tetovo University." Much to the international community's concern, radical demands to establish an ethnically based "federal system" in Macedonia had resumed in some ethnic Albanian communities.[43]

The summer of 1997 saw a serious setback in Macedonia's interethnic relations as a result of a controversy over the public display of foreign flags by national minorities. On June 4, 1997, the country's Constitutional Court decided that Albanian national flags should not be displayed in front of the town halls of Gostivar and Tetovo. The mayors of the two towns defied the ruling. On July 8, the National Assembly adopted a new compromise law on the use of flags by ethnic nationalities. On the following day, the government launched a massive law-enforcement operation in Gostivar to remove Albanian and Turkish flags hoisted in front of the town's municipal building. The municipality of Tetovo was also partly affected by a similar action. During clashes with the police in Gostivar, three demonstrators died and many were wounded in what appeared to be an excessive use of force by government special police forces. In the wake of those events, the police called a number of demonstrators in for "informative talks," a practice restricted by the law. Some of the demonstrators complained of brutal methods of interrogation. A few days before the events in Gostivar, two major ethnic Albanian political parties, Party for Democratic Prosperity of Albanians (PDPA) and the NDP, held a unification congress in an atmosphere of nationalist fervor.[44] The congress called for parallel government structures along communal lines, autonomous institutions, a pan-Albanian parliament, and ethnic regionalization. The appearance of black-shirted ethnic Albanian paramilitary guards in Tetovo while the congress was in session was a disquieting manifestation of ethnic extremism.[45]

The aftermath of the Gostivar drama gave rise to events discussed in successive reports of the UN secretary-general. In September 1997, the

Gostivar Municipal Court sentenced the city's mayor, Rufi Osmani, to thirteen years and eight months' imprisonment on charges of inciting national, racial, and religious hatred; of organizing resistance against the state; and of failing to comply with the Constitutional Court ruling on the flag issue. Three other politicians from Gostivar and Tetovo were also sentenced to prison terms.[46] On appeal, Osmani's sentence was reduced to seven years, but his imprisonment sparked a series of protest marches launched by the DPA. That action, in turn, provoked withdrawal or suspension of DPA mayors, municipal councilors, and MPs from the relevant state institutions, thus adding to the complexity of Macedonia's interethnic relations.[47] Following the formation of Ljubcio Georgievski's new government in the fall of 1998, and in keeping with his declared policy of seeking interethnic harmony, the newly constituted parliament's first legislative act was to pave the way for the release of the ethnic Albanian mayors and chairmen of the municipal councils in Gostivar and Tetovo. The UN secretary-general hoped the releases would contribute further to the easing of interethnic tension in the country.[48]

One of the most notable positive developments on the political scene in 1997, UN secretary-general Kofi Annan noted, had been an interparty dialogue started by President Gligorov on issues most vital to the nation. He likewise highlighted the recommendation by the Special Rapporteur of the UN Commission on Human Rights, Elizabeth Rehn, that Macedonia be removed from the commission's mandate in light of the considerable progress that had been made in the protection of human rights. She noted, though, that some important legal provisions continued to be violated with disturbing frequency, most specifically in the form of abuse of police authority. Accordingly, she recommended human rights training programs for the police.[49]

As the Kosovo tragedy started unfolding, Secretary-General Annan again warned the international community that the continuing uncertainties in the region might exacerbate domestic problems—particularly ethnic ones—within Macedonia. In mid-1998 a sustainable trend toward an easing in interethnic tensions in a spirit of mutual understanding seemed to be lacking. Over the past few years, a number of international entities, notably those of the United Nations system, the OSCE, European governmental structures, and governments of UN member states, had been actively engaged in bilateral efforts to strengthen pluralism and democratic reforms in the country. Although progress had been made in that direction, it still could have been reversed under the pressure of external developments.[50] Similar fears were expressed in the secretary-general's last report, just prior to UNPREDEP's termination.[51]

PILLAR ONE IN ACTION: THE PRIMACY OF BLUE HELMETS

Although Macedonian authorities had not expected UNPREDEP to defend the country's territory from an armed attack, the government was painfully aware of its army's weaknesses. When it left Macedonia, the Yugoslav army took home practically everything that could be considered defense-related. An unverified story has it that the Yugoslavs actually left four tanks behind, but only because they could not start them. Under the circumstances, Macedonia's potential adversaries would not have paid much attention to Article 123 of its constitution, which stipulates that "no person is authorized to recognize occupation of the Republic of Macedonia or of part thereof."[52] While there were many threats to Macedonia's security, the country needed time and protection to strengthen its defense capabilities. Its difficulties were further compounded by the embargo on imports of military equipment.

In the mid-1990s, when UNPREDEP's activities were at their peak and Macedonia was intensifying its efforts to gain membership in NATO, the government pointed out a number of threats to the republic, including Macedonia's possible entanglement in a broader regional conflict; the recurrence of conflicts along the lines of separation between Bosnia's Croat-Moslem and Serb entities; tensions resulting from unpredictable developments in Kosovo; and tendencies to create ethnically cleansed states. The peacetime component of Macedonia's armed forces was projected at the level of 20,000 troops, 35 percent of whom were professional servicemen. The country had four tanks (as noted), four airplanes, and five helicopters.[53] Its wartime capability was estimated at 120,000 soldiers and officers, including units of regular and reserve police (22,000 men and women). Yet at the same time, the government did not hide its defense problems: lack of equipment, including aircraft and helicopters; deficiencies in training methods; and an obsolete and inadequate communications infrastructure.[54]

Macedonia has long considered that its future lies with linkages to NATO as the guarantor of peace and stability in Europe and as a major pillar of the modern European security architecture. The government's White Paper on the country's defense capabilities declared that the Republic of Macedonia considered its future membership in NATO "as a permanent obligation for which there is a broad political and social consensus in the country. The decision is a result of our strategic determination for an active participation in creating a broader security structure in the North Atlantic region."[55] From that point of view, it was particularly important for Macedonia that three full-fledged NATO members—Denmark, Norway, and the United States—were troop-contributing countries to UNPREDEP. No less significant for our hosts was the status of the Nordic countries—Finland, Denmark, and Sweden—in the European Union. The addition of an Indonesian engineering platoon in early 1996 provided for continued infrastructure capability in support of the operation.[56]

The ten commandments

The success of any peacekeeping mission relies heavily on having competent personnel with high professional and moral standards. Throughout its existence, UNPREDEP was lucky enough to have first-rate commanders and highly professional troops. Special credit is due to the six successive commanding officers, later force commanders. According to a tacit agreement, UNPREDEP's most senior commanding officer would normally come from one of the Nordic countries at the rank of brigadier-general. The chief of staff at UNPREDEP's Skopje headquarters, however, would be a U.S. colonel. All of them served with unusual commitment, devotion, and distinction. One important effect of their work was a relatively small number of disciplinary problems. Indeed, for more than six years, the "ten commandments" of personal conduct for the UN's Blue Helmets remained high on our operational agenda:

◆ Dress, think, talk, act and behave in a manner befitting the dignity of a disciplined, caring, considerate, mature, respected and trusted soldier, displaying the highest integrity and impartiality. Have pride in your position as a peacekeeper and do not abuse or misuse your authority.

◆ Respect the law of the land of the host country, their local culture, traditions, customs, and practices.

◆ Treat the inhabitants of the host country with respect, courtesy, and consideration. You are there as a guest to help them and in so doing will be welcomed with admiration. Neither solicit nor accept any material reward, honor, or gift.

◆ Do not indulge in immoral acts of sexual, physical, or psychological abuse or exploitation of the local population or United Nations staff, especially women and children.

◆ Respect and regard the human rights of all. Support and aid the infirm, sick, and weak. Do not act in revenge or with malice, in particular when dealing with prisoners, detainees, or people in your custody.

◆ Properly care for and account for all United Nations money, vehicles, equipment, and property assigned to you and do not trade or barter with them to seek personal benefits.

◆ Show military courtesy and pay appropriate compliments to all members of the mission, including other United Nations contingents regardless of their creed, gender, rank, or origin.

◆ Show respect for and promote the environment, including the flora and fauna of the host country.

◆ Do not engage in excessive consumption of alcohol or traffic in drugs.

◆ Exercise the utmost discretion in handling confidential information and matters of official business which can put lives in danger or soil the image of the United Nations.[57]

Consolidating the troops

The essence of the philosophy underlying diplomacy and preventive deployment was straightforward: Ease tensions before they erupt into conflict. If conflict occurs, act swiftly to contain it. Resolve the underlying causes. In other words, every level of the operation required its own degree of diplomatic skills. Whether a force commander, an officer of the political component, or just a soldier on patrol, the emphasis on negotiation and mediation skills was of paramount importance for all UNPREDEP personnel. Prevention requires patience; patience calls for self-restraint; self-restraint enhances credibility, which in turn would bring us closer to mandate implementation. In the unanimous opinion of the mission's staff and many observers, UNPREDEP had been fortunate to possess first-rate military personnel with the highest professional standards. It was always fascinating to watch troops in the Nordic and U.S Battalions work together, recruited and trained as they were in entirely different circumstances. In carrying out their tasks, they would perhaps use different modes of operation but would still accomplish their common peacekeeping objectives. The composite NORDBAT was a novelty in UN peacekeeping and in military cooperation among Nordic countries. The Scandinavian Company (ScanCoy), similarly, comprised troops from three Nordic nations. The U.S. Army task force, Able Sentry, consisted of professional soldiers, trained mainly for combat, otherwise stationed in Germany. A former chief of staff of UNPRO-FOR/UNPREDEP reminisced that putting Nordic and American troops together in one preventive operation had been an inspiration; their countries demonstrated the highest degree of professionalism, competence, and technical sophistication in military matters.[58]

The diversity of troops allowed for stationing the right mix of soldiers in the right locations and for patrolling areas within UNPREDEP's theatre with maximum vigilance and efficiency.[59] The force drew on a blend of professional skills that allowed for the highest levels of readiness and proficiency. It also provided for a modest reserve capacity to meet a wide range of contingencies in adverse terrain and climatic conditions. These responses included foot patrols and the manning of temporary observation posts (OPTs); maintaining a self-defense capability for the OPs; holding in reserve a quick reaction force; monitoring the borders; conducting cross-border meetings and community patrols; and, if necessary, demonstrating a "show of force." The same was true of preserving logistical self-sufficiency for longer periods of time at OPs in the event of unfavorable weather or terrain conditions, preparing for troop withdrawal on short notice, and preparing support for humanitarian action, as required.[60] As noted, the force's high visibility along the borders had a calming and stabilizing effect throughout the area.

Along Macedonia's borders: deployments and diplomacy

The basic task of patrolling, monitoring, and reporting on the situation along Macedonia's northern and western borders proceeded without interruptions. Permanent OPs and OPTs operated along the 420-kilometer stretch on the Macedonian side of the borders with the FRY and Albania. Permanent OPs were staffed around the clock by up to a dozen soldiers each. At different points in time, the number of OPs would change, depending on the actual strength of troops or according to the military and political exigencies of the situation. At the peak of its operations in 1995 and 1996, UNPREDEP had twenty-four permanent and thirty-three temporary OPs. In late 1996, their number dropped to twenty-one: NORDBAT operated eleven, and USBAT staffed ten. A year later, following a Security Council decision to start a two-month phased reduction of the military component by three hundred of all ranks as of October 1, 1997, the number of OPs had to be reduced to sixteen and, subsequently, to eight.[61] The troop reduction was insisted on by some members of the Security Council, notably the Russian Federation, which believed that threats to Macedonia's internal and external security had been receding. Only in late 1998, in the face of the deteriorating situation in Kosovo, did the Council authorize an increase in the troop strength by the previously withdrawn three hundred.

The Security Council also extended the mandate of UNPREDEP for a period of six months, until February 28, 1999, and raised the number of OPs to fifteen.[62] Contingent upon circumstances and troop availability, UNPROFOR/UNPREDEP military personnel conducted between one hundred fifty and four hundred patrols per week, observing on average ninety to some one hundred sixty patrols weekly by the armed forces of Albania, the FRY, and Macedonia. Direct meetings with local officials and representatives of the ethnic Albanian communities in the border areas greatly helped to overcome some initial concerns over UNPROFOR's presence. UN patrols constantly reported illegal smuggling incidents, but at no stage did the force's mandate authorize the patrols to interdict, search, or seize the objects of illegal trafficking; this was the prerogative of the Macedonian army or the armies of the neighboring states in their respective territories. Even Security Council Resolution 1186 (1998), which entrusted UNPREDEP with the additional task of monitoring and reporting on illicit arms flows and other activities that had been prohibited under Resolution 1160 (1998), failed to empower the force to stop smugglers' convoys or to check on what the convoys were carrying.

Thus the first and only confirmed case of illicit arms traffic UNPREDEP discovered took place as late as February 25, 1999, along the southwestern part of the Macedonian-Albanian border, near the village of Spas. One of UNPREDEP's OPs had spotted six men on horseback, each horse carrying two wooden boxes, trying to cross from Albania to Macedonia. When a patrol was dispatched to take a closer look at the intruders, the six turned around and headed back to Albania, leaving behind one wooden box. The box contained a hundred hand grenades, forty empty 7.62mm magazines, two antitank mines, one rocket-propelled grenade, and one mortar grenade. Numerous earlier movements of a similar nature observed along the Macedonian-Albanian border and the Kosovo section of the Macedonian-FRY border also offered strong indications of arms embargo violations. Mandate restrictions aside, it has to be recognized that the very presence of UNPREDEP along the borders did have a deterrent effect on cross-border smuggling and contributed to reducing incidents of violence among smugglers, illegal immigrants, and Macedonia's border patrols.

As border demarcation negotiations between Macedonia and the FRY dragged on, more military units from both armies actively patrolled what they considered their territory, up to the old administrative border of the former Socialist Federal Republic of Yugoslavia. Although neither side acknowledged the administrative line as a legitimate international border, both of them used it for reporting and controlling border-crossing incidents. Aware as they were of the potential for possible encounters along borders to create unnecessary friction, UNPROFOR's first General Officer Commanding took special care when talking to military authorities of Macedonia's neighbors to the north and west; lines of communication with the FRY army were established as early as 1993. Following some tense incidents in the disputed border area between Macedonia and the FRY in the summer of 1994, UNPROFOR negotiated a military administrative boundary between the two countries that determined the northern limit of the UN troops' area of operation.[63]

As a result of further negotiations conducted by the force commander and the military authorities of Macedonia and FRY, a United Nations Patrol Line (UNPL) was agreed upon in 1995 and was accepted by the two parties as a "gentleman's agreement" with the aim of preventing "incidents by accident" along their border. This unwritten understanding was a purely military measure to augment the 1994 formula, with no relation to the pending issue of delineating the official international border between the two countries. According to the agreement, each party would respect the UNPL as the northern and southern limit for military operations, including patrolling, and it provided allowances for what were defined as "honest mistakes" to avoid unwarranted violence or harassment. The new line followed more manageable and visible terrain features and facilitated UN troop patrols. In some sections, the UNPL would allow UNPREDEP patrols to cross north of the old administrative border; in others, south of it. Regular visits by the FCs and their staff to Belgrade as well as cross-border meetings at the battalion level significantly contributed to reducing the risk of incidents. While for the Nordic soldiers, crossborder meetings were a matter of routine, for U.S. troops they represented quite a novel way of conducting the business of peacekeeping.

For a considerable period, the "gentleman's agreement" worked. Problems emerged with the successive phases of work by the Joint Macedonia-FRY Border Commission, both at the time of the commission's establishment in May 1996 and when the two parties submitted their respective territorial claims in early 1997. Several months earlier, UNPREDEP patrols had discovered four new fighting and observation positions of unknown origin in their area of responsibility, both south and north of the UNPL. On a few occasions, Macedonian troops would try to tell our patrols to leave their customary observation point at Tupan Hill, located along the Macedonian-FRY border. Both the FRY and Macedonia were gradually becoming very sensitive to "possession rights" in connection with their border negotiations. Still, it was unclear to us what advantage Macedonia might have gained by resisting the UN presence at that location.

The generally functional and even respectful patrolling regime that loosely governed the line began to fray in March 1997, when FRY patrols stopped greeting their UN counterparts or treating them with due courtesy. Instead, they tried to make them leave what they called FRY territory. A number of troubling incidents followed: FRY troops not only intensified their patrols of the disputed border areas but, in a few cases, also acted aggressively in sight of UNPREDEP patrols. On one occasion, a FRY patrol stopped an UNMO team and told the observers to dismount their vehicle. One FRY soldier pointed his rifle at the UNMOs and ordered them to raise their arms. The FRY troops then searched the UNMOs, their bags, and their vehicle. The FRY patrol insisted that the UNMOs were not within Macedonian territory. The Macedonian army reacted to such FRY provocations by dispatching its own patrols north of the UNPL, which could not but increase the risk of "incidents by accident." Tensions escalated following the appearance of reinforced Macedonian and FRY patrols at Kudra Fura Hill and, at a later date, the discovery by UN patrols of land mines at spots along the Kosovo section of the border.

UNPREDEP military negotiators were hard at work on all such occasions, but our interventions in the minefield incidents did not prove successful. The General Staff of the Yugoslav army admitted the existence of these mines "to prevent the infiltration of the Albanian diversion-terrorist groups via the territory of the Republic of Macedonia." Interestingly, in mid-1997 both FRY and Macedonian authorities indicated to UNPREDEP that they no longer felt bound by the UNPL "gentleman's agreement" and had allowed their patrols to cross south and north of it, respectively.[64] Likewise, UNPREDEP's offer to the two parties to lend—if so requested—its logistical and technical assistance in delineating their common border had never been accepted. In July 1998, the FRY army erected ten roadblocks along a fifteen-kilometer stretch of the border within the USBAT's area of operation. At least one of the roadblocks had been located squarely within Macedonian territory, and their positioning led many to speculate that the FRY action might have had the tacit approval of Macedonian authorities—yet for what reason, more speculation we heard revolved around the two countries' shared "Albanian problem."

Perhaps not so ironically, a better climate prevailed—at least for a short while—along Macedonia's western border, as the country's security officials initiated mutually beneficial contacts with Albania's military authorities. An agreement held that each side would display more tolerance during border encounters and that relatively shallow but potentially explosive border crossings on patrol would be considered "honest mistakes." Initially, the number of border incidents between Macedonian and Albanian patrols significantly decreased. That situation changed dramatically in 1997: during the "pyramid scheme" crisis in Albania, the border became exceptionally porous and was suddenly rife with dangerous encounters—among them, frequent crossborder shooting incidents involving UNPREDEP soldiers being fired at from the Albanian side. On a few occasions, UNPREDEP observation towers were deliberately shot at. In the course of their December 1997 visit to Tirana, the SRSG and UNPREDEP's force commander re-established earlier contacts with Albania's political and military leaders. Consequently, channels of communication were extended to all regional border area commanders, and they were actively pursued through regular meetings between the Albanian military and NORDBAT Company commanders, UNMOs, and UNCIVPOL officers. Also, meetings with mayors of Macedonian

and Albanian towns in the area of the city of Debar were held on a regular basis under the sponsorship of UNPREDEP's military component. In
the specific circumstances of the time, the value of such a dialogue—particularly as a confidence-building measure—could hardly have been over-
estimated.

The eyes and ears of the mission

The contingent of thirty-five UN military observers complemented the
work of UNPROFOR/UNPREDEP's formed units. UNMOs hold a
prominent position in UN peacekeeping operations; they are high-ranking
officers with special personal qualities, and they are expected to perform a
variety of delicate and not-so-delicate tasks, whose diversity and complexity
largely depend upon the mandate of the peacekeeping operation.[65]

In the case of UNPROFOR/UNPREDEP, the UNMOs' main concern
consisted of border and community patrols and contacts with the local population and with the military of the host country in the field. Supporting the
work of the mission's armed units, the UNMOs monitored some five thousand square kilometers of territory and constantly assessed its military situation. Their community visits and meetings with municipal leaders
contributed to a better understanding of problems facing the local residents.
UNMOs also ran a continuous program of visits to border villages aimed at
gaining the confidence of villagers and assisting in diffusing possible
interethnic tensions. Quite often, while carrying out their border areas visiting program, the UNMOs were approached by representatives of the ethnic
Albanian population with various complaints about alleged discriminatory
practices by local Macedonian government officials. In cases when the complaints were relevant to the force's mandate, they were brought to the attention of higher-level bodies, such as the International Conference on the
Former Yugoslavia's Working Group on Ethnic Communities and Minorities or the UN Commission on Human Rights.

Most of the time, UNMOs constituted the main UN presence along
Macedonia's western border area south of Debar, down to Ohrid. They also
operated from headquarters in Skopje and had teams in George Petrov,
Kumanovo, and Tetovo. UNMOs' mobile and helicopter patrols along the
UNPL and Macedonian-Albanian border provided us with an invaluable
source of information—much of it military, but most of it relayed from dis-
tressed villages.

UNCIVPOL: a few good cops

On the basis of the report of the exploratory mission to Macedonia in November–December 1992, and following the recommendation of the Secretary-General, the Security Council approved a small group of UN civilian police to be deployed in Macedonia.[66] Dispatching the twenty-six-person team of policemen and policewomen to Macedonia coincided with a significant evolution of UNCIVPOL's role in peacekeeping operations. To be sure, some experts believe that civilian police emerged as co-equal with, rather than subordinate to, military peacekeepers. The authors of the Brahimi Report have gone as far as recommending a doctrinal shift in the use of civilian police in peacekeeping operations.[67]

The mandate given the civilian police team for their mission in Macedonia went somewhat farther than UNCIVPOL's traditional role of only monitoring the local police. Of the gamut of tasks UNCIVPOL traditionally performed, our team was authorized

◆ to conduct independent patrols and observe the presence or absence of local police

◆ to observe and monitor the movement of refugees and displaced persons

◆ to observe gatherings, rallies, and demonstrations

◆ to visit prisons and observe treatment of prisoners

◆ to follow investigations against minorities through the judicial system and monitor the final result

◆ to assist humanitarian aid agencies and Civil Affairs components

◆ to help defuse intercommunal tensions

◆ to record and report all incidents as directed

◆ to monitor the tranquility and the maintenance of law and order in the vicinity of polling stations

◆ to assist in the reorganization and training of the local police

◆ to conduct on-the-job training of the local police.[68]

Attached to the civil and political component of the mission and in close cooperation with the UNMOs, the police team operated along Macedonia's northern and western borders with Serbia, including Kosovo and Albania. UNPREDEP's civilian police monitored the work of Macedonian border police at twelve border crossings, eight along the northern border and four along the western frontier; they visited the border crossings on a daily basis and, in cooperation with the border police, compiled statistics on cross-border traffic. Very sensitive problems would emerge with smuggling and illegal crossings at the border with Albania. Investigations in connection with fatal incidents there called for diplomatic skills and, above all, considerable police experience in investigative work on the part of UNCIVPOL monitors. As early as six months after the arrival of UNCIVPOL to the mission area, Secretary-General Boutros-Ghali was able to inform the Security Council that "since the commencement of their activities, UNCIVPOL had enjoyed a good working relationship with the local border police and other border personnel. The cooperation extended by the local authorities had also been most satisfactory."[69]

In all UNCIVPOL contacts, their message was consistently clear: "Police are to serve and help people and not to intimidate them." Their presence had considerably strengthened the mission's outreach to the local civil authorities and institutions. During their patrols, the police monitors emphasized the rule of law and respect for human rights as they maintained liaison with local police authorities, notably in politically and ethnically sensitive areas. In order to facilitate contacts with Macedonian police during their patrols, we jointly published with Macedonia's Ministry of Internal Affairs a pocket-size dual-language booklet with parallel English and Macedonian texts of United Nations Criminal Justice Standards for Law Enforcement Officials, and we distributed eight thousand copies of the booklet to all police stations in the country.[70] The booklet provided a compact overview of the relevant international standards binding upon law enforcement officials. Its contents covered the role of the police in arrest; the use of force and firearms; trials; relationships with victims, detainees, and prisoners; the practice of torture and other forms of cruel treatment; illegal executions; genocide; humanitarian rules; and protection of refugees. The Macedonian government was not initially enthusiastic about UNCIVPOL's presence on its territory and had been slow to provide the consent needed for the team's arrival. Yet over time, it was apparent that on most occasions the authorities accepted and even appreciated their work. In a letter to SRSG Yasushi Akashi in early 1995, Foreign Minister Stevo Crvenkovski thanked UNPREDEP for clear and objective interventions during recent interethnic tensions, including the outbreak of violence in Tetovo on February 17, 1995.

The host country's sensitivity to UNCIVPOL's work, however, would resurface periodically. For instance, since UNPREDEP's inception, local authorities had allowed UN civilian police to visit prisons to monitor the functioning of the rule of law. Until late 1997, all such visits required a routine clearance from the Ministry of Justice. From that point on, however, the government introduced new and more cumbersome procedures whereby UNCIVPOL officers were required to seek clearance for their visits through the Ministry of Foreign Affairs, which acted as an intermediary between the UN police and the Ministry of Justice. For the first few months this procedure worked, albeit slowly, but following the major unrest in Gostivar in July 1997, a UNCIVPOL request to visit the prison where the city's mayor, Rufi Osmani, had been temporarily confined was denied.[71]

Throughout their mandate in Macedonia, UNCIVPOL monitors had excellent relations with all segments of the population, regardless of ethnicity. They planned some projects precisely with the intention of reaching a broad public. For instance, in early 1996, in cooperation with Macedonia's Ministry of Education, UNCIVPOL initiated a road safety instruction program for schoolchildren in accident-prone and hazardous areas of the country. Children attending special classes on traffic safety received UNPREDEP safety reflectors to wear on their clothes. Later that same year, UNCIVPOL and UNMO monitors assisted Macedonian medical teams in polio vaccination programs in communities largely populated by ethnic Albanians. Their presence contributed significantly to restoring confidence in the vaccination campaign and in the teams of medical personnel composed largely of ethnic Macedonians. UNCIVPOL actively participated in UNPREDEP's training programs for law enforcement officials, as discussed in the next chapter.

The humanitarian face

Contemporary peacekeeping entails interacting with the people under the peacekeepers' protection. In the case of UNPREDEP's preventive mandate, such interactions had to take on a much more service-oriented rationale. Since its inception, UNPREDEP's military component had a somewhat informal liaison with a number of civilian agencies and, capacity permitting, offered various community services and humanitarian assistance to the local population in its areas of deployment. Wherever possible, so long as it did not jeopardize their mandated tasks, UNPREDEP's military contingents helped in the construction of roads,

telecommunication facilities, and water-distribution systems. With humanitarian assistance in mind, the force joined a number of international NGOs
to form an informal humanitarian-relief committee; soon, aid was delivered
to some one thousand people all across the country.

UNPREDEP initiated and hosted monthly informal roundtable discussions with interested NGOs for the purpose of getting a clearer picture
of Macedonia's basic human needs. Every year, between one hundred and
two hundred soldiers of the force reported to offer blood at the annual
blood donation campaigns organized by the Macedonian Red Cross.
Local civilians in different parts of the area of operation would regularly
approach UNPROFOR/UNPREDEP battalions and even OPs for medical aid. The Nordic peacekeepers, through the Macedonian Red Cross,
distributed a large consignment of winter clothing, received from the
Finnish Red Cross, to socially and economically disadvantaged families in
the villages of NORDBAT's area of operations. The military engineers
unit conducted a mine awareness training program for children of
Bosnian refugees who were soon to leave for Bosnia.

We had a special concern for Macedonia's children—the youngest, and
most innocent, victims of the country's precarious transition. Blue Berets
could be regularly seen participating in "Clean up the World" campaigns,
in special events at orphanages and homes for disabled children, and in
traffic awareness and road safety programs. At the request of some ethnic
Albanian political leaders, UNPREDEP dispatched a NORDBAT medical doctor to assist in the investigation of the allegedly deliberate food poi-
soning of schoolchildren in Tetovo. One village urgently appealed to
UNPREDEP to assist in recovering the body of a girl who had been pre-
sumed drowned in a local river, and USBAT members operated a light set
and generator to help with the search at night. Individual acts, usually of
a civilian police nature, also went a long way in fostering a sense of trust
in the mission's special concern for the country's youth. A Swedish peacekeeper, seeing a child hit by a local car, was able to stop the vehicle and
hand the driver over to the police. A U.S. peacekeeper who witnessed a car
accident offered help to the injured driver.

Many peacekeepers, upon invitation by the Macedonian army, contributed their knowledge of disaster preparedness and civil defense in their
respective countries. In the first months of UNPROFOR's mission, on
March 5, 1993, a tragic air crash occurred in Skopje. The mission extended

its immediate assistance to the victims. This act alone did much to foster a positive perception of UNPROFOR among the Macedonian public. In the summer of 1995, severe floods hit Macedonia, causing damage estimated at over half a billion dollars, and UNPREDEP was there with heavy equipment backup for affected villages.

Our Macedonian hosts were rather reluctant to get involved in discussions on possible consequences of refugee flows or similar calamities; yet they liked the idea of discussing general civil defense issues, which overlapped with topics of our interest. In May 1996, UNPREDEP and the Skopje University's Institute of Civil Defense jointly organized a seminar on "Civil Defense as a Major Component of National Defensive Capacity," at which senior officers from the four Nordic troop-contributing countries gave presentations on their countries' experiences in disaster planning and civil defense. Some two hundred representatives of various Macedonian ministries and other relevant institutions attended the seminar, all raising interesting questions and welcoming the seminar as a novel and helpful idea in a new country that, prior to independence, largely left such issues to Belgrade's federal purview. The seminar generated several byproducts of its own: a compilation of models of civil defense in the Nordic countries and the United States, including the latter's "Federal Response Plan" of the Federal Emergency Management Agency. A few countries supplied professional literature, established links with other civil defense institutions in Western Europe and the United States, and promoted Macedonians' participation in training programs abroad.

Unity of command and control?

Some writers on UNPROFOR/UNPREDEP have focused on one internal aspect of the force—namely, that of cooperation between the two battalions in light of the peacekeeping principle of unity of command. In his enlightening paper on prevention in Macedonia, an American scholar concluded that

> while the fruitful relationship and cooperation between the United States and Nordic military forces has been cited as one reason for the mission's success, some problems were noted with a lack of even distribution of tasks between the two contingents. These have included a self-imposed restriction preventing U.S. forces from coming within three hundred meters of the border, as well as general command and control problems arising from

the fact that, although nominally part of a UN force, U.S. troops continued to receive orders from their national authorities.[72]

Howard Kuenning offers a similar line of reasoning. In his view, the
operational limitations of the use of USBAT were the most complex challenges of the mission. According to U.S. regulations, the battalion was
under only a limited operational control of the UN force commander.
U.S. law grants U.S. command primacy over UN command. Consequently, U.S. soldiers in UNPREDEP's peacekeeping component could
not be placed on one particular observation point (Hilltop 1703), where
the most tense Serbian-Macedonian confrontation occurred in the summer of 1994; could not approach closer than 300 meters to the UN-
defined border's Northern Limit of the Area of Operations in their sector;
could not patrol at night; and could not deviate from their patrol route.
NORDBAT, Kuenning continues, had none of these restrictions and
seemed even more involved and cooperative in most operational, administrative, and logistical matters.[73]

Kuenning notes that in terms of military command and control, all U.S.
commanders wanted the mission to succeed and were uncomfortable with
the restrictions on USBAT operations. Yet, decisions made by U.S. officials
in Washington had indicated that the political costs resulting from American
casualties or even embarrassing incidents would be too high—enough to
warrant such policies of risk-avoidance that they themselves would not
accept if they had been leading missions under such circumstances.[74]

The question of unity of command and control in UN peacekeeping
operations did not concern UNPREDEP alone. Various UN organs and
secretaries-general had addressed the issue of how much authority United
Nations commanders exercised over national contingents assigned to their
peacekeeping operations. In one of his reports, Boutros-Ghali noted some
exceptional cases in which countries had offered troops but with prior
restrictions on their use that would have severely compromised the contingent's usefulness to the peacekeeping mission. Such offers had to be declined.
The secretary-general did not deny that United Nations command was not
full command but, rather, suggested it was closer in meaning to the generally recognized military concept of "operational command." An additional
limitation, in his view, is that the organization does not discipline or promote members of military contingents; such functions remain the purview
of their national authorities. Most important, when command in the field is

divided, the difficulties inherent in an international operation are maximized and the risk of casualties rises.[75]

The concepts in question were further developed in the supplement to *An Agenda for Peace,* which lists three levels of authority in peacekeeping: overall political direction, which belongs to the Security Council; executive direction and command, for which the secretary-general is responsible; and command in the field, which is entrusted by the secretary-general to the chief of the mission (the SRSG or FC/chief military observer).[76] In Boutros-Ghali's view, the experience in Somalia had underlined again the necessity for a peacekeeping operation to function as an integrated whole—all the more imperative when the mission is operating in dangerous conditions. Boutros-Ghali believed that singling out some contingents for favorable treatment, and others for unfavorable treatment, may undermine the mission's cohesion; troop-contributing countries' attempts to give orders to their contingents on operational matters creates both division within the force and an impression that the mission is serving the policy objectives of the contributing governments.[77]

The history of UN peacekeeping operations abounds with cases in which troop-contributing nations were reluctant to delegate full authority over their national contingents to the United Nations. Obviously, operations under the UN Charter's Chapter VII have generated stronger reluctance than those under Chapter VI. Moreover, "large troop-contributing countries interfere more than smaller ones do."[78] The interests and interference of troop-contributing countries often seriously disturb the role of the mission FC's command and control. Unfortunately, "it seems as though contributing countries normally delegate the authority of *operational control* of troops and personnel to UN forces. The authority of *command* is normally not delegated at all. In this respect, it is the contingent commander who is appointed to be the link to national command."[79] According to some experts, "unity of command is virtually impossible to attain in UN Chapter VII operations. Command arrangements may not and perhaps should not involve command authority—another reason why the UN can't succeed in Chapter VII operations. The best we can hope for is unity of effort."[80]

It would be inaccurate to claim that UNPREDEP did not have its own command and control problems; they normally surfaced when the situation called for a quick reaction to developments in the field. Particularly, problems emerged during the 1997 "pyramid scheme" crisis in Albania and at the initial stages of the Kosovo conflict. Successive UNPREDEP force commanders were for all practical purposes unable to redeploy U.S. troops from USBAT's area of responsibility to that of NORDBAT's area of operation along the border with Albania and the section of the border between Macedonia and Kosovo. American peacekeepers also needed some sort of command approval from their national authorities to conduct cross-border meetings. Periodically, therefore, NORDBAT was stretched to the limit, while the U.S. troops most likely felt uneasy about not being in a position to help their Nordic colleagues. In the fray, USBAT's commander was forced to juggle loyalties to several commanders outside of his own nation's chain of authority. Obviously, problems were bound to ensue.[81]

The self-imposed restrictions on U.S. participation in UNPREDEP seem to have been influenced by three important factors: the discouraging experience, shortcomings, and failures of peacekeeping operations of the early 1990s, particularly in Somalia; the conception of the Macedonian operation—in security and military terms—as one at a risk level equal to peace enforcement under the UN Charter's Chapter VII; and President Clinton's signing of Presidential Decision Directive 25 (PDD 25), establishing "U.S. Policy on Reforming Multilateral Peace Operations."

PDD 25 contains an exhaustive U.S. strategy regarding these types of missions, including definitions of command and operational control, based on the principle that a given multilateral action "best serves U.S. interests in preserving or restoring peace."[82] The document determines that "the President retains and will never relinquish command authority over U.S. forces. On a case by case basis, the President will consider placing appropriate U.S. forces under the operational control of a competent UN commander for specific UN operations authorized by the Security Council." The directive also stipulates that "within the limits of operational control, a foreign UN commander *cannot:* change the mission or deploy U.S. forces outside the area of responsibility agreed to by the President, separate units, divide their supplies, administer discipline, promote anyone, or change their internal organization."

Naturally, Boutros-Ghali had a harsh view of PDD 25, asserting that the document "dealt a deadly blow to cooperative multilateral action to maintain peace and security."[83] However, the situation was not entirely hopeless for UNPREDEP under the U.S. presidential directive. As the day-to-day functioning of the operation revealed, much of the U.S. position proceeded precisely from an overinterpretation of the serious threat to peace-keepers in Macedonia, which was far below that of other peacekeeping ventures. The unprecedented nature of the operation in Macedonia had fully warranted a more lenient approach to its command and control aspects. One of the best UNPREDEP chiefs of staff, Colonel Charles Seland (U.S. Army, ret.), has offered the following reflections on the matter:

> Who can command a soldier to perform a high risk action which has the real potential for conflict and possibly death? "Command" equals "direct," which equals "you must obey or be punished." Who punishes? Who can control a soldier by issuing regulations, directives, rules, policies, and standards which unite the force into one cohesive body designed to achieve one mission?
>
> Let's face it, the United States is in no mood to relinquish command to a non-American. It can and has been done, but a lot of work must precede this with the mandating body and the U.S. command authorities in Washington prior to deployment or as soon thereafter as practical. Trying to figure it out on the ground is fruitless. . . . Like it or not, if the force commander is not given "command" authority—which must be clearly spelled out, so that in time of crisis it can be assumed easily—then he does not have it.[84]

PILLAR TWO IN ACTION: BROKERING DIALOGUE

The record of UN political action in Macedonia shows a determined, continuous process. Right from its inception, the Macedonia Command paid keen attention to the political side of the UN presence in the country. The very stationing of a United Nations force had already been an act of profound political significance, but an operation like this—without a proper political backdrop and regular political analysis—would seriously handicap mandate implementation. Also, the Zagreb and New York headquarters expected reports on the political situation relevant to the mission's mandate. In fact, first to arrive in Skopje following the adoption of the December 1992 Security Council resolution mandating the mission was a competent civil affairs officer, Janusz Sznajder of Poland, who established the initial contacts with the authorities at different levels and prepared the ground for the reception of the military contingents.

More than a year later, when the status and mandate of the operation were evolving and the Security Council added the "good offices" component, the SRSG in Zagreb, Yasushi Akashi, decided to strengthen the political dimension of the mission. He dispatched to Skopje an experienced international civil servant, Hugo Anson, as his delegate. Both Anson and Sznajder made an outstanding contribution to establishing cooperative relations and starting a fruitful dialogue with the Macedonian authorities, political parties, and the public at large. Anson's arrival coincided with the preparations for Macedonia's 1994 presidential and parliamentary elections. The political scene was divided, and the election campaign was fierce and acrimonious. Local politicians were not used to foreign political brokers. Yet, Anson took a risk—and rightly so—to launch an initiative meant to calm emotions and create a better climate among various political rivals: the signing of a joint declaration by Macedonia's political parties. Following active contacts, discussions, and negotiations on the draft under the sponsorship of National Assembly speaker Stojan Andov, leaders of some dozen major political parties (but, significantly, not VMRO-DPMNE, the Democratic Party, and the ethnic Albanian PDP) signed the following text on October 6, 1994:

> We, the leaders of political parties in the Republic of Macedonia, jointly declare our commitment to ensuring that the presidential and parliamentary elections in October 1994 will be free and fair, and to respect the results of the elections.
>
> Both during and after the election campaign, we shall emphasize Macedonia's special tradition of interethnic cooperation, so important in the Balkan region, as the only sure way of moving towards a stable and prosperous future for all people of this country.
>
> In particular, we shall ensure that the members and supporters of our political parties avoid activities and language which could encourage interethnic and religious hatred or intolerance.
>
> We share the conviction that all citizens of the Republic of Macedonia, no matter what their ethnic origin, have equal rights and equal obligations. All citizens of the Republic of Macedonia, whose territorial integrity and sovereignty are recognized and ensured by the United Nations, are entitled to enjoy and strive for their equal rights, and are also bound to fulfill their equal obligations towards their state, the Republic of Macedonia.
>
> We, the leaders of political parties, will jointly do our utmost to ensure that whatever difficulties or provocations may arise, this Declaration will be respected throughout the Republic before, during, and after the October 1994 elections.

Although some signatories seemed to forget its existence the moment they signed it, the initiative was a useful exercise in good offices, notwithstanding accusations by others that the parliamentary elections were neither free nor fair. First, the declaration manifested the UN's genuine willingness to contribute an element of political tranquility to a divided pre-election landscape. Second, it demonstrated what the mandate of good offices might mean in practical terms. Third, the initiative tested the seriousness and reliability of some major political subjects on the national scene. Regrettably, two major opposition ethnic Macedonian parties that did not sign the declaration—VMRO-DPMNE and the Democratic Party—boycotted the second round of parliamentary elections.

Shortly before the 1994 elections, the Macedonian government had conducted a nationwide census to establish accurate estimates of the country's ethnic composition.[85] The census was financed, partly organized, and monitored by the Council of Europe and the European Union, with the assistance of a number of other international bodies, including the civilian component of UNPROFOR. The general impression of forty observers from nineteen European countries was that the overall results of the census were of acceptable reliability, despite difficulties in some areas—particularly those with a large ethnic Albanian population, poor quality maps, or some confusion regarding citizenship status.[86] The results of the census showed that 67 percent of the resident population of Macedonia were ethnic Macedonians, 23 percent were ethnic Albanians, and the remaining 10 percent comprised Turks, Serbs, Vlachs, Romas, and persons of nonidentified ethnicity.[87]

Reinforcing the mission

In 1995, with the operation's enhanced status as an independent mission operating under a full head of mission and subsequently the SRSG, several new elements of the civilian political component came to fruition. A seasoned diplomat, Ambassador Ataul Karim of Bangladesh, joined the team as deputy to the SRSG. The Political and Humanitarian Affairs and the Public Information Units were strengthened. UNPREDEP's administrative divisions, which consisted of some two hundred staff members, mostly Macedonian citizens, received Myrna Johnston of the United States as chief administrative officer to meet the requirements of the mission's new independent status. Quickly adopting UNPREDEP's proactive approach, the political and humanitarian affairs component was soon systematically monitoring developments and possible conflict-prone areas, with a view to promoting reconciliation among various ethnic groups. This small unit formed the link between peacekeeping on the ground and the country's political and interethnic levels. The mission thus succeeded in developing active contacts with the country's authorities and political forces at all levels. The unit closely interacted with the mission's team of UNCIVPOL.

In pursuing the good offices mandate, we concentrated on three broad areas of action: promoting cross-party political dialogue; building consensus on the fundamental political tenets of the state; and fostering interethnic dialogue, mutual trust, moderation, and compromise. This general framework was translated into more specific tasks, including maintaining active contacts and dialogue with the host country authorities at all levels; monitoring and reporting current developments; assessing political, interethnic, and other potentially conflict-prone situations; developing contacts with governments, international organizations, and the General Staffs of the Albanian and Yugoslav Armies; encouraging progress toward civil society; and developing the concept of early preventive action. In all our discussions with ethnic Macedonian and ethnic Albanian interlocutors on interethnic issues, we kept stressing that for the sake of progress in reconciliation, the inflammatory rhetoric had to cease; major differences had to be identified in a civilized discussion; points of agreement had to be found as overriding principles for the country's raison d'être, including a full consensus on its sovereignty and territorial integrity; and a patient dialogue had to begin, with a view to finding long-term solutions, and that in such a dialogue, every participant would have to demonstrate a give-and-take approach.

A useful attempt that failed

In January 1996, we began to invite leaders of Macedonia's major political parties to monthly working luncheons in order to acquaint them more closely with UNPREDEP's activities and to foster mutual relations among them. As there had been several dozen registered political parties in the country, we used a simple formula to select our invitees: the key leaders of the twelve political parties that had been represented in the parliament since independence in 1991. For almost three years, UNPREDEP's modest premises constituted the only place in town where an informal dialogue took place among the group of leading Macedonian politicians of various political and ethnic stripes. At that time, the two opposition parties outside the parliament, VMRO-DPMNE and the Democratic Party, were still ostracizing the government after boycotting the second round of the 1994 elections; UNPREDEP offered them a forum to air their political grievances.[88] In addition, smaller ethnic parties that had been outside the parliament in 1996–98 appreciated the opportunity to participate in the discussions. Above all, the informal luncheons (with modest menus from UNPREDEP's canteen) consolidated fellowship among the participants and helped to foster understanding of the many intricacies of world and domestic politics.

For the first several months, we tried to impart to our guests as much information as we could about the functioning of our preventive operation. We were also seeking in their political assessments elements that might contribute to a possible consensus on the fundamental tenets of Macedonia's existence as an independent state. Surprisingly, and contrary to popular belief, we managed to identify several important points that we thought might lend themselves to bringing about a nonpartisan national consensus. Encouraged, we decided to go a step further: to put on paper the major points of convergence and to try to negotiate a text that the participating political parties might eventually accept as their joint document. The task was daunting but, at least from our vantage point, not impossible. In early June 1996, I started shuttling between Skopje and Tetovo, where the ethnic Albanian party leaders had their offices, and conducted individual consultations with the leaders of twelve political parties. My purpose was to encourage the evolution of an agreed draft of a joint declaration, the signing and publication of which might ameliorate the country's sorely strained political climate. Following three rounds of separate and very constructive meetings, a balanced draft emerged that, in principle, was ready for final discussion and approval. The draft Joint Declaration on the Fundamental Consensus for Macedonia read:

> We the undersigned, representatives of the major political parties of the Republic of Macedonia,
>
> *Guided* by the best interest of the country,
>
> *Aware* of the differences in our respective programs, philosophies, and approaches as to how to run the affairs of the Republic,
>
> *Determined* to build the country the way we have mapped it out in our respective political programs,

Agreeing, at the same time, that certain overriding values of the Republic, regardless of our affiliation, are above political partisanship, and constitute a fundamental consensus on which we can build an independent and democratic Macedonia, guaranteeing all the rights to its ethnic communities,

Therefore, notwithstanding our differing approaches as to the means and ways of their implementation, we solemnly confirm the inviolable nature and the lasting validity of the following principles and objectives of major significance to Macedonia's statehood:

◆ Inviolability of the country's sovereignty and territorial integrity.

◆ Development of democracy, pluralism, and democratic institutions, in multiethnic realities and a civil society of equal opportunity.

◆ Maintenance of the country's internal and external stability.

◆ Membership in collective security arrangements, notably in NATO.

◆ Respect for human rights, based on international standards and principles of social justice.

◆ Commitment to free market economy and entrepreneurship.

◆ Integration into the European Union and other European regional institutions.

◆ Furtherance of good relations with the neighboring countries.

◆ Preservation of a healthy environment.

Before convening a meeting with all the prospective signatories, I decided to inform President Gligorov of the initiative and ask his reaction to it. I met the president on July 5 and explained to him the rationale behind the initiative as part of UNPREDEP's good offices mandate in search of common ground among different forces that were divided along both political and ethnic lines. Having read the draft text, Gligorov reacted very encouragingly. He said that in arriving at the text before he did, UNPREDEP proved to be more successful than he himself had been, because some political parties had thus far refused to participate in a dialogue under his auspices. He added: "Such a declaration could constitute a major pillar of stability in Macedonia."

Heartened by both the president's reaction and the results of my personal consultations with the concerned political parties, we convened a meeting four days later with the potential signatories to the joint declaration in order to finalize the initiative. The leading representatives of nine political parties—including two important ethnic Albanian groupings, PDP and NDP—attended the meeting. But three major parties were missing: Arben Xhaferi's PDPA, the Socialist Party, and the Party for the Complete Emancipation of Romas (PCER).

Ilinka Mitreva is a prominent Macedonian politician. She was the chairperson of the parliament's Foreign Affairs Committee and Macedonia's would-be foreign minister. At the time of the meeting, she was also the representative of the SDSM—the largest and strongest partner in the governing coalition—and asked to be given the floor first. Having commended the draft as one reflecting the realities of the political situation in the country, Mitreva pointed out that the initiative had been advanced by an international mission, commonly perceived by the local population as a military entity. This fact alone in the eyes of the Macedonian public might work against the signatories in general and the SDSM in particular. People might wonder, she said, why Macedonia's political forces had to resort to an external body with military connotations in order to arrive at such an important domestic political agreement. Hence, we discovered on the spot that the SDSM was not in a position to become a signatory to the draft declaration. During a nearly two-hour discussion, some participants questioned SDSM's arguments while others encouraged us to continue to pursue the initiative as a meaningful signal to the international community of Macedonia's commitment to democratic reform.

We often wondered why the SDSM felt motivated to thwart the initiative. The argument that, as a catalyst of this major nonpartisan accord, UNPREDEP had a military image was rather irrelevant—after all, at every stage of the joint consultations, we emphasized that the initiative, if successful, could be attributed to the declaration's signers; the text belonged to the participants of the working luncheons, and our consultations proceeded out of public view. One likely reason for SDSM's position might have been the long-standing reluctance of the Macedonian government to accept the SRSG's "good offices" mandate when it touched on internal developments in Macedonia—an activity the host government tolerated but did not encourage. Essentially, the government was very uncomfortable with foreign intermediaries raising domestic issues, unless absolutely necessary, particularly with intermediaries whose parent organizations or governments did not have enough leverage to offer or were unable to resort to some forms of conditionality.

Another possible cause for the turn of events might have stemmed from the general state of relations between the governing coalition parties and those of the opposition. Following the 1994 elections and in the face of growing international support for Macedonia, SDSM and its other coalition partners felt quite confident in running the affairs of the state. Except for the ethnic Albanian PDPA, there was no other opposition party in the parliament. Relations between SDSM and VMRO-DPMNE had their own tortured history and were more than strained; the two seldom went beyond trading accusations. Tactically, the government might not have been keen to confer legitimacy to the main opposition parties. Strategically, failure to rise above party divisions and join the initiative, many believed, was a mistake.

The search for a mutually acceptable consensus had definitely played a positive role in promoting stability in Macedonia. It fostered the development of a regular interparty dialogue at the highest level, something never before practiced in Macedonia's political arena. UNPREDEP's working luncheons for party leaders continued until late 1998, covering a host of domestic and international issues and keeping their participants abreast of what the international community was doing in Macedonia. They helped to establish friendships among people who would otherwise find such relationships hardly conceivable. Between January 1996 and September 1998, UNPREDEP hosted twenty-six such informal meetings. Altogether, at different points in time, forty-two party leaders attended them.

Youth: a hopeful future

Youth leaders were more receptive to joint cooperative ventures. In the Macedonia of the 1990s, there were two categories of youth organizations: political, which were direct extensions or wings of the major political parties, and nonpolitical NGOs under the umbrella of the Youth Council, which consisted of ethnic Macedonian organizations only. Following on our positive record of bilateral contacts with individual youth groups, in March 1997 we started inviting leaders from political youth organizations to monthly informal meetings devoted to current issues and the discussion of tolerance in civil society. During fifteen such working discussions, attended by a total of forty-six leaders, the young participants proved to be excellent and imaginative partners who—regardless of their ethnicity— saw their past, present, and future as citizens of Macedonia, and they seemed to understand well that tolerance was the very starting point on the path to civil society. With each successive meeting, we could observe signs of a more amicable political culture. In the spring of 1998, they came up with the idea of signing a "Joint Declaration of Youth Organizations of the Political Parties in Support of Tolerance in the Republic of Macedonia." They did not need any intermediaries. The entire negotiating process on the text was in the hands of the president of the Liberal-Democratic Youth. On April 2, 1998, eight major political youth organizations put their signatures on this joint declaration:

Guided by our genuine intentions and actions, with a view to creating and promoting the Republic of Macedonia as a contemporary, civil, and modern state with a European orientation, and giving due consideration to:

◆ the historic background and circumstances of the past that have shaped Macedonia into a State with political, ethnic, religious, cultural, and other differences;

◆ the constitutional provisions whereby the rights of the citizen as an individual are the main pillars and principles of a civil society;

◆ the need for a practical implementation of the spirit of the Constitution;

◆ the essential requirement of promoting positive sentiments among the citizens of the Republic of Macedonia;

We, the undersigned youth organizations of the political parties, do firmly stand and strive for:

◆ an inviolable development of individual rights, irrespective of gender, age, religion, nationality, political or any other distinguishing features that make us different from others;

◆ uncompromising resistance to any idea that forces us into mutual intolerance;

◆ the creation of space to foster positive ideas and projects, no matter where they may come from;

◆ the creation of conditions for equal opportunities according to personal capabilities of the individual;

◆ development of an economic base as the most important foundation for the fulfillment of citizens;

◆ constant efforts toward achieving the standards of advanced democracies; and

◆ upholding respect for the differences of others, without prejudice of any kind.[89]

DPA Youth was the only organization that did not sign the declaration.[90] Interestingly, in spite of its sponsors' efforts to publicize this unprecedented document, only one newspaper reported the signing.

The markedly better political and social climate among youth leaders was the result of a longer process of mutual cooperation. A number of joint seminars, workshops, and other projects had preceded the declaration on tolerance. We started off in spring 1996 with a seminar on "Youth as Agents of Social Change," together with the EU's PHARE program and Skopje's University of Sts. Cyril and Methodius. UNPREDEP then cosponsored a meeting on the "Implementation of the United Nations Standards and Rights of Persons Belonging to National or Ethnic, Religious, and Linguistic Minorities." Asbjorn Eide, director of the Norwegian Institute of Human Rights in Oslo, delivered the keynote address on the subject of "United Nations Standards: A Divisive Scheme or an Invitation to Civil Society?" The motto of the seminar, "Tolerance, Trust, Dialogue, and Equal Opportunity," reflected the challenges that all political, social, and ethnic forces in transitional states will have to face through concerted action. Financial support from the Open Society Institute–Macedonia allowed for a follow-up publication on the event.[91]

Another symposium was devoted to "Youth as Bridge-Builders in Multiethnic Communities," marking the first time that so many groups in the country came together on a common discussion platform. A publication under the same title was made possible thanks to the United Nations Children's Fund (UNICEF), Skopje.[92] Germany's Friedrich Ebert Foundation financed the seminar on "Youth: The Young Promoters of Tolerance" and an intensive training seminar on youth leadership. The participants discussed four major topics: promoting unity among the citizens of the country, guaranteeing individual rights, fostering equal opportunities for human development, and achieving basic standards of democracy and civil society. Much attention was also devoted to strengthening youth organizations, goal formulation, planning and implementation, and capacity building. Prominent experts from other countries or international organizations addressed most of these seminars. A grant from the Norwegian government enabled UNPREDEP and the youth organizations to launch an interethnic income-generating project for computer and foreign language skills in Gostivar.[93] Resources permitting, a similar undertaking was planned for the city of Stip.

Tirana

UNPROFOR/UNPREDEP's good offices extended to some external actors as well—notably the government of Albania. Such ramifications of at least one component of the mission were in keeping with the preventive aspect of our deployment and, in this case, had some strong reasons to support it. In the first place, UN troops were patrolling the Macedonian-Albanian border; although our mandate covered the Macedonian side of the border only, we encountered a number of practical issues that required direct contacts with the Albanian authorities. Second, because of Macedonia's sizeable ethnic Albanian minority and because of certain problems in the two countries' bilateral relations, it was essential to know first-hand the respective positions of the parties. With this in mind, UN representatives from Skopje paid several visits to Tirana, normally at the level of the commanding officer, the FC, or the SRSG. The commanding officer, Brigadier General Juha Engstrøm, and Hugo Anson visited Tirana in March 1995. Six months after my arrival in Skopje, we decided to avail ourselves of the invitation of the Albanian authorities and pay a visit to Tirana.

During January 23–25, 1996, General Engstrøm and I held a series of meetings with Albanian politicians and high-ranking military officials. We were also received by President Sali Berisha, who sounded constructive and forward-looking. Berisha admitted that originally Albania had doubts as to the utility of the UN's monitoring Macedonia's western border. Yet it had respected Security Council decisions and concentrated on the positive aspects of UNPREDEP's presence in Macedonia. The real future, though, lay in cooperation and friendly relations between Albania and Macedonia. According to President Berisha, "problems that took fifty years to accumulate cannot be solved immediately." That observation was true enough, but Berisha pointed out the need for Macedonia to change its approach to its ethnic issues, particularly in relation to educational opportunities for ethnic Albanians. He underlined that UNPREDEP should be terminated only as a result of normalization of relations with the FRY, Macedonia's acquisition of its own defense deterrent, and visible progress in the implementation of the Dayton Accords. On a practical level, our visit resulted in an agreement to hold regular joint meetings of Albanian and Macedonian border authorities with the participation of UNPREDEP personnel.

On our next visit to Tirana with Force Commander Bo Wranker, on December 13, 1996, our interlocutors had nothing but praise for

UNPREDEP's role in Macedonia and the region; their attitude toward the operation had further evolved since my last visit there, which was a good sign. President Berisha reiterated his position on the grievances of the ethnic Albanians in Macedonia. He saw the question of the university for ethnic Albanians in Macedonia as the major stumbling block in Albanian-Macedonian relations. At the same time, he spoke highly of his earlier meeting with President Gligorov in Lisbon, and he and his colleagues were generally optimistic as to the bilateral future of the two countries. The Albanian officials at the meeting repeatedly stressed the need for "a democratic Serbia" as a stabilizing factor in the Balkans, and they sounded certain that Milosevic would not be able to keep developments there from spinning out of control. It was quite evident that for the Albanian politicians, the real priorities remained in Kosovo. Sadly, three months later, Albania's "pyramid scheme" crisis exploded, which threw the country's very existence into question.

My third visit to Tirana, this time with Force Commander Bent Sohnemann, took place exactly a year later, on December 13–14, 1997. Albania had a new government in the aftermath of the pyramid scheme crisis, and the new team spoke a different political language with regard to Albania's neighbors, as well as to other matters. We discussed Albanian-Macedonian relations at length; postcrisis internal security in Albania after the crisis; the regional situation, including the role of UNPREDEP; the situation in border areas; and cooperation between UNPREDEP and the Albanian authorities. The visit resulted in the resumption of regular consultative meetings between UNPREDEP personnel and representatives of the Albanian and Macedonian armies after Albania's crisis. Direct lines of communication were reestablished between Albanian border guards and UNPREDEP in order to ease tensions and avoid incidents in the border areas.

Our Albanian hosts realized well that smuggling was a major problem of the day. The region's main drug route was from Turkey, via Macedonia, to Albania, and then across the Adriatic to Italy. Within the last four months of 1997, not a single box of cigarettes had been declared at customs—extremely odd for a Balkan country. Smuggling was costing the Albanian treasury some U.S. $80 million a year—one-tenth of the national budget in lost revenue. A few days after our visit to Tirana, a coordination meeting took place at the Albanian border town of Pogradec. The force commander, UNCIVPOL chiefs, military observers, representatives of NORDBAT, and senior representatives from the concerned Albanian ministries and other institutions attended the meeting.

HELPING TO CONSTRUCT A CIVIL SOCIETY

Throughout its existence, UNPREDEP tried to be equally useful in extending its channels of assistance in other crucial functions of the newly democratizing state. We drew on our contacts with troop-contributing and other countries to offer international experience to Macedonia's newly established Office of the Ombudsman. We sought help from the United Nations Electoral Assistance Division for the Macedonian Ministry of Justice and the National Election Commission in drafting a new electoral law for the country. Indeed, the United Nations has had extensive experience in electoral advisory services. At the time, the number of requests from governments was steadily growing, while resources to meet them were stretched to the limit: in 1998, there were twenty-one requests for such services, and the next year registered eight more; in 2000, they increased to forty-seven.[94] Still, UNPREDEP managed to obtain the services of a special consultant to come to Macedonia during the preparation of the new electoral law in 1998. Together with experts from the OSCE, the Council of Europe, and the National Democratic Institute in Washington, D.C., they made an important contribution to the drafting of the new law. Prime Minister Crvenkovski's government had consulted with the opposition parties on the text and included a number of their comments in the final draft.

Mobilizing political support

Because one of my main tasks as the SRSG in this new country was to mobilize political and material support relevant to the terms of the mission's mandate, UNPREDEP placed considerable emphasis on establishing an overall policy to guide peacebuilding activities in Macedonia. We realized only too well that, to a large extent, the country's peace and stability—the cornerstones of our mandate—hinged upon a more rapid program of socioeconomic development. This was an issue of major political significance, which the international donor community did not seem to grasp properly. With this conviction, I decided to attend the World Bank and EU Consultative Group Meeting for Macedonia, held on February

25–26, 1997 in Brussels. The group's task was to discuss levels of international development assistance to Macedonia and accept new pledges from governments and international organizations.

In my statement at the meeting, I sought to explain that UNPRE-DEP—unlike a conventional peacekeeping operation—had been established not to restore peace and stability in the host country but, rather, to consolidate them. "Consolidating" versus "restoring" was not just a matter of semantics but one of profound political essence. The former was proactive—the other, reactive. If democratization was a process that led to a more open, more participatory, and less authoritarian society, such a process, notwithstanding difficulties, was consistently making headway in Macedonia. Naturally, each society determines its nature and pace of democratization. However, a country in such a profound transformation as Macedonia could not accomplish its goal of full democratization immediately or singlehandedly. Democratization, therefore, should be conceived as a new and important area of technical assistance. Yet, support for democratization could not but be coupled with support for Macedonia's social and economic development. Strengthening civil society without concurrently addressing state capacity could very well undermine governability or overwhelm brittle state institutions. External assistance in that last regard constituted at the same time an acid test for the progress of democratization at the international level.

My plea was urgent and direct: The failure of the international community to come forward with timely and effective interventions in the former Yugoslavia had consequently gotten it much more involved with an inconceivably heavy price to pay. Prevention, as a cost-effective antidote to the intractability of conflicts, remained the call of the day for the young republic. Regrettably, the meeting did not generate an impressive amount of pledges for development assistance to Macedonia. The donor community again showed little understanding for Macedonia's special position or for its requirements as a major factor in regional peace and stability.

Exploring preventive action

When UNPREDEP became an independent mission, the science of prevention had been a nascent branch of international statecraft. We knew that a mission like ours could make a contribution to exploring the pros and cons of prevention, particularly in terms of relationships between its practical and scholarly considerations. The idea of an international gathering to discuss the subject in detail at the venue of the first comprehensive preventive operation seemed a natural course to follow. The main problem to solve, however, boiled down to finances. We were fortunate to draw the attention of our distinguished colleague, Ambassador Tore Bøgh, head of the OSCE Spillover Monitor Mission in Skopje, who helped us identify an interested implementing institution—the Norwegian Institute of International Affairs in Oslo. We soon obtained agreement for sponsorship of the meeting by Macedonia's Ministry of Foreign Affairs and the Center for Democracy in Washington, D.C. A fundraising campaign started to provide sufficient resources to bring several dozen leading experts in peacekeeping and preventive diplomacy to Skopje. In less than a year, we collected enough money to start intensive preparations for the meeting. Our generous contributors were the governments of Japan, Norway, Sweden, and Switzerland, as well as the Friedrich Ebert Foundation and the Furth Family Foundation in the United States. On October 16, 1996, we opened a four-day international workshop, "An Agenda for Preventive Diplomacy: Theory and Practice."

The workshop was one of the first international meetings of this size and political significance in Macedonia since independence. Its opening ceremony assembled the entire political leadership of the country, academics, and numerous supporters of UNPREDEP. In his message to the workshop, Secretary-General Boutros-Ghali stated that

> it was not enough for the international community to pay lip service to preventive diplomacy. . . . Rhetoric must be matched with deeds, theory must be clearly linked with practice. . . . UNPREDEP is an effective demonstration of what can be accomplished in the realm of conflict prevention when the international community demonstrates political will and acts decisively and promptly.[95]

Addressing the meeting, President Gligorov emphasized that the Security Council's decision to deploy peacekeeping troops in 1992 had been fully justified by subsequent events in the region, adding that the presence of the UN's Blue Berets clearly demonstrated the international community's interest in the security of his country.

More than seventy leading scholars and practitioners of preventive diplomacy participated in the workshop, whose discussions focused on the history of preventive diplomacy and its contemporary application, high-lighted the Macedonian experience, and examined other examples from Burundi, the Caucasus, Haiti, and the Baltic states.[96] One of the proposals advanced at the meeting was the establishment in Skopje of an International Center for Preventive Action and Conflict Resolution. Thanks to the efforts of committed people in Macedonia and the United Nations, the initiative became a reality, when in the fall of 2000, the center was officially launched at Skopje University.

Macedonia's Ministry of Culture and UNPREDEP organized a special concert, "Living Together," to celebrate the convocation of the workshop. A leading Macedonian producer, Nikola Dimushevski, produced the per-formance, which consisted of songs and dances of all of Macedonia's eth-nic groups. The program of the event stressed the following:

> The aim of "Living Together" is to combine folk, classical, and modern music and dance, representing the whole range of Macedonian ethnic tra-ditions. It also aims to be an expression of cultural tolerance without polit-ical boundaries and an illustration of how people, regardless of race, color, gender, or ethnic or religious background, can understand and appreciate each other's similarities and differences.

Unavoidable differences

Successive UN secretaries-general closely followed the work of UNPREDEP's political component, especially in connection with the SRSG's good offices mandate. Their interest was duly reflected in their reports to the Security Council. In the mid-point of the operation, Secretary-General Boutros-Ghali informed council members that com-ponents of UNPREDEP with responsibility for political and humanitar-ian matters had maintained an active dialogue with all political forces and ethnic groups in the country. As a result, UNPREDEP had been recog-nized as a significant instrument for facilitating dialogue, restraint, and practical compromise between different segments of Macedonian socie-ty.[97] A year later, the Security Council was told that the civilian compo-nent of the mission had utilized the good offices mandate vested in the SRSG: UNPREDEP's purpose was to bring together the various com-munities in an effort to promote mutual understanding, strengthen respect for human rights, and ease political and interethnic tensions in the country.[98]

In the latter half of 1997, we began receiving more frequent signals from sources in the Macedonian government strongly discouraging us from pursuing activities beyond tasks directly related to troop deployment and border monitoring. The secretary-general reacted promptly, informing the council:

In meetings with my Special Representative, officials of the host government have made it clear to him that there would be a very limited scope for the extension of his good offices role into the area of interethnic relations, considering that there are already several parallel initiatives dealing with the related issues. While my Special Representative has, therefore, not been able to pursue a more active role in this regard, he has continued to report on interethnic issues and developments with a bearing on internal peace and stability. In general, there seems to be growing recognition of the need for traditional steps to be taken to harmonize interethnic relations in order to enhance internal stability which, in turn, would have positive effects on the stability of the Balkan region as a whole.[99]

Ultimately, the Macedonian government's reservations did not have much negative impact on UNPREDEP's mandate implementation. The formula of its political part to use good offices "in cooperation with the authorities" of Macedonia and "as appropriate" had in itself implied a certain degree of contention. UNPREDEP's well-established cooperative relations at all levels of the political scene were extremely helpful and mitigating in this regard. Yet it is true that consecutive coalitions that ruled Macedonia during UNPREDEP's six-year presence in the country failed to use the time to work out a sufficiently constructive interethnic rapprochement.

If UNPREDEP's first two pillars encountered some resistance in the attempt to tackle Macedonia's fundamental cause of conflict, we could always rely on a broader approach that would seek interethnic rapprochement through developmental goals—that is, steering the new country's government services and social institutions toward more inclusiveness by bringing them in line with international standards and making them more efficient and equitable. Indeed, troop deployments (peacekeeping) and good offices (peacemaking) are highly visible and directed modalities to bring about peace and stability. The broader technique of fostering civil society through social and economic development (peacebuilding) is certainly more unobtrusive, but it is also a much more difficult method of trying to resolve economic and social inequalities, first and foremost because its scope is so wide: after all, how does a small UN mission try to set an entire society aright? This is the basic question—and task—examined in the next chapter.

5

THE HUMAN DIMENSION

THE DEBATES IN THE SECURITY COUNCIL on peacebuilding and Kofi Annan's report on "Prevention of Armed Conflict" have in many respects revolutionized the traditional approach to, and the practice of, preventive peacekeeping.[1] As if in anticipation of these new approaches, UNPREDEP acted on the assumption that "for early prevention to be effective, the multidimensional root causes of conflict need to be identified and addressed" and that "conflict prevention and sustainable development are mutually reinforcing."[2] Also, the Brahimi Report reinforced the conviction that "effective peacebuilding is, in effect, a hybrid of political and development activities targeted at the sources of conflict."[3] These assumptions formed the plinth of UNPREDEP's third pillar.

In our specific case, the human dimension of the conflict assumed a focus of its own. There was much to be done in the area of social integration and institution building, especially in the context of implementing duly approved international standards. The impact of Macedonia's transition could not but directly affect the social peace in a country recovering from the ills of a planned economy, and one that was reckoned to be the poorest among the former Yugoslav federation's republics. The attention devoted to the "human dimension" added greatly to the multiplier effect generated by the development of other preventive techniques and was an important confidence-building measure between the host country and the international community. It placed the preventive operation in the forefront of the development process rather than in the role of a passive observer. Finally, it constituted part of the preparations for successor arrangements to be instituted once the preventive peacekeeping mission left the host country. It was obvious to us that most of the projects and activities would, in the longer term, be much more effectively taken over by other international organizations and agencies, particularly by the Bretton Woods institutions, the United Nations Development Program (UNDP), and other relevant agencies of the UN system. Their programs represented macro-scale development, whereas ours would not go beyond its micro counterpart. This is why UNPREDEP was so vitally interested in establishing a UNDP office in Skopje, an effort that succeeded only in 1998.

Three points should be borne in mind to set our human dimension component in its proper perspective. First, we had no budget at all for peacebuilding projects.[4] Second, even though some funds could be raised from extrabudgetary sources, there was little hope of adding staff to the operation to address issues that, at the time, had not been given due international priority. Third, our notion of the human dimension should not be confused with the same term used by the OSCE. The two notions are complementary but differ somewhat in the scope of their substance.[5]

With respect to the first point, every time we had an interesting project, we would embark on an active fundraising campaign among interested member states, international organizations, or NGOs. In many instances, our efforts proved successful: UNPREDEP garnered close to U.S. $8 million in cash and kind to support various projects benefiting Macedonia.[6] Because we could not count on additional staff for these projects, we relied heavily on cooperating institutions and organizations in most cases. Moreover, for most projects, we had the full support and active involvement of Macedonia's Ministries of Foreign Affairs, Labor and Social Affairs, and Justice, as well as the Ministry of Internal Affairs; Macedonian authorities reviewed and endorsed every initiative. The tireless efforts of my special assistant, Vera Mehta, were part and parcel of the human dimension component—so much so that, among our hosts in Macedonia, she had been known as the SRSG's "secret weapon."

THE THIRD PILLAR IN ACTION

In all its actions under the human dimension pillar, UNPREDEP mapped out a clear path—toward civil society. First and foremost, the effort concentrated on bringing home the message that state and society were two complementary forces. In pursuing this objective, we resorted to various forms of both structural and operational prevention. Social development and crime prevention were the two major areas that called for priority treatment. Thanks to the generous financial contribution by the government of Finland in cooperation with the UN-affiliated European Center for Social Policy and Research, we managed to bring to Skopje a team of experts on social policy. Under the leadership of Professor Vappu Taipale, director-general of Finland's National Research and Development Center (STAKES), the team—known as the Intersectoral Mission on Developmental Social Issues—visited Macedonia from May 27 to June 5, 1996, with the following tasks assigned to it:[7]

◆ To evaluate the existing levels of programs and services in the country and to make recommendations on how they could be gradually upgraded to the norms prescribed by international standards, particularly in the Plan of Action laid down by the 1995 Summit for Social Development in Copenhagen and its major components—the elimination of poverty and the creation of employment and social integration.

◆ To outline policy directions for the future.

◆ To suggest specific model programs and services that could be undertaken as pilot projects through international assistance.

◆ To identify the areas of the action plan that Macedonia could embark on with its own resources and those that would require international support.

◆ To recommend human resource requirements and training approaches essential for the preparation of the needed cadre and personnel.

◆ To assess the potential for civil society and make recommendations for its effective development so as to complement governmental plans of action.

The Intersectoral Mission submitted a comprehensive report covering social policy and developmental welfare in Macedonia, the existing involvement of international organizations, job creation, and approaches to overcoming poverty and facilitating social integration, including a list of priorities and principles to inform change.[8] The report contained ten policy recommendations and ten model projects to advance Macedonia's social development processes: establishing a social development commission, expanding the scope of collaboration with international organizations, effectively monitoring and analyzing public policy, founding an equal opportunities commission, decentralizing service provision, developing a continuum of care facilities and policies, improving educational standards, empowering and involving local NGOs in civil society, offering job creation schemes for the unemployed, and reassessing the population policy.

The ten model projects, which were meant to demonstrate how certain policy recommendations could be implemented in practice, included the creation of a social policy and social care think tank; training of trainers in social policy, social work, and social development; professional practice in social welfare institutions; home-based early childhood education; welfare for the elderly; community development in the Roma district; nonviolent conflict resolution in schools and teacher-training programs and training specialists in interethnic relations; NGO incubators; micro-credit assistance for women; and establishing cooperation in social care.

The total cost of the projects' implementation was estimated at about U.S. $4 million within a period of up to four years. The Intersectoral Mission identified the projects as examples of small-scale initiatives that either the government or appropriate local authorities or NGOs could undertake. The mission believed the projects were cost-effective enough to demonstrate how changes in policies and practices brought about by these small-scale initiatives might be subsequently institutionalized by the Macedonian government. In the initial phase, a time-consuming fundraising provided resources for launching six projects under the overall program "Action for Social Change":

Establishing a social policy and social care think tank. Finland's STAKES made a financial contribution that allowed us to start this proj-

the International Crime (Victim) Survey. The project was jointly undertaken by Macedonia's Institute of Sociological, Political, and Legal Studies; the Law Faculty of the Skopje University; and the Republican Institute for the Advancement of Justice and Internal Affairs. Macedonia thus became the fifty-first country to participate in the project. The findings of the survey, as well as Macedonian police involvement in it, helped in the development of integrated criminal justice information data and the introduction of improved services to victims.

Another joint project, "Policing and Human Rights, 1997–2000," developed within a forty-country program of the Council of Europe, incorporated a comprehensive strategy on human rights in police work. In addition, two training courses were organized for senior departmental heads and chiefs of various police units in May and June 1998 in Skopje and Tetovo; thirty officials participated in each. The courses covered subjects such as modern management techniques, the human rights dimension of police work, and community policing, as well as values and ethics for police personnel. A third course on the same topic took place June 23–25 in Kumanovo, another town with a multiethnic population.

On UNPREDEP's initiative, several other projects were formulated on issues vital to domestic crime prevention and criminal justice and submitted to prospective donors. Upon the termination of UNPREDEP's mandate, follow-up on these as well as new initiatives was taken over by the United Nations Office for Drug Control and Crime Prevention in Vienna and the newly established UNDP office in Skopje.

Continuous action

Success in peacebuilding can be assured only if action on its behalf is consistent and carried out in a continuum of action. In the conditions surrounding UNPREDEP, this was a giant task. One major obstacle, for example, was the international community's underestimation of the need for peacebuilding initiatives in preventive actions and the consequent failure to organize a large-scale conference of donors in support of more developmental policy projects in Macedonia. In spite of this major hurdle, we took up the challenge.

First, we decided to make the basic international standards on social issues available to Macedonian policymakers, academics, practitioners, and local authorities in their own language. Through the joint effort of

Finland's STAKES, the government of Slovenia, and UNICEF–Skopje, we translated and published the following major global standards in Macedonian: the Vienna International Plan of Action on Aging (1982); United Nations Principles for Older Person (1991); Strategy for the Year 2000 on Aging (1992); World Program of Action Concerning Disabled Persons (1982); Standard Rules on the Equalization of Opportunities of People with Disability (1993); Agenda 21: Program of Action for Sustainable Development; the Rio Declaration on Environment and Development (1992); Program of Action on Population and Development, Cairo (1994); Copenhagen Declaration and Program of Action of the World Summit for Social Development (1995); Platform of Action for Women and the Beijing Declaration (1995); Global Program of Action for Youth to the Year 2000 and Beyond (1995); and An Agenda for Development.[10] The global plans and programs of action proved to be most valuable tools in helping Macedonian officials at all levels understand the significance of UN standards for countries trying to establish or re-establish civil society.

UNPREDEP also initiated and pursued an active program in which foreign experts and guest speakers on social policy issues shared their experience with Macedonian colleagues. The series started with Swanee Hunt, U.S. ambassador to Austria. She made three important appearances while in Skopje, addressing the subjects of "Women in Transitional Societies: Passive Observers or Dynamic Agents," "Working Together on Women's Issues," and "By Women, For Women: An Agenda for the Future." These meetings, which brought together some three hundred women's leaders, helped raise the awareness of women's groups and their need to work together. Professor Charles Garvin of the University of Michigan held a two-day intensive training seminar on the methods of service delivery and strategies of social action and social change; a few hundred participants attended his lectures.

As part of a project on training activities for national capacity-building, Professor Colin Pritchard of the University of Southampton conducted a series of seminars focusing on social welfare services; more than two hundred professionals attended his seminars in different parts of the country. Helen Clemenshaw, director of the Center for Family Studies and the Center for Family Friendly Cities of the University of Akron, advised professional audiences on family issues and family-based intervention strategies. Professor

Hubert Campfens of the Wilfrid Laurier University's Faculty of Social Work offered a series of seminars on community development, popular participation, and mobilization of local resources; he also addressed women's groups on "Women's Leadership Roles in Promoting Social Development and Community Change." Professor Arline Prigoff of the University of California visited several regions of the country, conducting seminars for more than a dozen major women's NGOs; the seminars focused on needs assessment, project planning, and the evaluation and monitoring of programs as they affect women, their families, and communities. Professor Shimon Spiro of the Paul Boerwald School of Social Work in Tel Aviv made a similar contribution to the promotion of social policy issues. Altogether, between July 1996 and May 1997 these eminent experts conducted twenty-five workshops and seminars for fifteen hundred professionals throughout the country. They also had an important share in helping to establish postgraduate studies at Skopje University's Institute of Social Work and Social Policy.

The empowerment of women figured prominently in UNPREDEP's human dimension outreach. For two years running, we organized the March 8 observance of International Women's Day with local NGOs and representatives of relevant government agencies. The 1997 observance coincided with a symposium we organized with an interethnic panel of speakers, "Gender Equality: Fact or Fiction?" which reviewed women's position in Macedonian society regarding political participation, health, employment, law, social status, and mass media. In subsequent years, UNPREDEP joined Macedonian organizations in observing International Women's Day at the national level.

Out of concern over the situation of other vulnerable social groups, we encouraged the preparation of a report on the situation of persons with disabilities in Macedonia. The Macedonian Union of Associations for Persons with Disabilities prepared the analysis and, together with the Ministry of Labor and Social Policy, we invited the special rapporteur of the United Nations Commission for Social Development, Bengt Lindquist, to visit Macedonia. Using the report and its recommendations as a starting point, Lindquist assessed the needs of and problems facing persons with disabilities. He made a number of his own practical recommendations and advocated a closer dialogue between the government and citizens' action groups. His discussions at the highest government level and meetings with professional groups considerably raised the awareness of disability issues among Macedonia's social policymakers. The Macedonian government and NGOs representing people with various disabilities agreed to establish an intersectoral coordinating body as well as a monitoring mechanism for the implementation of the Standard Rules on the Equalization of Opportunities of Persons with Disabilities.

A unique project was generated by a grant from the Voluntary Fund for the International Year of the Family. On UNPREDEP's initiative, the Fund granted the Republican Bureau of Employment and the Skopje City Employment Bureau the sum of U.S. $50,000 to launch a self-employment and income-generating project for unemployed families. Grants of up to $5,000 each were given to families, all of which had been on social assistance, selected through a public competition for credit awards. Twelve micro-scale businesses were established, including cosmetics production and sales, a café, taxi and transport services, a bakery and pastry shop, computer data services, polyester and concrete mould casting, a restaurant, a bookshop, and a lawyer's office. The credits were repayable in installments within a few years, to a fund that offered support for projects of newly selected unemployed families. We also obtained several scholarships for Macedonian citizens to be trained in NGO development, agriculture, and higher medical education at the Golda Meir Mount Carmel Training Center in Haifa, Israel. Finally, having launched a worldwide book collection drive, we managed to offer more than five hundred books on professional issues to the Institute of Social Work and Social Policy. The books had been donated by academic institutions in the United States and Europe, specialized agencies of the UN system, the STAKES of Finland, and individual academics.

PUBLIC OUTREACH AND UNPREDEP'S IMAGE

Public relations and public information may seem like incidental concerns, given the somewhat urgent nature of UNPREDEP's mandate, but they represent one of peacekeeping's main arms of action; to a considerable extent, they condition the degree of a mission's success—especially if the mission has a preventive aspect that touches on all the institutions and integument of a country's society. In her excellent book on peacekeeping and public information, Ingrid Lehmann distinguishes six principles of communication for peacekeeping operations:

◆ Public perceptions are a strategic factor that affect conflict resolution and peacekeeping operations at all levels.

◆ International public opinion and local public concerns interact to create images of UN peacekeeping operations that, once established, become inseparable from, and exercise continuing influence on, the political process.

◆ To be effective in implementing their mandates, field missions must, from the outset, include external (public) and internal information programs as a strategic and operational-level management function.

◆ In the peacekeeping environment of the 1990s, education campaigns on specific issues, such as human rights, electoral processes, and the rule of law, were important components of peacekeeping operations.

◆ Information campaigns in peacekeeping missions must be culturally sensitive to the host country's information environment without compromising principles such as freedom of the press and human rights.

◆ Peacekeeping operations are conducted in an open environment in which transparency of policy and objectives is a principal characteristic of the management of the mission.[11]

Indeed, these principles are equally applicable to both preventive and post-conflict situations. Both UNPROFOR's Macedonian branch and UNPREDEP always had a small public information unit run by an international staff member and, during the first few years, assisted by a larger office at UNPROFOR headquarters in Zagreb. Because of its unique preventive mandate, the early years of the operation received a great and rather uncommon interest from national and international media, and the mission's small staff and officers in its military component made tireless efforts to cope with the daily demand for information. At the outset, the Civil Affairs Office established an information program to explain the role of UNPROFOR in Macedonia; its focus was to ensure that the public be given a variety of opportunities to understand the reasons for UNPROFOR's presence and the nature of its deployment. Initially, the public at large did not fully understand the rationale for deployment, so UNPROFOR formulated and pursued an open information policy involving close and constant contacts with the local media.[12]

The mission's evolution to independent status also benefited its public information activities. The operation gradually evolved from a narrowly conceived, psychological disincentive into a significant factor for regional stability: its monitoring, reporting, and good offices functions provided a new and different kind of deterrent, and this evolution had a substantial impact on the public perception of the operation. Particularly at the local level, this evolution was very positive, as the public profile of the mission gradually changed from peacekeeping at Macedonia's borders to include peacebuilding throughout the country's interior.

To ensure the required transparency of the mission's functioning, we consistently followed these precepts underlying our information strategy:

♦ UNPREDEP was an integrated United Nations operation functioning in a sovereign country.

♦ The final responsibility for public information policy rested with the SRSG.

♦ As with all UN operations, public information was an intrinsic element of the mission's political strategy and deserved the highest priority.

♦ All public information activities should maintain a balance between UNPREDEP's paramount international interest and those of the national contingents.

♦ Careful coordination between national battalions and UNPREDEP headquarters on all media-related matters ensured that the mission spoke with one voice, which was essential to a coherent public information program.

♦ Media inquiries regarding the activities of the United Nations, the mandate of the mission, and the role of the different components of the operation—both political and military—were directed through the spokesperson/press and information officer (PIO) at UNPREDEP headquarters.

♦ Media inquiries regarding the military duties of individual national contingents were directed through the battalion PIOs.

♦ The battalion PIOs played an important role in keeping their own national media informed about the tasks and functions of their contingents in UNPREDEP and their day-to-day operations.

The small UNPREDEP Press and Information Unit, effectively headed by Clair Grimes and, subsequently, Marc McEvoy, provided timely information to the media and promoted good relations between the operation and the local community through outreach programs and dissemination of public information materials. In close consultation with the SRSG and the FC, the PIO/spokesperson daily informed the media of significant developments and ongoing operations in the mission area. The spokesperson used several communication tools to carry out this vital function, including interviews, press releases, and ad hoc press conferences. The PIO produced and disseminated a range of UNPREDEP promotional items, including brochures, posters, stickers, calendars, bookmarks, greeting cards, and folders. In addition, the unit translated and distributed printed materials that promoted the work of the United Nations and produced information packets with Security Council resolutions, reports of the UN secretary-general, biographies of the commanding officers, and fact sheets. The PIO's local staff summarized and analyzed the daily Macedonian press, in both Macedonian and Albanian, as well as the content of current affairs programming in the broadcast media.[13]

Consistency of action is as important in public information activities as it is in the substance of peacekeeping, which is why we tried to pursue a continuous program of public relations to promote the mission's objectives. The mood regarding UNPREDEP among the Macedonian media was receptive: The main broadcaster in particular, Macedonian Radio and Television, was very supportive of UNPREDEP and usually endorsed its public information ventures. Occasional problems arose with media ventures just entering Macedonia's new market economy. For instance, *Dnevnik,* the country's first independent daily set up in 1996 by disgruntled journalists from the main government-controlled newspaper group, sometimes misreported on our activities, clearly out of a desire to appear different from the established press and to promote its own independent reporting. *Vecer,* a daily tabloid—influential because of its leading circulation figures—carried sensationalized stories on UNPREDEP.

The mission's change in status in 1995 coincided with worldwide preparations for the observance of the fiftieth anniversary of the United Nations, and there could hardly have been a better opportunity to bring the image of the world organization closer to the attention of the people of Macedonia. President Gligorov headed Macedonia's national committee for the anniversary; its executive secretary was Ilinka Mitreva, then chairperson of the National Assembly's Foreign Affairs Committee. A single conversation with President Gligorov was all it took to gain acceptance of our offer to join the observances at the national level and to approve a number of our ideas for joint celebrations, which continued from mid-October 1995 through Human Rights Day on December 10.

Hosted by USBAT, a special public concert by the U.S. Army Band preceded the major Macedonian observance of the anniversary, held on October 17 in the Skopje National Theatre. On that latter occasion, the host country's national committee announced an unprecedented publication: a collection of texts of the UN Charter and the International Bill of Human Rights in all six languages spoken in Macedonia—Macedonian, Albanian, Turkish, Serbian, Roma, and Vlach.[14] Locating the texts of these historic documents in the first four languages was rather easy, but we encountered some difficulties in finding Roma and Vlach versions; it took considerable effort to complete the impressive publication. In tribute to the fiftieth anniversary of the United Nations, the delegation of the Union of Veterans of Macedonia called on the chief of mission and the commanding officer to express their appreciation of the organization's work. The veterans union included veterans of the Macedonian resistance movement, which, particularly in the final phases of the Second World War, had been a strong element of the anti-Nazi coalition.

At the same time, UNPREDEP was carrying out an intensive school visitation program. UNPREDEP teams consisting of UN civilian staff, UNCIVPOL officers, and military personnel visited thirty-one schools across the country. A few days later, all of Macedonia's elementary and secondary schools devoted forty-five minutes of their history classes to the United Nations.

Much credit is due to UNPREDEP's publication program for covering as it did each of the mission's three pillars of action. In addition to publications mentioned earlier in this chapter, one major project was the translation and distribution to schools of a Macedonian version of *Everything You Always Wanted to Know about the United Nations* and *The UN in Our Daily Lives*. On UNPREDEP's third pillar alone, we published seventeen special publications on social policy issues, which were widely disseminated to numerous institutions, government agencies, and university faculties. Peacekeepers from the two battalions, UNMOs, and UNCIVPOL officers, along with UNPREDEP's civilians, were active in meeting schoolchildren and organizing and addressing seminars on United Nations.

As anniversary observances continued, Macedonian Public Television, as well as newly established private stations, offered wide coverage of UN issues and anniversary events. On October 27, 1995, we opened a photo exhibition, entitled "Visions," honoring the "UN50" in Skopje's municipal museum. During the following year, the same exhibit was shown in other cities, including Bitola and Tetovo. Toward the end of November, UNPREDEP opened another major photo exhibition, entitled "Working Together for Peace," consisting of numerous vivid photographs of UNPREDEP and UNPF in action; it also depicted the work of UNPREDEP peacekeepers in the field of community services. Finally, on the occasion of Human Rights Day, we cosponsored several additional public events, including a special function at Skopje University and a concert to raise funds for the Macedonian Red Cross.

Unexpected backlashes and joys of prevention

Every peacekeeping operation will be particularly sensitive to its public perception in the host country. UNPREDEP had a positive image in Macedonia, but from time to time we had to deal with unexpected backlashes. In UNPREDEP's case, one came from a group of Macedonia's filmmakers.

In the latter half of 1997, Macedonia released its sixth film since independence, *Gypsy Magic,* depicting the dire poverty of the ethnic Roma community portrayed through the life of a gypsy family. References to UNPREDEP's presence in the country could be found in earlier film productions; this time, however, the element of fiction had been brought down to the level of a degrading presentation that had nothing to do with reality. One of the key characters in the film—an UNPREDEP medical doctor from India—was shown as engaging in alcohol and drug abuse, as well as in some rather perverse behavior. The film portrayed other peacekeepers as shooting and threatening violence, along with other unbecoming and abusive actions. These portrayals of United Nations peacekeepers were distasteful, creating an outright derogatory image of UNPREDEP among the people we were trying to serve. Having seen the film, I decided to write a letter to the minister of culture, whose ministry had actually covered the bulk of the film's total costs of U.S. $1.2 million. Regrettably, the reply was far from satisfactory and confined merely to the defense of artistic license.

In the latter half of 1996 two popular songs in honor of UNPREDEP appeared in two public concerts. One, "UNPREDEP in Macedonia," was sung at the concert "Living Together," on the occasion of the international workshop on preventive diplomacy in mid-October.[15] The other, "The Peacekeepers of UNPREDEP," was performed at the closing concert of the Third Festival of Army Songs in late November.[16] Their lyrics read as follows:

"UNPREDEP in Macedonia"
We are here every day
To keep the peace night and day
To keep it and defend it from all sides
Our ship has sailed out
To stop the dark and dreadful storm
Before it comes and gathers in the sky
All the children are in us
All their games are our arms
We prefer the noisy playgrounds to the fronts

> *Refrain:* To keep the peace here, in the world
> To see the people free to smile
> Our mission brings you back your safety and your dreams
> UNPREDEP IN MACEDONIA.

"The Peacekeepers of UNPREDEP"
The borderlines of this small land,
Valleys, rivers and mountain peaks,
Defended are by soldiers young
Macedonia and UNPREDEP
They came to us from all the world
The peacemakers from UNPREDEP
To our land, the holy land,
Peacekeepers for many years.

> *Refrain:* Only peace we bring to Macedonia
> Only peace for such a place of sun and warmth,
> Only peace we bring to Macedonia,
> Only peace for such a place of sun and warmth,
> Such a place of sun and warmth.

We were also aware that the prominent Macedonian sculptor, Tome

Serafimovski, had donated a sculpture in honor of peacekeeping. The government planned to place the impressive sculpture in Skopje's city park. These and other small joys compensated greatly for the occasional misunderstandings of UNPREDEP's role or its intentions.

The public image

What counted most, however, were the effects of UNPREDEP's public outreach programs and the overall image the mission had among the Macedonian populace. Our own contacts with various groups indicated that the operation enjoyed much respect and was considered an innovative deterrent against possible external threats. Unfortunately, our modest budget did not allow us to explore these attitudes in greater detail by, for example, commissioning public opinion polls. Some polling was conducted by institutions affiliated with the Macedonian government, and Olga Murdzeva-Skarik and Svetomir Skarik have analyzed some of these results.[17]

The first such poll was taken as early as December 21–24, 1992 by the Agency for Public Opinion Survey of the Republic of Macedonia. In an at-random and anonymous telephone survey, more than six hundred respondents replied to questions regarding the early United Nations presence in the young republic. According to the Skariks' analysis, public opinion was very diverse, with few replies to the questionnaire revealing much unanimity. As much as 48 percent of respondents were not convinced there was a real danger of war in Macedonia, while 50.74 percent did not believe the UN presence would reduce the risk of war. Only 20.50 percent thought that the UN force had arrived to keep peace in Macedonia, and a relatively high percentage (15.87) believed that other reasons were behind UNPROFOR's presence. Close to half (43.47 percent) of the respondents believed that there should have been a national referendum to decide on whether to invite an international force, while only 21.49 percent would have granted the president the right to ask for United Nations peacekeepers.

In the spring of 1996, the Agency for Public Opinion Survey conducted another poll on public perceptions of UNPREDEP, this time using a much more representative sample of twenty-eight hundred respondents, and again, the same survey analysts summarized the results. As much as 73.28 percent of those participating in the poll believed that UNPREDEP represented a new technique in UN peacekeeping; 37.58 percent agreed that the force served Macedonia's interests. Respondents also thought the mission served U.S. interests (21.71 percent), UN interests (16.29 percent) and the interests of the European Union (13.71 percent). Strikingly, 51.29 percent responded that there was no current need for UNPREDEP in Macedonia, and 50.29 percent of respondents thought peace would be preserved regardless of UNPREDEP's presence. Forty percent believed that UNPRDEP would not be able to prevent a war in Macedonia; 36.86 percent disagreed with this opinion.

In her paper, "Preventive Deployment: The Missing Link between Conflict Prevention and Peacebuilding," Skopje University's Lidija Georgieva quotes the results of a 1997 survey based on a random sample of 1,136 respondents.[18] The group consisted of 460 ethnic Macedonians, 233 ethnic Albanians, 152 ethnic Turks, 119 Romas, 112 ethnic Serbs, and 24 others. To the question, "Has UNPREDEP been successful in accomplishing its mandate?" 26.41 percent of the respondents said yes, 14.88 percent thought it was partially successful, 9.07 percent saw the mission as unsuccessful, and 37.06 percent did not know. Responding to the question of whether UNPREDEP should be continued and, if so, in what way, 35.56 percent of those polled said the mission should continue under its existing mandate, 9.07 percent would expand the mandate to interethnic relations, 19.89 would broaden the scope of the tasks to economic and social matters, and 22.53 percent favored UNPREDEP's termination.

The attention we devoted to UNPREDEP's public image may sound self-serving in a way, but there were vital reasons for doing so. Unlike other peacekeeping missions, our mandate was really dependent not only on the international community—which essentially orders a country to stop a conflict with the installation of a peacekeeping mission—but also on Macedonians themselves. We realized that we were supplementing some of the functions a government and a country's leadership should be undertaking, the most visible of which was trying to foster a civil society in which *all* of Macedonia's various ethnic groups could participate.

Of course, a small mission such as UNPREDEP could not possibly handle the task alone: We had many experienced partners in the endeavor, attempting to heal or shore up many social institutions throughout the entire country. In its third pillar, UNPREDEP encompassed many NGOs and UN agencies, and the challenge of coordination was imperative, lest different partners found it advantageous for whatever reason to stray from the steady and directed agenda we formulated for the preventive mission's human dimension component. We all knew the tremendous challenges befalling heads of peacekeeping missions who try to coordinate NGOs' relief work in a postconflict environment, but, again, our mission was different: we didn't have the underlying unity of despair that makes the mission's command, NGOs, and the victims of mass violence find some sort of natural concordance. UNPREDEP was in what amounted to a "preconflict" environment, and departures or separate agendas could undermine the mission's credibility and sense of trust we constantly tried to instill among all Macedonians. That is why we were so concerned about UNPREDEP's public image: every organizational component of the mission's third pillar tasks had to work as an ensemble, and we all had to share our benefits and burdens. Otherwise, we could easily find events spinning out of control and into an abyss we constantly feared.

POOLING TOGETHER

In most instances, successful conflict prevention is not a craft to be undertaken single-handedly, no matter how effective the main actor may be. Indeed, complementary partnerships are precisely what a preventive operation must seek in order to consolidate its accomplishments on behalf of peace and stability; the wider the scope of the mission's work, the more international partners it will need. According to Lund, "no one initiative or actor alone is likely to be able to alter the course of a conflict; what is needed is combinations and mutually supportive interactions of many actors' efforts that all contribute toward an overall peace process."[19] He also stresses that "to a great extent, preventive diplomacy will always require the spontaneous energy and unique ingenuity of many kinds of actors in the different regions who assume responsibility and decide how to take action in their own ways."[20] He rightly concludes that preventive diplomacy is typically and necessarily a multilateral endeavor. Yet he notes that the participants in this endeavor all too often follow divergent approaches and consequently leave gaps in overall preventive coverage.[21]

Successive UN secretaries-general—no doubt the most qualified practitioners of preventive diplomacy—have advanced similar views. Boutros-

Ghali believed that if United Nations efforts are to succeed, the roles of the various actors must be carefully coordinated in an integrated approach to human security.[22] Kofi Annan, in turn, early in his tenure convened the first-ever meeting between the United Nations and regional organizations to be devoted exclusively to "Cooperation in Conflict Prevention."[23] In his view, in an era when the principal threat to human security comes from new, more diverse, and more deadly forms of conflict, the United Nations and regional organizations had an obligation to enhance their cooperation for conflict prevention. The meeting suggested various practical measures to promote such collaboration, including regular consultations, better flows of information, exchanges of liaison officers, extended working-level visits between headquarters, and similar measures as determined on a case-by-case basis.

The major challenge, however, remained marshalling member states' political will for prevention, for ultimately it is they who must undertake the fulfillment of the promise of multilateral conflict prevention. Looking to the experience of the early prevention ventures at that time, including UNPREDEP, the secretary-general and his counterparts from regional organizations mapped out several overriding tenets for effective prevention. These were, most notably, meeting the challenges of early warning and conflict prevention in the twenty-first century, building the capabilities of the United Nations and regional organizations in the field to provide early warning and conflict prevention, and launching collaborative interaction between the United Nations and regional organizations for early warning and preventive action. This marked a first step, as the secretary-general phrased it, in a "journey from a 'culture of reaction' to a 'culture of prevention,'" and laid important groundwork for establishing an organic link between conflict prevention and peacebuilding.[24]

When UNPREDEP was first established in Macedonia, global deliberations on new concepts of preventive action, and the collective approach they called for, were only in their infancy. Indeed, the main features of the overall international effort in Macedonia at the time were its fragmentation and lack of coordination. The effort even appeared counterproductive at times, with the mandates of various actors overlapping but the required complementarity conspicuously missing. This gap was particularly evident in the brief visits to Macedonia by some ad hoc envoys representing individual governments or international organizations. All too often, they based their conclusions on a superficial analysis of domestic developments, consequently engendering prejudice from one or more of the parties in local disputes. A certain tendency on the part of these representatives to overestimate situations and to make sweeping statements did not go without leaving their mark on certain aspects of UNPREDEP's political work. They also enabled the authorities and other political forces to offer conflicting interpretations of developments, depending on momentary political expediency.

The need for greater coordination and complementarity was particularly evident to international actors conducting political and economic programs in Macedonia; three factors seem to have helped them gradually reach such an understanding. First was the reality that "no one person or organization is able to become expert in every dimension of Macedonian society, and thus, all benefit from the perspectives and experiences of others working in the field."[25] The second factor stemmed from Macedonia's growing role in international affairs: the country's entry into the OSCE and the Council of Europe made it a party to those organizations' human rights instruments and standards and to their relevant monitoring procedures. The new state ratified all United Nations standards on human rights and the status of minorities. Macedonia also became bound by certain important political conditions and by requirements for external monitoring as part of its aspirations to join NATO and the European Union. The third factor was that most of us at UNPREDEP became convinced that a preventive action such as ours would have to address issues by implementing effective development activities through what some experts termed "a conflict prevention lens."[26]

Right from the start, we had been aware that we would need partners to pool resources for the tasks ahead. We first sought and found support from United Nations headquarters. Through this crucial relationship we learned that the less micromanagement and the more mutual confidence, the better—particularly between our preventive mission and the Departments of Political Affairs and Peacekeeping Operations. This vital liaison resulted in more effective program delivery, leaving us more time to conceive and plan peacebuilding initiatives. As the first peacekeeping operation of its kind, UNPREDEP had a particular need for all the trust and encouragement that headquarters could provide to be able to establish and develop the concept of early preventive action in an innovative and effective manner.

THE UN FAMILY: TOWARD A COMMON UN HOUSE

Organizations, programs, and agencies of the United Nations system are normally the first allies of action on behalf of peace. Yet at the field level, individual UN entities involved in operational activities all too often pursued their programs independently and without sufficient regard to, or benefit from, one another's presence. Until the mid-1990s, these organizations had only a modest level of representation in Skopje. To carry out the SRSG's responsibility for the coordination of United Nations activities in Macedonia, a mechanism of consultations had been established to implement effectively the terms of reference of the existing representations.[27] At the same time, UNPREDEP actively sought greater involvement by UN agencies not based in Skopje by directly approaching the agencies' headquarters.

Cooperation from members of the UN family was especially important because of their statutory obligations to support the quest for peace, democracy, and stability worldwide. In addition, the UN system offered a unique legal authority for addressing ethnic conflicts.[28] The UN system's contribution counted immensely, too, because of its role in possible exit strategies and successor arrangements that UNPREDEP had always had on the horizon in the eventuality that the operation would one day terminate. In this regard, we pinned our primary hopes on the possibility that the UNDP would establish a presence in Skopje and play a coordinating role. We hoped that, in the wake of UNPREDEP's eventual departure, UNDP would be able to set in place successor arrangements that would reassure the host country of the international community's continued commitment to Macedonia's peace and stability. It took a serious effort on the part of our peacekeeping mission to persuade UNDP to open a country office in Skopje, from which it could run its own program of activities, and which could also continue some of UNPREDEP's "third pillar" projects. Ultimately, the UNDP administrator agreed to establish a small office in Macedonia in August 1995. However, because of the unavoidable bureaucratic procedures involved, such as those in the decision-making process and the shortage of funds, the office did not start functioning until June 1998, under the experienced leadership of Raquel Ragragio. Ironically, some of our less patient Macedonian interlocutors, unaware of the difficulties involved in UNDP's establishing a Skopje office, had suspected UNPREDEP of deliberately delaying UNDP's representation for the alleged purpose of being left free to run its own peacebuilding projects.

UNPREDEP's active mobilization of interagency support for developmental assistance to Macedonia culminated in early 1998 with our decision to convene a "Consultative Meeting of the Entities of the United Nations System on Their Activities in the FY Republic of Macedonia." In initiating the idea of such a meeting, UNPREDEP was guided by the need to enhance the feasibility of actions already under way, to strengthen the UN's presence in the young republic, and to establish closer working relations with host government counterparts. Prior to the meeting we published a summary of UN projects and activities in or on behalf of Macedonia.[29] The inventory consisted of two sections: the first catalogued an impressive array of directed resources from thirty UN system entities, which had readily responded to the initiative.[30] The other section reflected UNPREDEP's track record in proving that a comprehensive operation in early preventive action can mobilize development resources and offer a series of catalytic activities leading toward social peace, human security, and social integration—in addition to providing the invaluable voluntary humanitarian work contributed by its troop component. Because of our restricted mandate and lack of funds, we always stressed the *catalytic* nature of our "human dimension" projects.

The interagency meeting on Macedonia convened in Skopje on March 10, 1998; thirty-one representatives from twenty-two agencies participated. The meeting consisted of a bilateral and an interagency segment. During the first segment, representatives of Macedonia's seventeen government ministries and other institutions made presentations on their cooperation with the United Nations system. The second segment was devoted to reports by the participating UN agencies on how their programs were benefiting Macedonia. Following these segments was a discussion of major issues of concern, including an overall strategy for the future. Participants were also given time to hold individual meetings with their counterpart ministries and to acquaint themselves with the functioning of UNPREDEP.[31]

In opening the meeting, I pointed out that in order to protect peace and stability in the region, notably in Macedonia, it was very important that what we called UNPREDEP's future "exit strategies" did not pre-empt the effectiveness of the earlier "entry strategies," and that the successor arrangements proved to be at least as effective as their predecessors. What we needed at this juncture was a battery of viable collateral arrangements by the entire United Nations system to reinforce the existing types of international presence in the country. This inventory could be achieved primarily in close cooperation with specialized partners in the political, economic, and social fields. Macedonia's small size gave investors in its developmental efforts the advantage of being able to see positive results much more rapidly and effectively than could be done with projects in other states.

The participants in this unprecedented meeting agreed upon a program of action for a consolidated approach to developmental issues, in the form of findings and conclusions meant to guide future activities by concerned entities from the United Nations system in Macedonia (see figure 1).[32] One of the meeting's immediate follow-up activities was a joint effort to implement in Skopje Secretary-General Annan's idea that UN system entities with ongoing missions at the country level, throughout the world, endeavor to enhance interagency coordination and efficiency by using common premises and operating under a single United Nations flag. The government of Prime Minister Crvenkovski had given preliminary agreement to support the project by providing adequate physical accommodations. During his May 1999 visit to Macedonia, Secretary-General Annan thanked Crvenkovski's successor, Prime Minister Georgievski, and his government for having agreed to establish such a "UN House" and to make the premises of UNPREDEP's headquarters available for the purpose.[33]

THE UN CHARTER'S CHAPTER VIII IN THE FIELD

The second source we turned to in our quest for partnership in action was a regional organization—the Conference on (subsequently, Organization for) Security and Cooperation in Europe (CSCE, later OSCE). The United Nations peacekeeping operation in Macedonia had been preceded by the inception in 1992 of the CSCE's Spillover Monitor Mission in Skopje, one of its first field missions.[34] When it established a UN presence in Macedonia, the Security Council took due note of that fact by "welcoming the presence of a mission of the Conference on Security and Cooperation in Europe" in Macedonia and urging "the force presence in the former Yugoslav Republic of Macedonia to coordinate closely with the Conference on Security and Cooperation there."[35]

Figure 1. Findings and Conclusions of the Consultative Meeting of the Entities of the UN System on Their Activties in the Former Yugoslav Republic of Macedonia

1. In line with the evolving philosophy of preventive diplomacy and peacebuilding, as expressed in several pronouncements of the secretary-general and the Security Council, the United Nations Preventive Deployment Force (UNPREDEP) has successfully combined troop deployment, political action, and good offices with the promotion of human development.

2. The government's pronouncements at the consultative meeting have shown that it has charted a course that leads to vigorous actions to address the pressing problems of a difficult transition and has laid the foundation for sustained economic recovery. During the past six years, the Former Yugoslav Republic of Macedonia has made substantial strides in a multiple transition to independent statehood, a free market economy, a pluralist democracy, and an *etat de droit*. Considerable progress has been accomplished in spite of many difficulties encountered in a turbulent environment.

3. The challenges confronting the country in the short run include a substantial reduction of productive capacity and growth in unemployment and its attendant social ills, often exacerbated by the country's exposed geographic position. The problems of drug trafficking, corruption, and criminality are symptoms of deeper underlying social and economic problems that a coherent strategy of the government can effectively address, supported by consistent efforts on the part of the international community.

4. The deliberations of the consultative meting have pointed to a consensus on the main components of a strategy contributing to the preservation and further consolidation of peace, stability, and sustainable development, namely:
   a. regional and international cooperation based on expanded trade, economic, political, and cultural relations, including the exchange of experience on issues of transition;

b. confidence-building measures, including macroeconomic stability, essential to the development of a propitious climate for
business initiatives and for attracting foreign and domestic
investment in agriculture, industry, and services sectors, and
thereby promoting employment;

c. measures to establish an enabling legislative framework for
private sector development;

d. structural reforms and modernization required to prepare the
ground for a competitive export-oriented economy;

e. administrative reforms to strengthen public administration,
corporate governance, and transparency and professionalism
in public sector management, which complement the measures in (b), (c), and (d) above, including the promotion of
human resources development and training;

f. consolidation of an *etat de droit* based on the rule of law, good
governance, social dialogue, an active civil society, and respect
for human rights, underpinning the Office of the Ombudsman;

g. upgrading of physical infrastructure required for the development of industry, including civil aviation, roads and railroads,
and communication networks, tourism, and trade;

h. protection of the environment and health as well as the country's diversified cultural heritage;

i. promotion and facilitation of social service reform, notably
education, social protection, and security and health, consistent with the country's goal of integration into the European
Union.

The participants emphasized that the United Nations system, in
tandem with its partners in the international community, can
facilitate the government's efforts to overcome pressing economic and social problems and lay the foundation for sustainable development.

5. The mission of UNPREDEP has included an important
humanitarian and human development dimension, which has

complemented the military and political functions and served to build confidence between the host country and the United Nations. It has also proved to be catalytic in paving the road for initiatives that several United Nations agencies and other regional organizations have undertaken with considerable success.

6. Both on the side of the government and among the agencies represented at the meeting, there was strong support for the concept of a common "United Nations house," including a resource center of the entire United Nations system in Skopje. Specifically, the host government expressed its firm commitment to the implementation of this idea as a means of facilitating the pursuit of a joint interagency effort and sustainable course of action.

7. The participants welcomed the forthcoming establishment of a United Nations Development Program (UNDP) country office to continue and expand the social action program of UNPREDEP, which thus far has comprised mainly microdevelopment projects. In voicing strong support for an expanded role of the United Nations system, the participants stressed certain important factors that optimize delivery and secure long-term effectiveness. Foremost among these is the need for closer coordination and clear focus of United Nations activities in economic and social development.

8. The meeting participants were informed of the recommendations contained in the recently published national development strategy. They noted that the strategy provided a useful framework for integrating the various operational activities sponsored and undertaken by the United Nations and the wider international community in partnership with the government.

9. The participants recognized that the agencies of the United Nations system in the field needed to force closer operational linkages in the spirit of "one unified system operating under one flag." Every opportunity must be taken to build greater synergies among the programs of the agencies. Accordingly, the participants called for the establishment of a framework for

cooperation based on national priorities, agency complementarities, and shared goals.

10. In the above context, the participants believed that the establishment of a common "United Nations house," including a resource center about the United Nations system in Skopje, would enhance the value, efficiency, and effectiveness of their respective activities in support of national development.

11. To implement their strategy, United Nations agencies, supported by UNDP, as appropriate, should pay particular attention to the following:

   a. assisting the government in its efforts to mobilize resources in support of strategic national goals;

   b. emphasizing all crosscutting issues contained in the decisions and recommendations of the United Nations global conferences of the past two decades;

   c. helping to ensure the compatibility of national legislation with international standards and strengthening the capacity of national structures for their implementation;

   d. establishing a common "United Nations house."

12. In conclusion, the participants thanked UNPREDEP for its timely initiative in organizing the consultative meeting and expressed the hope that the meeting would assist, and pave the way for, a continued presence of the United Nations system, in line with the expressed wishes of the host government. They believed that such presence was necessary and would prove conducive to the consolidation of peace in the region and the successful completion of the process of transition, which would enable the country to meet the major challenges of globalization and integration into the wider European and world communities.

The first collaborative ventures coincided with our efforts to base relations between our two organizations on an effective platform of solid cooperation. At their 1992 Helsinki Summit, the heads of state or government of the CSCE members reached an understanding that the conference was a regional arrangement in the sense of Chapter VIII of the UN Charter, and that as such it provided an important link between European and global security.[36] Proceeding from this important statement, a framework for cooperation and coordination between the UN Secretariat and the CSCE was signed on May 26, 1993.[37] Soon after, the UN General Assembly granted the conference observer status.[38] Ever since, the agendas of the successive regular sessions of the General Assembly have contained an item on "Cooperation between the United Nations and the Organization for Security and Cooperation in Europe," under which it considers the UN secretary-general's periodic reports on the subject.

In one of his reports, the secretary-general referred to the practice of, and an informal understanding on, a division of labor between the two organizations, whereby "the United Nations has retained the lead in peacemaking efforts in Tajikistan and in Abkhazia, Georgia, while OSCE has had the lead on the question of the Nagorno-Karabakh region of Azerbaijan, the Republic of Moldova, and South Ossetia, Georgia."[39] This division alone indicated the extent of confidence and complementarity between the two organizations. On several occasions, the General Assembly acknowledged the OSCE's increasing contributions to the establishment and maintenance of international peace and security in its region through its activities in preventive diplomacy, crisis management, arms control and disarmament, and postcrisis stabilization and rehabilitation measures, as well as the crucial role the OSCE plays in the human dimension.

Under a general mandate "to monitor developments along the border of the Host Country with Serbia and in other areas of the Host Country which may suffer from spillover of the conflict in the former Yugoslavia, in order to promote respect for territorial integrity and the maintenance of peace, stability and security; and to help prevent possible conflict in the region," the Skopje CSCE Mission had been entrusted with a number of tasks, including

◆ continuing dialogue with government authorities of the host party;

◆ establishing contacts with representatives of political parties and other organizations, and with ordinary citizens;

◆ conducting trips to assess the level of stability and the possibility of conflict and unrest;

◆ engaging in other activities compatible with the OSCE goals of the mission as defined above;

◆ maintaining a high profile in the country;

◆ in case of incidents, assisting in establishing the facts.[40]

It takes no great leap of imagination to see that the principal political mandates of both OSCE and UNPREDEP were very much alike. Yet the two missions did not follow redundant programs of action; in fact, their actions were mutually reinforcing rather than overlapping, greatly facilitating their cooperation. Quite early on, the United Nations and CSCE agreed upon and signed the "Principles of Coordination between the United Nations Protection Force (UNPROFOR)–Macedonia Command and the Monitor Mission of the Conference on Security and Cooperation in Europe (CSCE) in the former Yugoslav Republic of Macedonia."[41] Having taken account of the respective mandates of the two missions, the crucial principles for cooperation and coordination compelled them to coordinate their activities closely and establish appropriate mechanisms of cooperation, which included weekly consultation meetings at the head-of-mission level; regular exchanges of situation reports and other relevant information; and coordination of movements. Both missions agreed to refrain from commenting on each other's functioning or activities, particularly in their public pronouncements. Separate commitments addressed the provision of mutual assistance in cases of emergency.

Both missions shared a genuine interest in moving things ahead, which led to our undertaking a number of joint activities. Boutros-Ghali had conceived of five forms of cooperation between the United Nations and regional organizations: consultation, diplomatic support, operational support, codeployment, and joint operations.[42] In Macedonia, neither of us deliberately tried to hold a lead in peacekeeping or peacemaking practice. Our joint methods of work and close cooperation, however, actively involved practicing at least the first three of the five forms on Boutros-Ghali's list. For example, OSCE had little capacity to effectively monitor Macedonia's border with Serbia; the difficult terrain and adverse weather conditions along the border meant that effective monitoring required a constant presence the OSCE could not maintain. UNPREDEP's observation posts and patrols were there permanently, and the UN mission was able to share some of its first-hand findings with its regional partner. To take another example, our respective capabilities in political action were correlative: OSCE's efforts on behalf of its "third basket" or "human dimension" mandates focused primarily on human rights and interethnic relations, allowing UNPREDEP to concentrate more on other elements of the broader notion of human security and to encourage member states, the entire United Nations system, and international NGOs to contribute their developmental share to Macedonia's progress.

Close cooperative relationships were established between the two missions from top to bottom. Frequent meetings between chiefs of mission, including UNPREDEP's force commander, became a common practice; our deputies and other officials would also meet as needed. The OSCE continued hosting weekly meetings among all the international actors in Macedonia, as it had since its inception, without interruption. The general policy on both sides was to encourage more exchanges of information and to arrive at a joint assessment of developments. In his periodic reports to the Security Council, the UN secretary-general would point out that "joint initiatives in good offices by my Special Representative and the head of the OSCE mission have been aimed at underscoring the determination of the international community further to strengthen peace and stability in the former Yugoslav Republic of Macedonia."[43]

Regular meetings of the two heads of mission with President Gligorov were another part of our joint strategy. In most cases, the meetings proved extremely helpful and enlightening. On one such occasion, however, our call on the president was used in a way that somewhat distorted its intention. On July 29, 1996, Ambassador Christian Faber-Rod of the OSCE mission and I met with President Gligorov to assist in the search for a political solution to problems in the aftermath of ethnic demonstrations in Tetovo and the sentencing of five leaders of the so-called Tetovo University. Faber-Rod and I had requested the meeting in order to seek the president's help in obtaining an early release of the ethnic Albanian activists on the grounds that they had been convicted under the old penal law while the new legislation excluded offenses with which the leaders were charged.

Gligorov was quite forthcoming but totally noncommittal, presenting to us a very optimistic picture of interethnic relations in Macedonia at a time when they were actually seriously strained. Following the meeting, the president's office put out a press release, which essentially concluded that "during the discussion, interethnic relations in the Republic of Macedonia were positively assessed, especially within the government coalition with PDP, as was the policy of an increasing participation of Albanians in the educational process at the Skopje and Bitola universities." A few critical comments that followed in some Macedonian-language media outlets, attributing political pressure to our intervention, shed more light on the reasons for President Gligorov's restraint in meeting our concerns.[44]

Several months later, Faber-Rod and I held another joint discussion with the Macedonian president on March 24, 1997. The meeting coincided with the political fallout and street demonstrations following the TAT banking scandal in Bitola. The president was quite open in expressing his disillusionment with some political parties and expressed his hope that the time leading up to the 1998 elections could be used to strengthen legal and democratic practices in the country, but only if all major political parties agreed to join the effort on a national scale. His experience in this regard, however, did not leave him encouraged. He recalled his unsuccessful attempt to involve one of the major opposition parties in negotiations with Greece on the Interim Accord. The only condition, he said, had been to respect the principle of confidentiality in such negotiations on matters vital to the state and to view them as being above party politics. His invitation was not accepted, and he regretted that an important opposition party had declined to assume responsibility for matters of national importance, even to such a small extent. In an extensive exchange of opinions, we encouraged the Macedonian president to take a more active and forthcoming nonpartisan posture toward political developments, which he could then afford, as he was nearing the end of his second term and not running for re-election. President Gligorov listened attentively but was obviously not prepared to make an above-party-politics commitment.

Macedonia's interethnic relations—as described in the preceding chapters—remained central to our common concerns, the core issues being those between ethnic Albanians and ethnic Macedonians. Coordination of the two missions' efforts in this regard certainly posed a challenge, for it was not unusual for both ethnic groups to try to impart conflicting information to one or both of our two missions. Exacerbating this tendency was the fact that ethnic Macedonians did not consider their country's interethnic relations to be a legitimate subject of international concern. In their view, if any international organization was to get involved, it was the OSCE, as it was an entirely civilian mission and, as such, better qualified to deal with the issue than was UNPREDEP. On the other hand, the United Nations, as a depositary of a number of important international human rights instruments, could not shun its own responsibilities in this area; UNPREDEP's mandate, and the secretary-general's reports on its work, were unambiguous on the matter. In such a situation, working together with OSCE eliminated overlaps and allowed for a better coordination of efforts than would have been the case if we had worked separately. In short, the OSCE mission proved to be a responsive ally.

The High Commissioner

Apart from providing day-to-day cooperation on interethnic relations at the level of our two missions, the OSCE had a distinct asset of its own—the office of the High Commissioner on National Minorities (HCNM). Originally conceived in response to developments in the former Yugoslavia, the post was established in 1992 as an instrument to prevent conflicts at the earliest possible stage and quickly became one of the most powerful instruments the OSCE could offer to mitigate inter-ethnic tensions elsewhere in Europe. UNPROFOR's arrival in Macedonia coincided with the January 1993 appointment of Max van der Stoel as the first OSCE High Commissioner on National Minorities.

There could hardly have been a better person for the post. An ardent human rights advocate who had previously served his country as a member of its parliament, minister of foreign affairs, and permanent representative to the United Nations, the Netherlands' van der Stoel combined all the qualities required for the position. Every inch a diplomat, he was straightforward, businesslike, and to the point. Patience and consistency characterized his actions, and his calm and gentle manners in imparting firm points of view impressed his interlocutors. UNPREDEP and his office established excellent relations and frequently exchanged views on current developments in Macedonia, particularly during the HCNM's regular visits to Skopje. The question of minority education, notably minority language education, was at the top of van der Stoel's agenda.[45]

The HCNM's mandate rested on a solid foundation of independence and impartiality, further enhanced by the strong support from major actors in the OSCE as well as from the NGO community. Soon after van der Stoel's appointment, the Foundation on Interethnic Relations was founded in the Hague as an NGO with a view to carrying out specialized activities in support of the HCNM. It proved extremely beneficial in facilitating the elaboration of a general framework to assist states in developing minority education policies. In October 1996, following participation in several international meetings and considerable research, the foundation completed and published *The Hague Recommendations Regarding the Education Rights of National Minorities.*[46] As the authors explain, the recommendations' purpose was to clarify, in relatively straightforward language, the content regarding the rights of minority education that would be generally applicable in situations in which the HCNM might become involved. The drafters of the recommendations had analyzed all of the major international human rights instruments from the point of view of the right of national minorities to education, and their effort proved particularly useful because most international human rights instruments making reference to minority language education are somewhat vague and general on the subject: they make no specific reference to degrees of access, nor do they stipulate which level of "mother tongue" education should be offered to minorities, nor by what means. The recommendations, however, proceed from several basic considerations behind the letter and spirit of such international instruments:

◆ One, that the right of persons belonging to national minorities to maintain their identity can be fully realized only if they acquire a proper knowledge of their mother tongue during the educational process.

◆ Two, that at the same time, persons belonging to national minorities have a responsibility to integrate into the wider national society through the acquisition of a proper knowledge of the state language.

◆ Three, that in applying international instruments that may benefit persons belonging to national minorities, states should consistently adhere to the fundamental principles of equality and nondiscrimination.

◆ Four, that it should be borne in mind that the relevant international obligations and commitments constitute international minimum standards. It would be contrary to their spirit and intent to interpret these obligations and commitments in a restrictive manner.

While the national minorities in Macedonia, notably the ethnic Albanians, insisted that the first of the foregoing points was crucial for their future as Macedonian citizens, their ethnic Macedonian counterparts saw more relevance in the responsibility to integrate into the wider national society through the acquisition of a proper command of the state's primary language. These two trends have constantly competed in Macedonia's public life and balancing them could be considered the greatest challenge to the country's educational process. We at UNPREDEP had no difficulty following the recommendations' line of reasoning and offered our full support to the HCNM in promoting them; after all, as a general framework, the recommendations were based on UN standards and consistent with the policies of the world organization.[47]

The mandates of our two organizations were rather restricted because in order to achieve any meaningful accommodation, we had to obtain full consensus of the parties concerned, which, to say the least, was a complex and time-consuming task under the circumstances. Yet both of our missions closely monitored current developments in interethnic relations and tried, within our restricted mandates, to help solve problems. Van der Stoel concentrated more on long-term solutions to Macedonia's interethnic problems, and chief among them was the question of education for the ethnic Albanian community. The fact that he was not stationed permanently in Skopje gave him more leeway in his numerous discussions with both Macedonia's authorities and leaders of its ethnic communities. During UNPREDEP's presence in Macedonia, from June 1993 to February 1999, the HCNM paid some forty visits to Skopje. From the substantive point of view, the HCNM acted on his own, but our mutual cooperation was also based on the Principles of Coordination between our two missions. What would bring the High Commissioner and us in UNPREDEP into closer interaction was mutual exchange of information on our respective findings and actions, as well as the fact that the HCNM's was a typical preventive repertoire of action that the United Nations also practiced. Even a sketchy chronology of his efforts offers an overview of the impressive gamut of initiatives that, one might expect, could have generated an equally impressive reaction from the parties to whom they were addressed.

On his initial visits to Skopje in 1993, van der Stoel quickly determined that the fundamental issue of Macedonia's interethnic relations was the status and grievances of the ethnic Albanian community, so he made a number of recommendations to both the OSCE and the Macedonian authorities regarding a new population census (to be held under international supervision), interethnic dialogue, minority language education, minority-group participation in public affairs and nondiscrimination in public service, the role of local self-government, and access to media and citizenship. (Ultimately, the census was held in 1994.) At the same time, van der Stoel came out with a project to establish a pedagogical faculty to train teachers, with courses given in Albanian. He also encouraged Macedonia's politicians to strengthen the role of the Council for Interethnic Relations, which had stood practically dormant since the adoption of the new constitution.

A year later, he prepared a report for the Macedonian government focusing on educational opportunities for children of Albanian extraction, particularly at the high school level. He made further comments on the new draft law on local self-government and on its provisions concerning the official use of the languages of national minorities in parts of the country where they constituted either a majority or a sizeable portion of the population. He encouraged the government to follow the lead of other OSCE states and reduce the fifteen-year residence requirement to obtain Macedonian citizenship and to expand the number of Albanian-language television networks and programs in the country.

In 1995, the HCNM concentrated on the major, divisive issue of education—specifically, the initiative of ethnic Albanians to establish "Tetovo University." The unilateral actions of the project's initiators had inflamed interethnic tensions, and the High Commissioner was quite explicit in telling both the government and the ethnic Albanians that international standards guaranteed the right of persons belonging to national minorities to establish their own educational institutions, but that such a prerogative could be exercised only within the framework of, and in conformity with, existing national laws. The HCNM's preventive action in the particular case of the "Tetovo University," as well as the presence of UNCIVPOL monitors during the riots in that city, greatly helped avert a wider confrontation. In the aftermath of these events, van der Stoel advanced a proposal to create a multilingual faculty for public administration and business, funded by foreign donors, that would have English, Macedonian, and Albanian as official languages of instruction. During his successive visits to Macedonia, he worked consistently and with good results to increase the number of ethnic Albanian youth attending secondary schools and the country's two universities. Several of the HCNM's projects had a tangible impact on increasing the number of ethnic Albanians available to serve in public administration.

The following year, van der Stoel convened and chaired the roundtable "Building Harmonious Interethnic Relations in Macedonia," bringing together prominent figures in Macedonia's political and academic life on both sides of the country's major ethnic divide and serving as another useful platform in the search for common ground. The meeting once again demonstrated that genuine dialogue and dignified compromise could ultimately prevent rising ethnic tensions from developing into an ongoing conflagration.

In March 1997 alone, the HCNM visited Macedonia twice on account of disquieting events then taking place, including demonstrations by ethnic Macedonian students against the Law on the Pedagogical Faculty, which had allowed some courses to be conducted in Albanian. He was back in Skopje a few months later in reaction to the tragic demonstrations and violence that had taken place in the town of Gostivar in early July. On that occasion, van der Stoel was allowed to visit the imprisoned mayor of Gostivar and his counterpart from Tetovo. He urged the authorities to conduct a thorough investigation of what had happened in Gostivar and strongly supported the idea of providing international training for the Macedonian police.

The High Commissioner visited Macedonia six times in 1998, firmly convinced that the deteriorating situation in Kosovo warranted paying more attention to Macedonia's interethnic climate. He intensified his efforts in quiet diplomacy, concentrating on the status of ethnic Albanians in Macedonian society; throughout the year, he continued his active involvement in exploring avenues to improve educational opportunities for the country's ethnic Albanians. The Foundation on Interethnic Relations offered its own project to serve this purpose, providing educational support to ethnic Albanian students preparing for entrance examinations to Skopje University. The HCNM also regularly followed up on the results of the investigation of the 1997 Gostivar episode.

On November 6, 1998, van der Stoel issued a statement on several significant aspects of Macedonia's ethnic situation, acknowledging the government's efforts to increase the number of ethnic Albanian students in secondary schools and universities, and calling for new reforms to sustain that process. He further recommended the establishment of an Albanian-language state college to train elementary and secondary school teachers who would use Albanian as their main language of instruction. The

HCNM urged the authorities to agree as well to the establishment of a private trilingual (English, Macedonian, and Albanian) higher education center for public administration and business, and he invited the new government following the 1998 elections to embark on a campaign to recruit ethnic Albanians who might be suitable candidates for public service. He was equally concerned about the need for strengthening local self-government, a step conceived as contributing to an environment conducive to minority rights in a modern state.[48]

The HCNM's visits to Skopje in December 1998 and March 1999 marked the beginning of another phase of cooperation that culminated in 2000 with the adoption of Macedonia's new law on higher education.[49] The importance of van der Stoel's contributions to the drafting of this law is unquestionable: for the first time, all of Macedonia's major political factors agreed that the country's higher education institutions could also be under either private or state administration, that both indigenous and foreign individuals and legal entities could establish institutions of learning, and that education at such private institutions could be performed in both the languages of national minority members and in world languages. These major provisions opened the way to launching Southeast European University in Tetovo, which has largely pre-empted the controversial case of "Tetovo University."

Finally, it was with regard to Macedonia that the HCNM resorted to an important part of his mandate for the first time in his term of office—namely, to

> provide "early warning" and, as appropriate, "early action" at the earliest possible stage in regard to tensions involving national minority issues which have not yet developed beyond an early warning stage, but, in the judgment of the High Commissioner, have the potential to develop into a conflict within the CSCE area, affecting peace, stability, or relations between participating states, requiring the attention of and action by the Council or the CSO [Committee of Senior Officials].[50]

The HCNM visited Macedonia during the 1999 refugee crisis, when some 350,000 ethnic Albanians had crossed the border from Kosovo and dramatically changed the country's ethnic balance. On May 12, 1999, in an address to the OSCE Permanent Council, van der Stoel issued an official early warning that the refugees represented "too big a burden for the country" and that the crisis increased the risk of social discontent and interethnic tensions.[51]

The ICFY

The International Conference on the Former Yugoslavia was another natural partner for UNPREDEP, which worked closely with the conference. Our cooperation centered on humanitarian issues and the promotion of dialogue on human rights matters involving ethnic communities and national minorities. UNPREDEP developed special ties with ICFY's Working Group on Humanitarian Issues and its Working Group on Ethnic and National Communities and Minorities, promoting legislative and administrative changes specifically aimed at improving the situation of all ethnic communities. A series of meetings concentrated on new legislation in the fields of education and self-government; we also held joint discussions on language issues and questions pertaining to citizenship and the display of national symbols by ethnic communities. The Working Group on Ethnic and National Communities and Minorities, under the dynamic chairmanship of a distinguished German diplomat, Ambassador Geert Ahrens, also addressed a number of matters pertaining to the media. Ultimately, this initiative resulted in an agreement between the governments of Denmark and Switzerland and Macedonian Radio and Television providing for the delivery of television equipment that would triple broadcast time in the Albanian language and considerably increase air time for languages of other nationalities.[52]

After the termination of ICFY, UNPREDEP continued to undertake certain tasks in areas where it had cooperated with the conference. Because ICFY had been sponsored by both the United Nations and the European Community (subsequently the European Union), the UN mission in Skopje paid due attention to collaborative ventures and exchange of information with the European Community's monitor mission, then attached to the OSCE Spillover Monitor Mission to Skopje.

Member states

In forging partnerships for prevention, UNPREDEP established special relationships with a number of governments that had shown interest in helping Macedonia on its way to stability and a secure existence.

First in this group were the troop-contributing countries, which were keenly interested in the safety and effectiveness of their soldiers. We maintained regular contacts and day-to-day cooperation with the U.S. mission in

Skopje—first the U.S. Liaison Office and then the American Embassy—headed by refined diplomats and supportive colleagues exemplified by, respectively, Victor Comras and Christopher Hill—the only diplomatic mission of a troop-contributing nation to Macedonia. Denmark, Finland, Indonesia, Norway, and Sweden did not have embassies in the mission area; however, ambassadors from the four Nordic countries accredited to Skopje from other capitals paid frequent visits to UNPREDEP's officials and to their respective troops. These countries were unquestionably leaders in responding to our fundraising efforts, especially on behalf of the "human dimension" pillar of the operation. The Nordic countries always displayed an unusual degree of sensitivity to social problems. They also trusted that UNPREDEP had the skill of selecting future project implementation agencies that would make good use of their financial contributions. Visits by Nordic government ministers added considerably to the value of our political dialogue. Numerous American politicians and high-level military officials were regular visitors to USBAT and UNPREDEP headquarters, yet they were less generous in supporting our projects. Most of the U.S. assistance to Macedonia was offered through bilateral channels, but American nongovernmental institutions and academics, however, lent a great deal of direct support to several UNPREDEP ventures.

The second group of states closely following UNPREDEP's performance were the UN Security Council's permanent members, all of which had embassies in Skopje that systematically sent reports to their capitals on our operation, as well as on all kinds of unconfirmed rumors regarding UNPREDEP's future and the reactions to them. The ambassadors from the Security Council's five permanent member states formed the core group for the visits we periodically organized for local diplomats to our OPs along the borders with the FRY and Albania.

Other interested governments represented a third group of states ready and willing to use UNPREDEP's channels to help Macedonia. Only a few states made up this category, yet they were consistent in their support for a dozen or so developmental projects. Those in the lead were Japan and Switzerland. The first is a country situated far away from Macedonia and the other was not even a member of the United Nations at the time, yet their interest in this small Balkan nation exemplified a welcome case of international solidarity in support of preventive action. Other coparticipants in this network were Austria, France, Italy, Poland, and Slovenia.

NGOS—CARRIERS OF THE SPIRIT OF PREVENTION

UNPREDEP's experience with nongovernmental organizations, both indigenous and international, was very satisfying; though we relied on these types of organizations a great deal in carrying out the mission's "human dimension" tasks, that modifier requires a bit of explanation: Our mutual cooperation began at a time when a global change in approach to the NGO community was taking place. Past experiences had left much prejudice toward NGOs among different political quarters. Yet the watershed change that took place in world affairs in the early 1990s provided a strong impetus for enhancing and recognizing NGOs' constructive roles as carriers of the spirit of prevention, barometers of early warning, and committed peacebuilders. As one observer put it:

> There are many ways that NGOs respond to early rumblings of conflict: They serve as silent witnesses, thus preserving their neutrality; they are annoying witnesses or bell ringers; they are political witnesses, with a mission to arouse an external response. Indigenous NGOs are the more capable of detecting early warning signs; international NGOs are best placed to encourage external intervention and to channel resources to local partners.[53]

The Carnegie Commission on Preventing Deadly Conflict concluded in its report that "NGOs are often the first to be aware of and to act in crisis areas, and they have a wealth of information regarding the conditions and grievances that give rise to violence."[54] To be sure, the role of NGOs is normally based on two crucial tenets of modern democratic society: freedom of association and freedom of expression. The secret of their impressive record lies in their effective application of developmental priorities to achieve political stability in the host society; hence, NGOs will be more successful in building bridges between an exclusive regime and an inclusive civil society, primarily within the framework of intrastate rather than interstate conflicts.

Most authors agree that, given their panoramic view and understanding of conditions "on the ground," NGOs possess several characteristic features that make it easier for them to pursue efforts in preventive action: They are often the first external witnesses that become aware of a possible conflict. They may have more flexibility and neutrality than any other actor on the scene, and their lack of coercive powers may generate more trust among the parties to conflicts. They can afford risks that governments or international organizations may find hard to justify. NGOs can act quickly and try new forms of action in an expeditious manner. Last but not least, they have considerable access to victims during "complex emergencies," as well as a considerable amount of leeway in responding to their needs. At the same time, international NGOs often become "schools" for their local and indigenous counterparts, thereby enhancing the important factor of networking and division of labor among them.

All in all, NGOs offer a unique capacity for exercising conflict resolution techniques of active tolerance building and the promotion of intercultural literacy, especially at the local level. Such capacity is, in fact, the crux of preventive action, extended to the grassroots level—the very place where international preventive operations should have their greatest effect. Aware of these unique NGOs' capacities, we offered much political support to national and international NGOs working in Macedonia on behalf of broadly conceived early conflict prevention. While fully recognizing the great merits NGOs offer in conflict prevention and preventive action, we also had to be aware of the inherent impediments to their work, as must all international civil servants in possible future preventive missions. Many such caveats stem from lingering suspicions and mistrust on the part of various governments toward NGOs' role in society and in the world at large. NGOs will take a lesser preventive role in places where a primary military action is simultaneously occurring, so one must be constantly aware of such problems to avoid unnecessary disillusionment and frustration and to adjust appropriate responses to the inescapable dilemmas involved in NGOs' missions in these areas of operation.

Nor can one exclude the possibility that there will be situations when some NGOs will tend to overestimate their own role. In other cases, there may be charges that NGOs are pursuing their own hidden agendas. In Macedonia, for instance, ethnic tensions led to perceptions that some international NGOs—rightly or wrongly—were partial protectors of, and advocates for, ethnic Albanians.

The local landscape

When the UN peacekeeping mission first arrived in Macedonia, a number of international NGOs were already there, working on their various programs. They had monitored the first general and presidential elections, launched projects to tackle national political and ethnic cleavages, and started conflict resolution training and the establishment of national

NGOs. Much credit for the continuous effort in this regard is due to the Open Society Institute–Macedonia, Search for Common Ground, and the Friedrich Ebert Foundation, as well as to the National Democratic Institute in Washington, D.C., Catholic Relief Services, the International Research and Exchanges Board (IREX), the Institute of Sustainable Communities, and the International Red Cross. There were very few indigenous NGOs in Macedonia that could be described as typical civil society NGOs. Traditional NGOs work there had just not been done; those that were called "nongovernmental" concerned themselves mainly with artistic or cultural activities. Notable exceptions were the war veterans organization and some women's groups. Moreover, registering an NGO with the authorities involved cumbersome formalities that discouraged such action. Thus the bulk of preventive work normally pursued by NGOs in conflict situations was performed by their international counterparts.[55]

Nonetheless, right from its inception UNPREDEP tried to reach out to the kind of important civic groups that normally would form a community of nongovernmental organizations or institutions. We organized a number of joint functions in cooperation with the Union of Women's Organizations in Macedonia and the Organization of Women of Macedonia. Ethnic Albanian women had their own organization, which also maintained relations with our civilian component. The Skopje-based Center for Ethnic Relations and the Center for Multicultural Understanding and Cooperation worked with UNPREDEP on several projects, including one on "Future Leaders: Catalysts of Tolerance."

Most active in our work with NGOs, of course, were the youth organizations, as discussed in the previous chapter. The youth wings of different political parties and the two student unions at the Universities of Skopje and Bitola all took part in our major projects on youth, such as the seminar and publication on "Youth as Bridge Builders in Multiethnic Communities," a workshop on "Youth: The Young Promoters of Tolerance," an intensive training seminar on youth leadership, and the establishment of language and computer centers.

UNPREDEP had equally fruitful contacts with the Association of War Veterans and the Macedonian Red Cross. All these actions proved to be effective instruments of raising awareness of NGOs' role in shaping up a civil society.

Our international allies

Several major international NGOs generously supported UNPREDEP's projects, both financially and professionally; a few of these stand out as giants in their respective fields. Their long-standing experience in conflict prevention and their confidence in the programs we ran together greatly facilitated our mutual cooperation, extending far beyond UNPREDEP's experience.

Search for Common Ground (SCG) was founded in 1982 as a modest NGO in Washington, D.C. Its first focus was on building bridges between East and West and it subsequently turned to helping prevent and resolve conflict in different parts of the world. In the past twenty years its staff, coming from more than two dozen countries, grew to more than two hundred, and there are thousands of people directly involved in its projects. The organization has developed a toolbox of twenty-four operational conflict resolution methods, such as mediation and facilitation, dialogue workshops, cross-ethnic cooperation within professions, community organizing, court-based mediation, conflict-resolution curricula in schools, interethnic kindergartens, debunking stereotypes, media and journalist training, publications, and arts and culture. SCG's comprehensive and innovative outreach activities to parties in need of mediation and conciliation have earned it well-deserved respect and acclaim.

The organization began work in Macedonia in 1993 with a view to strengthening interethnic relations and helping prevent violence. In the field of the media, the organization has helped to bridge ethno-linguistic divisions, facilitate cross-ethnic journalism, and engage dozens of journalist from various ethnic groups in the preparation of joint articles and other publications. At the end of the 1990s, SCG started production of *Nashe Maalo* (Our Neighborhood), a children's television series that promotes interethnic understanding. Consisting of twenty-four half-hour dramas, the series was aired at the peak of the war in Kosovo and, according to evaluation reports, contributed to increased understanding and acceptance of other ethnic groups. The organization took pride in announcing that as part of its media projects, it had worked closely with every newspaper and television station in the country, and with almost every reporter. Consequently, during the Kosovo crisis, rather than preaching hatred—as so often happens in the Balkans when conflict intensifies—Macedonia's media were relatively restrained.

In the field of education, SCG established effective ties with Skopje University's Ethnic Conflict Resolution Project to develop curricula on multiculturalism and conflict resolution. The curricula are used in several dozen schools and offer interactive games that deepen children's understanding of conflict and alternatives to violence. The organization also prided itself on the establishment of six bilingual, multiethnic kindergartens called "Mozaik," whose aim was to socialize young children in diversity and tolerance. An SCG publication recalls that with the war in Kosovo, most parents pulled their children from the kindergartens—only to return them to school within days.[56]

Creative thinking prompted SCG to launch original projects on environmental conflict resolution that crossed ethnic lines.[57] Besides producing ecological benefits, the purpose of such projects was to promote interethnic cooperation and to diminish the tendency of Macedonia's communities to blame each other over the sources of such problems rather than address their common concerns. Thus environmental protection also promotes grassroots initiative and convinces citizens that they can effect positive change, especially through active participation in organs of local self-government.

In early 1998, the Swiss government expressed readiness to offer, on UNPREDEP's recommendation, funding for a project called "Training for Nonviolent Conflict Resolution," which included promoting conflict awareness among schoolchildren, teachers and parents, and university students and professors of the Pedagogical Faculty; creating innovative conflict resolution games; and introducing bilingual interethnic kindergartens and community outreach activities. When asked about the best partner to implement the project, we did not hesitate to recommend Search for Common Ground. Within a few months, SCG successfully launched the Swiss initiative as the Ethnic Conflict Resolution Project, attached to Skopje University's Faculty of Philosophy.

The Friedrich Ebert Foundation (FES) is the oldest of the five German political foundations. Established in 1925 as the legacy of Germany's first democratically elected president, Friedrich Ebert, the foundation in the past few decades has supported processes of transformation in Central and Eastern Europe, focussing on democratization and the further development of a democratic political culture. In the mid-1990s, it opened offices in most southeastern European countries, including Macedonia. Here its focus has been on supporting social and economic transition, ethnic conflict resolution, and civic organizations—including trade unions and women's, youth, and students' organizations—as role models in building democratic and participatory societies. Part of this effort involves the recruitment and steady development of civic and political leadership. All in all, FES organizes more than fifty events or functions every year in Macedonia, such as seminars, conferences, training courses, and numerous publications.

FES has done impressive work on interethnic rapprochement. It has promoted greater professionalism in journalism by providing various training courses for journalists and by hosting meetings between Macedonian and German journalists. The foundation readily joined UNPREDEP's initiatives by sharing its rich experience and funds earmarked for international assistance, with its significant contribution going toward the organization of our Skopje international workshop "An Agenda for Preventive Diplomacy: Theory and Practice." FES also extended its support to the seminar "Youth: The Young Promoters of Tolerance" and to the Intensive Training Seminar on Youth Leadership. In following up on this involvement, the foundation established direct contacts between Macedonian and German youth and organized several seminars to raise awareness of tolerance and living together in an ethnically mixed environment.

SOS Children's Villages is a private nonpolitical and nondenominational welfare organization, offering a new permanent home to abandoned, orphaned, and destitute children, regardless of race, nationality, or creed, and prepares them for independent living. In 1949, Hermann Gmeimer of Austria established the first SOS village; eleven years later, as the network expanded, especially in Austria and other European countries, an umbrella organization for all national SOS children's villages came into being—the SOS-Kinderdorf International. Today, the organization is present in more than one hundred and thirty countries on all continents and has a consultative status with the UN Economic and Social Council. The idea behind SOS Villages has had a powerful impact on work with abandoned and orphaned children worldwide; it has long been considered the best alternative to the natural family environment.

A typical SOS children's village family consists of a group of five or more children, usually boys and girls of various ages who grow up together as brothers and sisters. New family members may be admitted up to the age of ten. The family is headed by an SOS children's village mother who is responsible for the upbringing of the children and for the management of the entire household. The children receive a good education and sound preparation for adult life; they normally stay with the village until they are able to live independently. Each family has a house of its own, with a combined living room as the center of its social life. Every village normally consists of ten to fifteen family houses and is run by an SOS children's village director and staff. The organization has accumulated a wealth of experience that has earned it global recognition.

There is no country in the world without orphans; neither children's homes nor adoption has solved that problem. The same was true of Macedonia. Having been aware of the track record of SOS Children's Villages in other countries, we invited a delegation from the organization's headquarters in Innsbruck, Austria to visit Skopje in the summer of 1996 and explore the feasibility of establishing an SOS children's village. Only after a few such fact-finding missions and three more years were all the obstacles surmounted. The new project required elaborate discussions with high-ranking officials and with the staff of relevant ministries on issues of legal guardianship and child custody. The arrangement called for some amendments in Macedonia's existing laws and the identification of a suitable building site, provided by the government. Following detailed and lengthy deliberations on the legal considerations of child care under this novel setup, previously unknown in Macedonia, the project reached its implementation phase. The ceremony of laying the cornerstone for the first Macedonian SOS children's village took place on April 14, 1999, at the height of the Kosovo refugee crisis. The unique village, situated in suburban Skopje and completed a few years later, has provided the country with a modern facility for eighty children and their new, specially trained mothers.

Open Society Institute–Macedonia, run by the Soros Foundation, was UNPREDEP's willing collaborator and staunch supporter, financing a number of our major projects, including in particular the seminar on the implementation of United Nations Standards and Rights of Persons Belonging to National or Ethnic, Religious, and Linguistic Minorities; publication of "Interethnicity: Turning Walls into Bridges"; building civil society in low-income multiethnic neighborhoods; training workshops and seminars on social welfare and social development; a seminar on prevention of drug trafficking and abuse; and training courses on police management.

Washington, D.C.'s Center for Democracy extended its generous financial support to the international workshop "An Agenda for Preventive

Diplomacy: Theory and Practice" and to the organization of the gala inter-cultural concert "Living Together."

UNPREDEP's initiatives on youth issues received support from the World Assembly of Youth and the European Youth Forum, while the project on home-based early childhood education attracted the interest of the Netherlands' Avarroes Foundation and Ireland's Focus on Children.

It is not incidental that I have devoted considerable attention to our most helpful interlinkages with other partners, notably governmental and nongovernmental organizations. Conflict prevention is a top-to-bottom and bottom-to-top process. Unless we understand this axiom in both word and deed, the chances for real success are pretty slim. Exercises in ethnic or political rapprochement start at the top with the United Nations, and NGOs initiate the crucial corresponding action at the bottom; individual governments and regional organizations normally add their projects and actions to fill the space in between. Whenever the United Nations is deprived of such supportive partnerships in pre- or postconflict prevention, its efforts will tend to wane. The significance of this truism has been forcefully underscored in both the Brahimi Report and the report of the International Commission on Intervention and State Sovereignty, *The Responsibility to Protect.*[58]

These peacebuilding techniques are complex and require much of the time of the head of the mission; there are many programs, people, and organizations to coordinate. In the quotidian, managerial diplomacy that goes on every day in a peacekeeping mission, the careful timing and sequencing of events can mean everything to the mission's success.

Unfortunately, timing was an inauspicious element of two apparently separate events revolving around the Security Council in early 1999: Taipei's enticing overtures to Macedonia in return for the new country's switching its recognition from the People's Republic of China (PRC) to the Asian power's "renegade province," and another six-month renewal of UNPREDEP's mandate. The former culminated in early February 1999, when the new Macedonian government announced that it was indeed granting official recognition to Taiwan. The latter was scheduled for the Security Council's agenda less than three weeks later.

Those of us in the diplomatic community who were well acquainted with Skopje's power circles grappled for an understanding of the Macedonian government's move—the country's urgent need for Taiwan's putative offers of aid and investment, perhaps, along with the sense that maybe UNPRE-DEP was no longer necessary since Macedonia seemed to be getting stronger, its government and civil society by now becoming mature. President Gligorov's exasperation over the decision and apparent inability to rescind his government's action led us to believe that Macedonia's governing institutions were perhaps still rent by factional feuds—the crucial checks and balances among government branches and division of powers in the executive were still being worked out, we surmised—and if that were true of the country's central government, what could be said about the more amorphous nature of local government and civil society?

Diplomats usually like certainty—or, unless ambiguity serves their purposes, at least they try to get as much information and arrive at as much clarity as possible, just as any decision maker would. In this case, though, the certainty that existed in the Security Council at the beginning of 1999 made many diplomats and Balkans-watchers concerned. Specifically, we were certain about two things that February: UNPREDEP's renewal would be on the Security Council's agenda within a few weeks and the People's Republic of China, as a permanent member of the Security Council, wielded a veto.

I had left Skopje, Macedonia, and UNPREDEP about four months before, but I continued to follow developments in the preventive mission and in Macedonia. My successor as SRSG, a distinguished Spanish diplomat and former ambassador to Canada, Fernando Valenzuela-Marzo, arrived in Skopje in the middle of January. In the first months of the new year, I shared my diplomatic colleagues' quiet astonishment over the Macedonian government's decision, and even though I then had an acute sense of that curious Balkan fatalism as March approached, I could not help but feel more than a bit apprehensive.

6

PRESERVING A HERITAGE

C HINA'S DELEGATION TO THE UN Security Council once coined a saying: "Every peacekeeping operation should have not only a beginning but also an end." The saying has often been repeated in the council, especially in the context of peacekeeping operations' economies of scale. After all, if an operation becomes too large or lasts too long, there are bound to be diminishing returns—however one measures them—on the international community's investment in the operation. With regard to UNPREDEP, however, the basic question remained throughout its mandate: How does one measure the success of an early preventive operation and, were it to be considerably reduced or withdrawn, judge whether peace and stability would continue to hold, threats and tensions disappear, and channels or institutions for defusing conflicts continue to grow and consolidate? Our consistent reply from the field was that the real litmus test of UNPREDEP's accomplishment would be seen only when and if, following the mission's withdrawal, peaceful conditions prevailed in the host country over the coming decades. At the same time, we strongly believed that an abrupt or premature termination of our effort would be dangerous, leaving behind a political or security vacuum that could very well spark a fire of recidivism in the region.[1]

The underlying justification for the successive extensions of the force's mandate had always been based on several weighty arguments, particularly that disturbing threats to stability persisted in the area, notably those engendered by the situation in Bosnia and Kosovo; by the lack of progress in the demarcation of the border with the FRY; by Macedonia's inadequate defensive capabilities; and by the country's internal stresses and strains, especially those arising from interethnic tensions complicated by the country's incomplete transition to a market economy and full-fledged representative democracy. For quite some time, none of these factors by itself had represented an immediate threat to peace and stability in the republic. Yet taken together, and in light of the level of unpredictability of regional developments, the sum total of their likely repercussions had to be treated with utmost seriousness. In fact, even in early 1999 none of the threats that had led to the UNPREDEP's deployment could be considered fully eliminated. Each of them was simmering on a back burner and could easily have been brought to a full boil again by changing circumstances. The Albanian lesson of 1997 and its protracted ramifications, as well as the subsequent story of Kosovo, had offered clear evidence of the risks that the international community would likely confront in this part of Europe for years to come.

By early 1998, it had become increasingly clear that Kosovo was heading toward an inevitable explosion. It was also evident that both Macedonia and UNPREDEP had assumed much greater significance in and for the region than anyone would have expected five years before. Few would disagree that the country was of major strategic importance to the region, "in which NATO has a strong interest through Greek and Turkish membership."[2] Similarly, against the backdrop of events elsewhere in the area, UNPREDEP—as the first United Nations operation in early preventive deployment—had gradually evolved from a kind of narrowly conceived deterrent into a factor contributing to regional stability. Its monitoring, reporting, and good offices functions had turned into a deterrent of a new kind and "to a certain extent, a textbook example of conflict prevention."[3]

In early 1999, few could have expected that UNPREDEP would be terminated abruptly—ended just for the sake of ending it—and at a time when it was most needed. On February 25, 1999, the Security Council met to consider "the situation in the former Yugoslav Republic of Macedonia" on the basis of the secretary-general's most recent report, which recommended an extension of the mission, with its existing mandate and composition, for a further six months, until August 31.[4] Macedonia's foreign affairs minister supported the recommendation, having presented in his letter to the secretary-general of January 29, 1999, a number of arguments for extending the mission's mandate for another six months.[5] The eight-power draft resolution concurred with those recommendations.[6] Yet, when the resolution was put to a vote, it was not adopted: the People's Republic of China, a permanent member of the Security Council, exercised its veto. As of March 1, 1999, UNPREDEP ceased to function.[7]

The mission's termination took many by surprise. Of course, every member of the Security Council has the right to vote the way it considers proper. In this particular case, though, the PRC's official arguments explaining the veto were not convincing. The Chinese argued that they had always maintained that UN peacekeeping operations, including preventive deployment missions, should not be open-ended. In their view, the situation in Macedonia had stabilized over the past few years, the country's relations with its neighbors had improved, and the Security Council's original objective in Macedonia had actually been accomplished. Finally, the PRC contended that the UN's already insufficient resources should be used where they were needed most—for instance, in Africa and other regions plagued by conflict and instability.[8]

Regarding Macedonia's relations with its neighbors, the PRC's delegate had a plausible argument on just a couple of fronts—but even then, just on the surface. On Bulgaria, a qualitative change in bilateral relations took place with the accession to power of the VMRO-DPMNE coalition. The very historical name of the party, not to mention its political leanings toward closer relations with Bulgaria, proved particularly helpful in forging new connections. Citizens and governments of both states have entered into many bilateral and multilateral projects together, particularly in the context of the Stability Pact for Southeastern Europe. Relations improved significantly following the meeting of the two prime ministers in Sofia on February 22, 1999. Both countries agreed to resolve their outstanding language dispute and further improve their bilateral relations. In February and March 2001, Bulgaria offered its western neighbor DM 16 million in military-technical assistance.[9] As of late, most of Bulgaria's restrictions on Macedonians' entry into the country have been lifted. On November 16, 2002, Presidents

Prvanov and Trajkovski held an unprecedented meeting in Melnik and Bansko, Bulgaria to pay homage to their countries' historical hero, Jane Sandanski—until recently, a figure to whom the Bulgarian government forbade Macedonians to pay homage.

Some Macedonians now complain of too active a Bulgarian presence in their country. The Bulgarian mind has not been easy to read with respect to future relations with Macedonia. However, if membership in NATO and the European Union should not prove a pipe dream, Bulgaria's relations with the sovereign Macedonia must follow the path of normalcy and mutual advantage.

Similarly, UNPREDEP's presence in Macedonia had an indirect impact on parallel international initiatives devoted to improving relations between the new country and its southern neighbor. On March 18, 1994, President Clinton appointed as his special emissary for Macedonia Matthew Nimetz, who initiated a series of shuttle diplomacy trips between Athens and Skopje. The two sides discussed different formulas regarding both the name issue and broader areas of mutual Greek-Macedonian relations. Meanwhile, Cyrus Vance actively pursued his UN mandate. In November, the Greek negotiators agreed to discuss a "small packet" of bilateral initiatives excluding the name issue. As negotiations at different levels continued, U.S. assistant secretary of state Richard Holbrooke announced progress in Greek-Macedonian relations on August 1, 1995, and that more details would become public by mid-September. On September 13, Macedonia and Greece signed their Interim Accord, addressing friendly relations and confidence-building measures; human and cultural rights; international and regional institutions; treaty relations; and economic, commercial, environmental, and legal issues. The agreement would remain in force until superseded by a definitive agreement.

The Interim Accord provided that through 2002, either party could withdraw from the accord by written notice, which would take effect twelve months after delivery to the other party. The agreement conspicuously omitted the parties' names; Article 11, paragraph 1 of the accord, for example, illustrates the intricate language in evidence throughout the agreement:

> Upon entry into force of this Interim Accord, the Party of the First Part [Greece] agrees not to object to the application by or the membership of the Party of the Second Part [Macedonia] in international, multilateral and regional organizations and institutions of which the Party of the First Part

is a member; however, the Party of the First Part reserves the right to object to any membership referred to above if and to the extent the Party of the Second Part is to be referred to in such organizations or institutions differently than in paragraph 2 of United Nations Security Council Resolution 817 (1993).[10]

Macedonian-Greek relations have consistently improved since the signing of the Interim Accord and the lifting of the Greek embargo. The name issue, however, remains unresolved. U.S. envoy Nimetz took over from Vance as the UN secretary-general's representative, extending good offices to the two parties. Officials from the two governments considered several different name formulas, but each caused problems for at least one party.[11] In yet another gesture of goodwill, Macedonia unilaterally waived a requirement for entry visas from Greek citizens. Both sides have demonstrated plenty of confidence building in the implementation of the Interim Accord. Greece has now become the number-one investor in Macedonia's economy and the main beneficiary of the Macedonian privatization process—only two other states enjoy larger trade flows with Macedonia. As a Skopje daily noted, "[I]t took five years for Greece to convert Macedonia from a 'twilight zone' into an El Dorado of Greek business, which had discovered fertile land for reproduction of boundless profit in its northern neighbour."[12]

People in Skopje say that Greeks have wasted much of their time by only recently trying to promote their image among the Macedonians. By initially concentrating all their energies on ostracizing Macedonia internationally, Greece missed a unique and early opportunity to become a significant contributor to regional cooperation in the Balkans: though belatedly, Greece definitely wants to play the role of a regional power, and Macedonia seems a key element of this strategy. One hopes that an observation from Norman Davies, a distinguished European historian, will help the two countries accommodate their main problem:

> To ask whether Macedonia is Greek is rather like asking whether Prussia was German. If one talks of distant origins, the answer in both cases must be "No." Ancient Macedonia started its career in the orbit of Illyrian or Thracian civilization. But, as shown by excavation of the royal tombs, it was subject to a high degree of hellenization before Philip of Macedon conquered Greece.[13]

Looking westward from Skopje, subsequent changes in the Albanian leadership have significantly altered both the climate and substance of

Macedonian-Albanian relations. In December 1997, Macedonian foreign minister Blagoj Handziski visited Tirana and signed six bilateral agreements, four on the regulation of the border regime and two on economic cooperation. The border agreements helped to reduce tensions across the frontier by preventing and resolving border incidents and reforming the visa regime, including a reduction of fees. Residents living within ten kilometers on either side of the border could spend two days twice a month in the other country without passports or visas. A month later, Skopje received the first visit ever of Albania's prime minister, Fatos Nano. On that occasion, Albanian and Macedonian officials concluded eight agreements on mutual cooperation, including judicial issues, finances, and customs. In June 1998, Prime Minister Branko Crvenkovski led a high-level Macedonian delegation to Tirana. Crvenkovski and Nano decided to meet regularly, every two or three months. The frequency of other cabinet-level visits between Skopje and Tirana also accelerated. On several occasions, Prime Minister Nano publicly attempted to mitigate some radical ethnic Albanian ambitions by describing Macedonia as an example of a joint multiethnic community.

Encouraging as these developments might appear, several unanswered questions still remained from the Macedonian standpoint: How long would the new trend of improved relations last? Must relations regress to the status quo ante with a possible change of successive governments in Albania? Would Albania's leaders rise above the radical demands of their brethren in Macedonia for the sake of regional peace, stability, and cooperation? The intensity of these concerns grew with the proliferation of uncertainty in the Balkans, as conflicting interests and outright mistrust rent societies in the region.

Political changes in the Federal Republic of Yugoslavia at the end of the twentieth century augured a new era in Macedonian-Yugoslav relations. The new leadership in Belgrade has recognized Macedonia's contribution to good-neighborly relations and to peace and stability in the Balkans. A dialogue at the highest state levels has become routine practice. Peaceful cooperation and expanded relations in many fields, slowly but gradually, have begun replacing the feuds of the past. If other unexpected developments in the region do not obscure the brighter horizon in relations between Macedonia and the FRY, the positive trends should firmly advance the cause of peaceful and stable Balkans.

Yet the situation we saw at Macedonia's northern border just before the withdrawal of the mission looked ominous, and we considered it a bit of cold comfort that our observations were backed up by Secretary-General Kofi Annan. In early 1999, in his last report before UNPREDEP's abrupt termination, Annan noted that relations between Macedonia and the FRY had been strained because of Macedonia's decision to allow the deployment of a NATO Extraction Force on its territory.[14] There had also been no progress on border demarcation. The report advised that developments in Kosovo could lead to a full-scale civil war in the Serbian province, which might have unpredictable repercussions for the entire region.[15]

Such was the diplomatic panorama from Skopje around the time of UNPREDEP's termination—markedly improved since Macedonia's independence, but certainly not free of concern from the vantage point of the Security Council. Indeed, most observers agreed that the real reason for China's veto was the establishment of diplomatic relations between Macedonia and Taiwan, and there is no question of a direct cause-and-effect relationship. Regrettably, on the Macedonian side the bilateral part of the case was handled in an unprofessional way, to say the least, without adequate understanding of either the intricacies of the matter or of its immediate and long-term ramifications. Canada's representative on the Security Council expressed profound disappointment that, despite the solid support for UNPREDEP's extension, the council failed to renew the mission: the arguments China advanced in support of its veto could not be sustained in the light of the facts; it was, in his view, "an unfortunate and inappropriate" use of the veto. He also deeply regretted action taken by the Macedonian government, which precipitated the dispute with China.[16]

UNPREDEP's untimely termination elicited a series of tributes to its role and record of achievement.[17] Many of them were expressed immediately after China cast its veto. Argentina's representative was convinced that UNPREDEP constituted "one of the Security Council's central efforts for peace in the region, particularly at a time when delicate and complex negotiations are taking place with regard to the situation in Kosovo." The fact that Macedonia had not felt the repercussions of the conflicts that affected and continued to affect its neighboring countries and regions was, he emphasized, "clear proof that UNPREDEP is fulfilling its mandate in a completely effective manner. Because the situation in Kosovo has not yet been resolved, the presence of UNPREDEP, which is a preventive force, constitutes an irreplaceable reassurance."[18] In the opinion of the Russian delegation, the force was making "an important contribution to stabilizing the situation in Kosovo and to the success of international efforts to achieve a peaceful political settlement of the crisis, as well as to guarantee the security and stability of the entire Balkan region."[19] The U.S. representative considered UNPREDEP "a vital actor in promoting stability in the region."[20] Slovenia called UNPREDEP "a success story of United Nations peacekeeping and of the United Nations in general. It is a model of preventive deployment which should inspire the United Nations in dealing with a variety of incipient crisis situations in various parts of the world."[21]

Speaking on behalf of the European Union and the Central and Eastern European countries associated with the EU, Germany's delegate called UNPREDEP a great success: "It can serve as a model for future such deployments. The European Union sees the value of UNPREDEP not only in its military component and its border monitoring, but also in its civilian efforts to promote understanding among the different ethnic groups in the former Yugoslav Republic of Macedonia."[22] In its presidential statement of November 30, 1999, nine months after the Chinese veto, the Security Council recalled that "the United Nations Preventive Deployment Force, as the first United Nations preventive deployment mission, has prevented the spillover of conflict and tensions from the region to the host country. The council will continue to consider the establishment of such preventive missions in appropriate circumstances."[23]

On UNPREDEP's departure from Macedonia, President Gligorov addressed a letter to the secretary-general in which he thanked him for the UN's outstanding contribution to the maintenance of peace and security in the Republic of Macedonia. In his opinion, UNPREDEP proved itself to be a barrier to wider destabilization and thus a "very successful mission."[24]

In his message to the opening ceremony of the International Center for Preventive Action and Conflict Resolution in Skopje on October 20, 2000, Secretary-General Kofi Annan added a new element of appraisal: "Eight years ago, at the visionary initiative of the Macedonian government, the mission that became UNPREDEP was deployed to prevent the violent conflict in other parts of the former Yugoslavia from spreading across your border. That mission was an unqualified success, not least because of the active partnership and cooperation between the government and the United Nations."[25]

To some observers, however, UNPREDEP did not warrant all those encomiums. Whereas politicians and diplomats have lavishly praised its role, some writers and academics take a more restrained—if not strongly critical—approach. One observer, for instance, alleges a number of drawbacks to the operation: UNPREDEP was powerless to affect the course of difficult events in the country; it was seen as ineffectual and too close to the government; the mixed troop contingents that replaced the U.S. soldiers were seen "as often openly anti-Albanian"; and it had little power to influence internal developments in the country.[26] Against the backdrop of UNPREDEP's mandate and its overall record, however, one is tempted to take issue with such views.

First of all, UNPREDEP did ease tensions in Macedonia. Its ability to do so should be measured not only against those events that assumed explosive proportions but also against those that, thanks to UNPREDEP's mitigating and preventive presence, were kept from reaching that point. This is, after all, the crux of prevention. The alleged perception of the mission's ineffectiveness had been denied by the deterrent functions of the operation, which—as long as it lasted—faithfully implemented its mandated tasks. If anything, UNPREDEP had been seen in some quarters, especially within Macedonia, as *too* effectual, to the point that we often had to remind our interlocutors of the stated objectives and limitations of the operation.

Second, throughout UNPREDEP's existence there were no other troop contingents that replaced U.S. soldiers on the force, and the peacekeepers were not "openly anti-Albanian." Areas inhabited by ethnic Albanians were regularly patrolled by NORDBAT, which maintained the best possible relations with the local population and authorities. The Finnish Company stationed in Tetovo proved to be an excellent ambassador for both the United Nations and Finland; in a gesture of goodwill, it conducted its periodic company ceremonies, such as marking a change of command or national holidays, not only in English and Macedonian but in Albanian as well. Ethnic Albanians in these towns and villages approached our UNMOs, UNCIVPOL teams, and regular troop patrols in full confidence, voicing their complaints against the authorities and other grievances, which we tried to investigate.

Finally, the charge of being "too close to the government" does not hold currency either. Cooperation with the host country's authorities in using "good offices, as appropriate," was the essence of our work. The very fact that the authorities were reluctant to fully reciprocate our mandated good-offices efforts would indicate that the force was, instead, not close enough to the government.

WHY DID UNPREDEP HAVE TO GO?

Politics and diplomacy always breed suspicions that hidden motives are at play. So, too, did the sudden manner in which UNPREDEP was brought to an end. The mere veto by a permanent member of the Security Council was not enough to convince some observers that "the Taiwan connection" might have been the only reason for the force's premature departure. Other likely motives have also been attributed to UNPREDEP's withdrawal, but one thing is certain: UNPREDEP came to an end not because the need ended, nor because it completed or failed its mission, but because of extraneous issues. Its termination in no way invalidates its work or its legacy. President Gligorov was very critical of his government's action, which he called "the direct trigger" of China's veto; he considered the move "wrong and, of course, the fault of our government."[27]

President Gligorov's reference to the Taiwan case as "the direct trigger" of the veto raises the question of whether there might have been an "indirect trigger" of the pullout as well. This question is difficult to answer. UNPREDEP was Gligorov's child, and he had always been its staunchest supporter. He understood best the intricate complexities of Balkan politics: even in the early days of Macedonia's independence, when he had invited United Nations troops to the country, some younger members of the country's leadership had mixed feelings about the project—for example, would it delay Macedonia's membership in NATO or negatively impact its regional and international position? Later, they viewed the protracted presence of UNPREDEP as a sign of the country's weakness. When Macedonia lost its 1997 bid for membership in the Security Council, some politicians suggested that the presence of an international peace-keeping operation on its soil had not been helpful, to say the least, in its attempt to beat the competition. As time passed and the situation in Kosovo deteriorated, Macedonian politicians started talking of the need for a more robust military presence, preferably one from NATO, which might also allow the country to advance one step ahead of the PfP formula and to facilitate accelerated access to the alliance. In short, they sought a transition to long-term security. In addition, both the authorities and the public—and perhaps the U.S. military—had grown somewhat fatigued with the constant effort required, every six months, to ensure successive extensions of UNPREDEP's mandate.

In the opinion of a leading and influential Macedonian politician whom I interviewed in Skopje in September 2000, UNPREDEP's termination presented both "a dilemma and a puzzle." Would it have been possible, he asked, to preserve peace during the Kosovo crisis under UNPREDEP's existing mandate alone? His answer was in the negative: the KLA had been active along the border between Macedonia and Kosovo continuously; had NATO not been involved, the Kosovo conflict would have lasted much longer and would have spread into Macedonia. Indeed, enormous efforts by the Macedonian government and the support of the international community eventually resolved the refugee problem satisfactorily. Gradually, with the arrival in Kosovo of the UN mission and NATO peacekeepers, the refugees either returned to their homes or moved to third countries. As a multiethnic society, Macedonia seemed to have passed an extraordinary test of political maturity and endurance. "Without NATO," continued the Macedonian politician, "we could have neither accepted nor returned the refugees in such a short time. Macedonia would have been involved in the war in various ways." My interlocutor presented in a nutshell what might be considered an "indirect trigger" of the veto:

> There was no way to avoid replacing UNPREDEP with NATO in its new role. Otherwise, the consequences would have been much graver. However, the manner in which this objective had been arrived at proved harmful to the country's interests. Formally, UNPREDEP terminated because of China's veto as a result of our recognition of Taiwan. We should have found a more sophisticated method. The one applied had negative consequences. Many Western states criticized the decision. Our move provoked China. This is not good for a small country like Macedonia. We now do not enjoy the sympathy we used to in the Security Council. To many governments, our move had been incomprehensible. It had not taken account of the credit due to UNPREDEP. Even if a step like this were unavoidable, someone else should have handled it.

Indeed, UNPREDEP's departure left a vacuum of its own. Before long, an increasing number of public figures realized that NATO was primarily preoccupied with Kosovo and had neither a mandate nor any immediate intention to operate in Macedonia. NATO's stationing of a logistical support base for the Kosovo operation fell far short of Macedonia's expectations for an active NATO presence in the country.[28] Nostalgia for UNPREDEP has subsequently surfaced in public discussions. The force had left a heritage that would be an error to ignore.

WHAT WAS UNPREDEP?

Preventive action is not a panacea for every crisis around the world. Even in the case of UNPREDEP, the mission was never meant to be a philosophers' stone to cure all of Macedonia's ills; measuring it against such a metric would lead to some spurious conclusions. The yardstick of its effectiveness is the extent to which it was able to implement its mandated tasks. Conversely, UNPREDEP was neither an ephemeral nor a watershed phenomenon. Some expected too much from it, while others expected far too little; neither group viewed the operation proportionally. What, then, was UNPREDEP, and what did it accomplish?

First and foremost, the mission showed that, under appropriate circumstances, prevention can work. It proved to skeptics that the United Nations "can do." As noted earlier, it would be imprudent to claim that the operation achieved a successful outcome through its efforts alone. We were only one part of a larger communications network in which several factors were at work. Decisive among these factors was that, throughout the 1990s, the international community and Macedonia's political forces had been able to prevent the recurrence of the tragedy early in the decade that befell countries elsewhere in the region. This important consideration does not in any way diminish the weight of preventive complementarity our presence promoted in both the host country and the region as a whole. Indeed, our partners in this great effort, notably the OSCE, NATO, the European Union, the Council of Europe, and numerous organizations and agencies of the United Nations system, as well as the NGO community, deserve full credit. What UNPREDEP did, then, was foster these partnerships and integrate their distinct and overlapping functions into an appropriate peace operation. As one observer notes, "The UNPREDEP mission can thus rightly be considered a significant step toward integrating preventive deployment into an effective overall approach to conflict prevention."[29]

Second, UNPREDEP demonstrated that a preventive operation can be an incubator in which newly independent or newly stable states can develop. In Macedonia, prevention was like incubation, a figurative illustration of what the international community can do to avert conflict. UNPREDEP's six years in service helped to give Macedonia an international personality; it helped the new country along in the maturing process. Internally, UNPRE-DEP became a symbol of facilitated dialogue among political parties; it provided a forum that had never before existed in Macedonia. The mission brought with it the space for the renewal of political culture in Macedonia and filled a substantial part of the political vacuum in the host country.[30] During the mission's presence, Macedonia made significant headway along the path to building a pluralist political arena based on democratic principles of civil society. We witnessed a profound evolution with respect to Macedonia's external and internal environments. The political climate along the young country's borders improved markedly, and UNPREDEP's first two pillars not only provided a tremendously symbolic commitment to Macedonia's sovereignty but also allowed some rather powerful bilateral initiatives to codify, as it were, the international community's equal commitment to the principle of the inviolability of borders. Domestically, however, the political actors involved in these processes were not able to turn their positive accomplishments during UNPREDEP's presence into a long-term peace or a real starting point for permanent cohabitation.[31] The abrupt termination of UNPREDEP inevitably had a negative effect on its program delivery in peacebuilding. A number of projects had to be frozen in the pipeline, though others have been completed or are continuing under new sponsors or implementing institutions. Still others have been taken over by the alliance of like-minded governments, organizations, and NGOs that have had a unique grasp of Macedonia's needs during its complex transition.

Third, through UNPREDEP, the United Nations succeeded in drawing a "thin blue line" of security, and, for six full years, helped to confine a conflict by building confidence in highly polarized communities. Although the highly polarized ethnic communities were both grudging and somewhat hostile in their mutual relations, we did seem able to at least manage the problems. The UN's presence allowed both groups to at least sleep better at night, knowing that the international community had a vested interest in their seeking to work together. Considering the nature of such combustible cohabitation, this process in itself was quite an accomplishment.

Fourth, UNPREDEP revealed that a multidimensional and integrated approach to prevention is not only feasible but also effective. According to one observer, UNPREDEP's mission clearly had precedent: "Not only was the United Nations to display a capacity for rapid and effective action prior to an eruption of hostilities, but the flexible expansion of the mandate has set a solid example of how various preventive strategies can be integrated successfully within one mission."[32] The comprehensive three-pillar formula for action (troop deployment, good offices, and the human dimension) proved to be a forerunner of the precepts for peacekeeping missions that the international community embarked upon on the threshold of the twenty-first century. In that regard, UNPREDEP was a unique laboratory of prevention that, thanks to the record of United Nations standard-setting in different areas of human endeavor, managed to do without trial-and-error experimentation. Consequently, the story of the mission could be defined as one of "soft peacekeeping," perhaps even "softer" than some of the stipulations of UN Charter's Chapter VI, under which such a preventive operation would normally be established. To many local politicians, this was a new and quite striking contribution by outsiders.

Fifth, the operation demonstrated—especially with respect to the root causes of conflict—that if more interventions readily resorted to tools such as those UNPREDEP used, the international community could reduce the opportunity cost of many political options it has failed to seize in good time—particularly true with regard to the material costs of conflicts that were not caught at an early stage. One scholar offers an interesting comparative analysis of UNPREDEP's costs against those that would have been incurred had there been an intermediate or large conflict there: assuming that the preventive operation lasted for six full years and its average budget amounted to some U.S. $55 million annually, its costs would total some U.S. $330 million (the sum of U.S. $55 million was about the same or even lower than the annual budget of the International Tribunal for the Former Yugoslavia).[33] Incomparably higher costs could have been involved had there been an intermediate conflict lasting two years, and the cost estimates of such a war would be in the neighborhood of U.S. $15 billion. A large conflict involving Macedonia and several other countries may cost as much as U.S. $144 billion. Hardly anything else can better illustrate the maxim that prevention is better—and indeed cheaper—than cure.

Finally, the United Nations preventive operation in Macedonia inspired and accelerated new efforts by the international community toward further expansion of preventive concepts and their practical application. Work on these important ideas is in full progress: they have expanded over the entire United Nations system and preoccupy the attention of most of the world organization's principal organs—and UNPREDEP provides them with a blueprint for early noncoercive prevention. In the years to come, however, the global community will have to face new, more complex challenges. Transnational terrorism is one such challenge that may increasingly call for more and more punitive forms of counterreaction and coercive prevention.

LESSONS LEARNED

The international community invested years of effort and resources in peacekeeping and conflict prevention in the former Yugoslavia and learned many lessons during that time. We learned that imposing an order does not necessarily lead to the establishment of one. We also learned that peacemaking can be plagued with difficulties, but that positive results can be achieved if we establish clearly defined mandates—with genuine support from all parties—and deploy missions rapidly. Most important, we relived the lesson that lives and money are saved by preventing conflict before it breaks out rather than by waiting to act until there is a costly and horribly destructive war to stop. UNPREDEP, the first major example of noncoercive prevention in UN history, has taught us that the premature withdrawal of an operation can prove harmful to its very purposes.

In the particular case of the preventive deployment experience of UNPREDEP, the UN secretary-general identified three major political lessons:

> First, preventive action can make a difference. The spread of a regional conflict and the rise of domestic ethnic violence were averted by timely action. Second, international preventive action is not a threat to national sovereignty. The deployment of UNPREDEP occurred at the urging of the government. And third, the United Nations increases the effectiveness of its efforts by working cooperatively with a regional organization, in this case the Organization for Security and Cooperation in Europe.[34]

These guideposts in learning draw on several important circumstances surrounding the establishment of UNPREDEP: prompt action on, and timing of, the operation; the mission's smooth and gradual transformation into a comprehensive and multifaceted vehicle for action; and a relatively high degree of readiness by the parties concerned to help in implementing the mission's mandate. Other lessons came to the fore relatively soon: international incentives and disincentives vis-à-vis the parties involved must be mutually complementary (UNPREDEP had practically no leverage for "conditionality"); a political or military vacuum in one part of the region may provoke a chain of negative events elsewhere; and peace and stability in Macedonia depended largely on developments in other parts of the region. At the same time, we learned that finding solutions would be neither easy nor quick, but that the very search for them could break the ongoing circle of mistrust that served as the crux of the country's instability.

We remained hopeful throughout 1998 that the seriously deteriorating conditions in Kosovo need not provoke an explosion in Macedonia. The gravity of Macedonia's situation was long-term and called for long-lasting solutions. In fact, the following factors seem to have mitigated an outbreak of violent conflict in the former Yugoslav republic:

◆ Preventive action was taken early enough to avert conflict.

◆ There was unanimity in the Security Council.

◆ Largely even-handed action was taken on behalf of the international community vis-à-vis both domestic and external major political forces.

◆ UNPREDEP played a deterrent role.

◆ There had been no "tradition" of armed struggle between the country's ethnic Macedonians and ethnic Albanians.

◆ There was gradual but effective progress of democratic reforms in the country.

◆ There was, and had always been, a strong ethnic Albanian component in Macedonia's postindependence period.

◆ Having joined the government, political leaders showed a readiness to make concessions on behalf of coalition partners representing other political camps.

We came to appreciate the fact that the longer UNPREDEP stayed in the country, and the more firmly the international community applied pressure for a solution to the existing interethnic conflict, the stronger the sense of security grew. That growth, in turn, allowed Macedonia's national deterrent potential to expand. We were absolutely certain that, on a macro scale, any further international action had to include an elaborate component of well-coordinated developmental programs, with a view to combating poverty and countering the social exclusion that lay at the roots of Macedonia's potential national conflict. Had sufficient international assistance been given to the country, a rapidly growing economy could have alleviated much of the interethnic tensions. Some notable beginnings had been made in that direction, but the overall effort was uncoordinated and plagued by what often appeared to be competing interests. Supporting more educational opportunities and better standards of living, especially for the country's ethnic minorities, would have offered women a dignified status as equal partners. Meanwhile, the country continued to face a situation illustrating a well-established axiom: whenever its underlying socioeconomic problems were neglected, political tensions were exacerbated.

On a micro scale, we learned that a preventive peacekeeping operation cannot be deprived of funding for humanitarian and developmental projects and still be fully effective; this lesson applies to both the military and the civilian components of the mission. Whether they promote either what is called peacebuilding or the human dimension, such projects serve as major confidence-building mechanisms between the mission and the host country. UNPREDEP's successive force commanders were often helpless to respond to requests from villagers in inaccessible areas for just a few hundred meters of roads, or for pipelines to provide a village with running water, or for insignificant amounts of wiring to provide another village with electricity, or for spare parts for pumps and generators. Assistance of this kind not only improves local living conditions but also boosts troop morale by giving peacekeepers concrete evidence that their efforts really do make a difference in people's lives. Such initiatives were equally important for force protection because they enhanced trust in the local population, which was frequently unaware of what UN peacekeepers were really doing in their country. The amount of seed money needed for such purposes need not be excessive if its use is well conceived and well utilized; the political "value added" of such projects' effectiveness always exceeds that of the money spent on them.

Quo Vadis Macedonia?

I departed Skopje in the fall of 1998, fully aware of Macedonia's continuing ethnic rifts. Like many other international representatives, I strongly believed that there was both room for and an urgent need to meet some of the basic concerns of the country's ethnic Albanians, and doing so would delineate the ultimate limits of what was, and what could not be, acceptable to the parties concerned. As I pointed out in my end-of-mission report, such a solution would require considerable concessions from both sides, just short of endangering the region's existing geopolitical status quo. Nonetheless, it appeared at the time that at least four measures, comprehensively treated, would lend themselves as the foundation of a peacefully negotiated agreement: increasing the number of ethnic Albanians in state and government structures, expanding opportunities for university education for ethnic Albanians, allowing the Albanian language to be used in the country's parliament, and relaxing the laws on citizenship (at that time Macedonia required the payment of high fees, in addition to fifteen years of legal residence, in order to obtain citizenship).

More progress might have been made on these issues had the country's governmental authorities promoted them forcefully enough. Certainly, doing so would have created an entirely new situation in the country. It would have earned Macedonia much international credit and further enhanced its democratic transformations. Internationally, the climate for reforms was encouraging. Macedonia enjoyed a high standing in European opinion, especially following the solution of the Kosovo refugee crisis: "The influx exerted immense pressure on the coalition government and Macedonia's population. Their willingness to rise to the challenge was a remarkable achievement that has not yet received the international recognition it deserves."[35] Analyzing the situation in Macedonia following UNPREDEP's departure, Andrew J. Pierre notes that, thus far, Macedonia had survived remarkably well. There has been good progress both domestically and in relations with its neighbors. Its aspirations to join NATO and the European Union should further consolidate this "spunky yet still fragile state."[36]

As much as the foregoing assessments were correct, neither the process of "incubation" nor the job of building a secure state had been completed at the termination of the UN mission—not, at least, to an extent that would warrant the removal of a preventive deployment; that action was based on both internal and external predicaments. Domestically, most of all, Macedonia's leaders did indeed embark on the path of democratic governance, but the necessary institutional framework for such an intricate political form was still in its infancy. If a democratic process of good governance is meant to be participatory, transparent, accountable, and effective, and if it is supposed to promote the rule of law and the principle of equal justice under the law, and to ensure that political, social, and economic priorities are based on a broad social consensus, then the Macedonia of 1999 still had a lot of work to do.[37] Effective institution-building, for instance, is a long and arduous process in any country; under the best of circumstances, it requires at least between one and two decades. Building civil society can be equally time consuming, to say the least. Yet in that regard, foreign visitors to Macedonia often compared that country's progress against the centuries-old record of civil societies in established Western democracies. They inevitably drew conclusions that Macedonia's progress was incomplete, if not disappointing, for as long as society is formed primarily along ethnic lines, construction of a truly *civil* society obviously will encounter formidable challenges.

Forward-looking strategies for solidifying Macedonia's gains in the latter half of the 1990s were also inhibited by psychological factors. How could all of the country's political forces be convinced that the different modalities of our preventive action were well intentioned and also in their best interest? In an early post-UNPREDEP conversation, a prominent Western diplomat who had been committed to Macedonia's cause for years shared his candid reflection with me: "I try to help Macedonians as much as I can, but I sometimes have an impression I am more concerned about their future than they are." It is probably too early to assess fully UNPREDEP's impact on Macedonian public opinion. It would take several sociological studies to arrive at a balanced picture of the mission's role, its accomplishments, and its failures. For such an assessment, which would also have to take due account of the "Balkan character," one would need time and the ability to employ unemotional yardsticks based on empirical findings and fair standards of comparison.

In more pragmatic terms, Macedonia still faced fundamental long-term problems at the time of UNPREDEP's departure, and their solution remained crucial to the country's future—not only as a full-fledged member of European political and economic structures but of its very existence as well. Squabbling between Macedonia's political and intellectual elites, tense interethnic relations, slow progress toward democratic reform, a deteriorating socioeconomic climate, and the continued precariousness of bilateral relations with neighboring states still ranked high among the country's fundamental problems at the time of UNPREDEP's withdrawal.

A pernicious byproduct of this situation, which was pointed out in chapter 3, was corruption—a practice that is certainly not alien to many countries today, notably in the Balkans. Macedonia had never combated it forcefully enough, and the prevailing mood in the country was that little could be changed in that regard. Hence, there has been practically no anticorruption constituency in the Macedonian public. Although it was seldom documented, there was a long history of suspicion regarding large-scale corruption in the country. The Skopje daily *Aktuel* raised the suspicion bluntly when it asked: Where did DM 3.5 billion in foreign aid go?[38] According to the newspaper, from the time of its independence until late 2001, Macedonia had received the equivalent of U.S. $1.8 billion in foreign aid; yet, notwithstanding this enormous amount of money, the economy not only failed to show any signs of recovery but, at the same time, was steadily deteriorating. *Aktuel* attributed this to several factors, including mismanagement, organized crime, and corruption. Other Macedonian sources have criticized the privatization process of state-owned companies and the insignificant amounts of money for which enterprises were sold.[39]

The international community's involvement in Macedonia's arduous journey into the future has represented what amounts to the other side of the uphill battle to consolidate its statehood. Despite all the tangible help they provided in charting the new country's course, the major Western powers played a role that was somewhat ambiguous. To be sure, they remained ambivalent on some issues. Throughout the 1990s, when Macedonia evinced few of the crises that plagued the region, it appeared that the country was left off the list of regional top priorities in several crucial respects. The benefits of the strong international vocal support for Macedonia and of UNPREDEP's mitigating presence was undercut by a number of factors: the belated state recognition accorded Macedonia, its delayed admission to the United Nations, international tolerance of the economic blockade from the south, the effects of sanctions against the former Yugoslavia, and the distant prospects for membership in NATO and the European Union.

In short, Macedonians did not believe their country was getting a square deal, and they felt they were being held in a kind of limbo. No wonder they initially viewed with suspicion the "regional approach" concept the

European Union developed in 1996 for addressing Bosnia and Herzegovina, Croatia, the FRY, Macedonia, and Albania. They were convinced—not without justification—that Macedonia should have been put in the same group with Bulgaria and Romania in its efforts to join the European Union. Even in early November 1997, during the Balkan Summit in Crete, President Gligorov was insisting that Macedonia was ready to develop regional cooperation actively in all fields, but not within the constraining and conditional regional institutional structures crafted by the European Union and the international community at large. In his view, a straight line between Skopje and Brussels was the only effective, and plausible, path toward Macedonia's development—a view shared among many other Macedonian politicians, who held deep-rooted fears that an institutionalization of Balkan cooperation might eventually be used as a pretext to delay Macedonia's membership in the European Union, or to bar it altogether.

Yet the relatively brief interregnum between the first wave of Balkan democratization and the present has shown that the European Union's regional approach was unavoidable. Macedonia and Albania formed a separate group among the five Balkan states by virtue of neither one having been involved in the 1991–95 Balkan wars and of both having more advanced relations with the EU. Political and economic conditionality became the salient feature of the regional approach, and it was further strengthened in the EU Common Strategy toward the Balkans, comprising the Stability Pact for Southeastern Europe and the stabilization and association agreements to be signed between the EU and the relevant Balkan states.[40] The functioning of the new framework was elaborated in greater detail in the November 27, 2000 Zagreb Declaration of the European Union, Albania, Macedonia, Bosnia and Herzegovina, Croatia, and the FRY.[41] The EU signed the first stabilization and association agreement in the region with Macedonia. On the occasion of its initialing during the Zagreb Summit, the European Union called upon the leaders of Macedonia to continue their reforms in line with the provisions of the accord. Once the agreement enters into force, it should involve the following for the first decade of the twenty-first century:

◆ Arrangements for establishing free trade areas with the European Union and bolstering regional cooperation.

◆ Commitment to bringing Macedonia's legislation in line with EU standards, notably in the key areas of the internal market, to encourage trade and investment.

◆ Close political dialogue between the EU and Macedonia, including dialogue between Macedonia's National Assembly and the European Parliament.

◆ Important provisions on cooperation in a wide range of other areas, such as justice and domestic affairs.

◆ The provision of financial assistance in support of concrete programs and projects.[42]

Regretfully (but perhaps not unexpectedly), some political and bureaucratic inhibitions encountered in the process of rapprochement with the European Union has not been free of mutual recrimination. For example, EU sources claimed that the union had provided Macedonia with some €422 million from 1991 to 1999 (including €215 million provided through the PHARE program for assistance in the transition to a market economy).[43] However, some Macedonian news outlets asserted that "the Stability Pact remained only a piece of paper."[44] According to the same media source, all the promises of financial aid made by the international community to Macedonia during the Kosovo crisis have thus far remained promises only. International financial institutions and the European Union apparently earmarked more than U.S. $200 million in nonreimbursable loans to assist Macedonia during the Kosovo refugee crisis "but have so far failed to grant a single penny for the realization of eight projects envisaged by the Stability Pact." A few months later, the acting deputy Stability Pact coordinator admitted that the EU was "aware of the disappointment in the region, since more was expected from the Stability Pact."[45]

At the time UNPREDEP was unexpectedly terminated, Macedonia seemed to be heading in the right direction domestically, albeit not without vicissitudes. Meanwhile, the conflict next door in the north was brewing with dramatic intensity. As long as the international community approached the Kosovo crisis in terms of endemic nationalist conflict and ethnic hatred rather than in terms of its own remediable policy failures, it was hard to believe that Macedonia would be unaffected.[46] The sudden removal of the protection force from the Macedonian side of the border left the country considerably more vulnerable. As one analyst noted, "A lessening of interest on the part of the West or a lack of a concerted plan of action could eventually leave the region as it is—weak, unstable, and a persistent security concern."[47] Carl Bildt, former UN special envoy for the Balkans and EU special representative to the former Yugoslavia, shared similar concerns: "If we approach Kosovo in isolation, we will never succeed. Any solution will have to take in the region as a whole. Our approach to Kosovo should be a consequence of our approach to the region as a whole—not the other way round."[48]

In early 1999, we were convinced that Macedonia ultimately had a place in a new democratic Europe. At the same time, we felt that the country's very independence, its peace, stability, and territorial integrity, had never been more threatened from the outside than it was upon UNPREDEP's departure. The country was in a dire need of a "Pact for Macedonia" that would address both domestic and international exigencies; developments had gone too far to be solved by internal political forces alone. The newly elected government coalition and the international actors most intimately involved with Macedonia shared this perception only halfheartedly. In the first place, the mistake of UNPREDEP's premature withdrawal should have been promptly and effectively redressed; at a minimum, the intensifying crisis to the north urgently called for a new international presence along Macedonia's side of the Kosovo border. Using UNPREDEP's record of achievement as a starting point, the international community should have acted more vigorously to bring Macedonia back on track, at least parallel to the levels of stability it had previously enjoyed under the UN operation. Such a reorientation could have been achieved by upgrading the status of Macedonia's relations with NATO; expanding military assistance to Macedonia, particularly in training and materiel; enhancing the level of the European Union's engagement; sponsoring a comprehensive and coherent peacebuilding program for the entire country; recognizing Macedonia's constitutional name—the Republic of Macedonia; and offering and helping to implement a broad educational public program on civil society and cohabitation at all levels of society.

At the same time, Macedonia was ripe for a social contract, which could have been facilitated by some sort of national roundtable or national reconciliation commission, bringing together the country's major civic and political forces. A document of this sort could have set in place a peacefully negotiated national consensus, rising above ethnic and political cleavages, on major issues of concern to all citizens of Macedonia, including the need for joint efforts to increase state capacity building and deeper integration in European and Euro-Atlantic structures, and the urgency of launching an effective nationwide campaign of "clean hands" to fight corruption and related crimes, as well as political scandals. Early efforts toward these ends would have contributed to the lessening of a dangerous polarization among myriad actors in Macedonia's increasingly fractious political arena. Unfortunately, none of these opportunities was exploited effectively, either because of the prejudices of the past or because of the sense that conciliatory action might allow one party, one day, to prevail over the other side's claims.

UNPREDEP is now history, of course, but the unprecedented operation has not yet taken its rightful place in annals of diplomatic history. One day it will, and hopefully it will contradict Aldous Huxley's ironic contention that the most important of all the lessons that history has to teach is that people do not learn very much from the lessons of history. UNPREDEP marked an unfinished but momentous episode in Macedonia's history, helping to chart its future along the path that starts with the present. The mission's heritage of prevention will continue to devolve through future national and international action as an effective way of taming the centrifugal forces of disunity and feuding in the Balkans and, perhaps, other parts of the world that suddenly find themselves at the precipice of a seemingly inevitable encounter with mass violence.

Meanwhile, in this still relatively young Balkan country, more than half of the populace believes it is going in the wrong direction, so the question, "Where are you heading Macedonia?" will still take some time to arrive at a clear and proper answer.

EPILOGUE

FOLLOWING UNPREDEP'S WITHDRAWAL, the former Yugoslavia's perplexing odyssey continued as new developments in the Balkans unfolded. The "unfinished peace" left over from a few years before had seemingly regressed into an "unfinished war," adversely affecting the region's numerous flash points. Observers rightly claimed that the Yugoslav federation's disintegration began in Kosovo, and with Kosovo it would have to come to a close. But why should the new and independent Macedonia pay part of the highest price for the sins of history?

In 2001, Macedonia went through its gravest crisis since independence. The first symptoms of trouble had appeared a year before, when unusually violent, ethnically motivated incidents took place in several locales. Three policemen, all ethnic Macedonians, were killed in an ambush in Aracinovo, an ethnic Albanian village located near Skopje and known for its involvement in illegal trafficking and other forms of organized crime. Eleven persons were arrested in the subsequent investigation; one of them died in police custody. Around the same time, three other police stations came under attack. Then, in July 2000, a Macedonian armored personnel carrier was severely damaged when it drove over a freshly laid landmine in the border area adjacent to Kosovo. Macedonian army patrols stationed along the same border also came under fire from the Kosovo side. Four soldiers in the area were even captured and detained (and subsequently released in exchange for a former KLA commander held in Macedonia). On January 22, 2001, three assailants attacked a Macedonian police station in the village of Tearce, near Tetovo. The attackers killed one policeman and injured two others.

In mid-February, a heretofore unknown armed ethnic Albanian group with direct ties to Kosovo made its presence known in the Macedonian border village of Tanusevci. The group called itself the National Liberation Army (NLA). Initially, it could not claim to control more than six square kilometers of land. The first armed clashes between the NLA and the Macedonian security forces took place in Tanusevci and moved east to other border villages, including Malina Mala, Brest, and Gosince—names all too familiar to us from UNPREDEP's daily border patrol reports. Three more Macedonian soldiers and another policeman were killed in the fighting.

This fresh and more resonant hail of bullets took everyone by surprise. Politicians—foreign and domestic alike—were equally shocked, and their immediate reactions were unequivocal. The government of Macedonia termed the incursion from Kosovo as an outright act of aggression and terrorism. Arben Xhaferi, leader of the DPA, the ethnic Albanian party belonging to the government coalition, argued that the violence in Tanusevci tarnished the image of all ethnic Albanians and threatened their natural alliance with the democratic nations of the West. Out of the recent violence, Xhaferi said, Albanians "emerged as villains, as the party at guilt and a destabilizing element in the region." Albanians throughout the region, he stated, did not support the NLA's extremists; to the contrary, the ethnic Albanians hoped that they would be isolated.[1] His colleague in the party's leadership, Menduh Thaci, directed his ire at Kosovo politician (elected the province's president at the end of the year) Ibrahim Rugova, who had proposed granting Macedonia's ethnic Albanians the status of a constituent nation as a condition of ending the insurgency. "It is not his business to interfere in Macedonia," said Thachi. "The Albanians in this country have their own political representatives."[2] A few weeks later, leaders of ethnic Albanian parties in Macedonia's parliament issued a joint declaration in which they called upon armed groups operating on Macedonian territory to lay down their weapons and peacefully return to their homes: "We condemn the use of force for achieving political goals. There is no room for violence in a democratic country and it makes political dialogue impossible. It blocks the road to Europe, which we, both as citizens of Macedonia and Albanians, have chosen. It could be tragic for us as Macedonian citizens and for the region at large."[3]

On March 4, 2001, Macedonia's minister for foreign affairs sent a letter to the president of the UN Security Council, requesting that he convene an urgent meeting of the council to consider measures to achieve the cessation of violence and a lasting stabilization of the area on the border with the FRY's Kosovo section and to prevent the spillover of violence into the Republic of Macedonia. Three days later, the council adopted a strongly worded statement condemning the "recent violence by ethnic Albanian armed extremists" in the north of Macedonia.[4] The Security Council also underlined "the responsibility of the government [of Macedonia] for the rule of law in its territory." Many other important declarations followed, including those by the presidency of the European Union and by NATO. Most of them deemed the attackers "terrorists," and the officials behind the declarations refused to negotiate with them.[5] Javier Solana, the EU's High Representative, considered that it would be "a mistake to negotiate with terrorists in this particular case. It is a mistake to do it and we do not recommend doing it."[6] Several weeks into the crisis, NATO secretary-general George Robertson still referred to the NLA as "a bunch of murderous thugs whose objective is to destroy a democratic Macedonia."[7]

The prime ministers of neighboring countries, notably those of Greece and Bulgaria, visited Skopje and offered their countries' military assistance. The government of Albania denounced the acts of violence "by extremist groups of individuals, acts which run counter to the aspirations of Albanians and Macedonian Albanians throughout the region." Albania's government was firm in its belief that "acts of violence contradict the interests of the Albanians and the position of the Albanian political faction in Macedonia. Such acts are aimed at damaging the image of the Albanian people all over the region and at depriving them of the international support and sympathy won during the war in Kosovo."[8] Regional analysts agreed that for the first time in Balkan history, the forces of disunity and disintegration had failed to attract support of either their ethnic kin or of the major political forces in the neighboring countries.

The violence entered a new phase in mid-March 2001, when fighting broke out in the immediate vicinity of Tetovo. The government of Macedonia started mobilizing reservists and undertook an arms buildup by purchasing large amounts of new weaponry. UN Security Council Resolution 1345 of March 21, 2001 strongly condemned "extremist violence, including terrorist activities" in certain parts of Macedonia. At the same time, Prime Minister Georgievski criticized NATO and the EU for insisting that his government wait before responding and show restraint in countermeasures. The international community's increasing appeals to the Macedonian government for restraint, the country's poor weapons supply, and inadequacies in the capabilities and training of government troops to conduct effective operations against the extremists all tended to keep Skopje from taking more determined action. Each passing week saw successive villages occupied by the extremists, who committed new acts of terror.

By summer, a sizeable part of Macedonia's northern and western territory, consisting of at least eighty mostly ethnically mixed villages, had fallen prey to NLA units. Some sixty Macedonian soldiers and policemen lost their lives in ambushes or in combat. Civilian victims, including thousands of displaced persons, have yet to be fully accounted for. The Macedonian air force and artillery inflicted particularly heavy losses on ethnic Albanian villages in the Kumanovo-Lipkovo area. NLA troops, in turn, deprived the entire town of Kumanovo of its regular water supply for weeks. "Cleansing" actions against ethnic Macedonians imposed their own toll of suffering and material destruction. In early June, an angry crowd in Bitola destroyed some fifty shops and twenty homes belonging to Albanians and Macedonian Muslims. In mid-2002, there were still some thirteen thousand internally displaced people as a result of the crisis.

Who were the NLA? Various explanations continue to be offered to this day, most all of which share a salient observation: they executed a well planned and meticulously organized conspiracy against Macedonia and peace in the region.[9] Undoubtedly there were ethnic Albanians from Macedonia among the insurgents right from the start, and others who joined the insurgency locally once it was under way. However, the NLA's initial core could not but come from outside Macedonia; they must have been war veterans, professionally trained for the operation, with a distinct "Made in Kosovo" trademark. At no stage of the insurgency could ethnic Albanians in Macedonia be said to have joined the fighting on a mass scale. Of those who did join, many were sons of ethnic Albanian families who did so under duress. This fact was of no small importance in view of the purpose of the terrorist attacks—to provoke the Macedonian government into a full-scale war. Some analysts see the origins of the insurgency as being at least partly intertwined with organized crime, especially with the various lucrative trafficking schemes taking place through both Macedonia and Kosovo. For organized crime, fishing is much easier in the troubled waters of destabilized and war-torn areas.[10]

What were the NLA demands? Observers found it hard to believe the leader of the NLA's political wing, Ali Ahmeti, who claimed that the insurgents respected Macedonia's territorial integrity and called only for changes in the constitution and for other measures that would put ethnic Albanians on par with their Macedonian countrymen. In principle, the demands did not question directly the nature of Macedonia as a unitary and multiethnic state; rather, the insurgents emphasized that their aim was to obtain only what the ethnic Albanian community had been striving for since Macedonia's independence: recognizing ethnic Albanians as one of the peoples forming the state of Macedonia; accepting Albanian as the country's second official language and allowing it to be used in parliament and public administration; extending higher education opportunities in the Albanian language to ethnic Albanian students; ensuring ethnic Albanians' proportionate representation in state administration, the police, and the judiciary; and expanding the role of local government to the advantage of localities inhabited by ethnic groups, notably ethnic Albanians. The presidents of the DPA and the PDP joined Ali Ahmeti in subsequently reiterating most of these claims in a highly controversial joint statement they signed during their unexpected meeting on May 22. Ethnic Macedonians viewed the joint statement as a severe provocation, while EU and NATO ministers agreed with President Trajkovski that the document was "no longer relevant."[11]

Why did the NLA launch its assault in February 2001? A host of external and internal factors accounted for the timing of the aggressive action against Macedonia and its democratically elected government. Some of these factors had been taking shape over a longer duration and their consequences might have been predicted. For one thing, developments in and around Kosovo had made the ethnic Albanian communities in the region feel that they had all the international support they needed. Their extremist leaders must have concluded that, if they wanted to gain anything, the time had come to act. For another, UNPREDEP's early withdrawal left the Kosovo section of the border with Macedonia virtually unprotected. NATO's Kosovo Force (KFOR) had been busy in Kosovo proper; its mandate could not have left any illusions regarding the defense of Macedonia. Under those circumstances, the preparation of a military action from across the border was only a matter of time. Time was also of the essence in order to establish hideouts and secret arms caches or to prepare supplies on the Macedonian side of the border. The absence of

UNPREDEP (or, for that matter, any similar international operation of formed troops), KFOR's exclusive concentration on Kosovo, and the inadequate resources of the Macedonian army created a haven for such activities and easy illegal crossborder traffic. UNPREDEP's experience had taught us that the scale of guerilla preparations of this magnitude could not have gone unnoticed. After all, our patrols had been frequent visitors to many border villages that were later listed as sites of the insurgents' violence.

The timing of the assault against free and sovereign Macedonia was likewise tied to a compounded range of economic and political factors that the perpetrators did not fail to exploit. Economically, the country was in dire straits. Militarily, its army was poorly equipped and badly trained. Politically, as the case of the DPA demonstrated, a number of ethnic Albanian radicals re-entered the political mainstream and, at least for the time being, were satisfied with the concessions they had obtained within the new ruling coalition. The new radicals, in turn, including those in Kosovo, were worried that the concessions might lull the ethnic Albanian population into at least a temporary peace. Formed only in late 1998, the government had to cope with a series of crises (most notably a phone tapping scandal) and quickly and visibly suffered from what might be defined as "leadership fatigue." Macedonians were also considerably disillusioned with the international community, especially following the Kosovo refugee crisis and its ramifications for Macedonia. Last but not least, the situation was further complicated by the weaknesses of Macedonia's civil society at both the national and the local levels.

Externally, Macedonia was bearing the brunt of the international community's past mistakes: the issue of the country's name, delays in establishing more effective relations with the European Union and NATO, failures to solve Macedonia's "hard security" problems, and the early withdrawal of UNPREDEP. The Kosovo-Macedonia portion of the border remained unguarded, and KFOR was not prepared to act; concern mounted among troop-contributing governments over possible casualties in KFOR's national contingents. The signing of the Macedonia-FRY agreement on the final demarcation of their mutual border irritated radical politicians in Kosovo, who believed that they should have been involved in the negotiation process and become part of the final agreement since some of the disputed territory was situated along the Kosovo section of the border. Following rancorous statements by Kosovo politicians, including a declaration by the province's parliament and several border incidents, Macedonia's National Assembly issued a counterdeclaration, rejecting the legality of Kosovo's claims. The matter was taken up by the UN Security Council, which reconfirmed the validity of its Resolution 1244 and the status of Kosovo under its terms.

The rebels remained keenly aware that the international community was still actively involved in the unfinished business in other parts of the Balkans and that it might be some time before it took up a response to the incursion. They must have entertained similar hopes in connection with possible reactions of the new U.S. administration. At the beginning of the crisis, Washington was rather noncommittal, deeply involved as it was in the transition of power. Initial signals that the Bush administration had not intended to increase U.S. involvement in the Balkans did not help to dispel concerns over the incipient emergency in Macedonia. To be sure, the international community essentially aggravated the crisis in the first weeks by letting it spread beyond the village of Tanusevci; given the Kosovo Albanians' standing debt of gratitude to NATO, an infantry battalion of peacekeepers and appropriate diplomatic persuasion might have been enough to contain it and lay the groundwork for a solution by preventive techniques, such as negotiation and effective conditionality. As the insurgency continued and the NLA occupied new territory—at the same time the Macedonian government was wrestling with its own internal crises—the process of identifying international trouble shooters and maximizing their role swallowed up precious time and more victims. All this played directly into the rebels' hands as the international community again acted too late and did too little, particularly in the critical first weeks of the crisis.

Although the role of the European Union, NATO, the OSCE, and U.S. diplomacy in containing the dramatic developments was of primary importance, historians and political analysts will keep busy in the years to come trying to find out why international pressure to end the conflict had gradually shifted from the perpetrators of aggression to the government of Macedonia. Indeed, the overall efforts of Javier Solana and Francois Leotard on behalf of the European Union, George Robertson on behalf of NATO, the Romanian chairmanship of the OSCE, and James Pardew on behalf of the United States eventually proved to be well-intentioned and laudable. At a certain point, however, some of these specific approaches changed, putting the onus of responsibility on the government to take

nonmilitary measures to end the escalating conflict. In some of their pronouncements and actions to end the conflict, the international facilitators
appeared to equate what they earlier branded as "a bunch of murderous
thugs" with the ultimate target of the insurgents' violence. This visible
shift, in turn, played right into the hands of hard liners and radicals on
both sides, and it actually strengthened a popular belief that the only point
of agreement between the ethnic Macedonians and ethnic Albanians was
their joint conviction that the international community was siding with
the Albanians. Moreover, in dealing with the government, the facilitators
were not above employing heavy-handedness and arm-twisting, which the
ethnic Macedonians believed to be arrogant and part of the international
community's prejudice against them, to say the least. Consequently,
national sentiment toward the international community is not very high
these days in Macedonia.

Whereas the representatives of the international community perceived
the solution of the crisis first and foremost in political terms, different factions in the government concentrated on military options. Political means
required time and patience. Military options were quick and bold; they
were also harder to restrain. Political means involved some contacts with
the other side that neither the government nor, in part, the international
community recognized as legitimate. But the insurgency could not be
defeated by force alone, and the international facilitators also seemed to
believe that because developments had gone as far as they did, progress on
the political front could bring about the inevitable changes in the rules of
Macedonia's interethnic relations that should have been made long ago
and in a peaceful manner. In a way, the facilitators chose to strike while
the iron was hot. But of course the iron was just too hot, so the question
remained, "How far do the ends justify the means?"

The loss of human lives and destruction, months of political wrangling
on Macedonia's political scene, several government crises, and uncertainty
regarding the country's future finally showed that patience and sacrifice
had not been in vain. In arriving at a solution, even the most radical politicians were able to yield to the spirit of compromise and accommodation.
While the cessation of military hostilities was handled mainly by international facilitators, unquestioned credit for the process of negotiations goes
to Macedonia's political leaders. Ultimately, both the ruling coalition and
the opposition were able to rise above party politics and work out an agree-

ment that, circumstances permitting, may stand a chance of holding for years to come.

On August 13, 2001, leaders of Macedonia's four major political parties—VMRO-DPMNE, SDSM, DPA and PDP—gathered at the resort town of Ohrid under the auspices of President Trajkovski and signed a Framework Agreement to secure "the future of Macedonia's democracy and [permit] the development of closer and more integrated relations between the Republic of Macedonia and the Euro-Atlantic community." In a mood of hope, but not without acrimony, Macedonia's parliament ratified the agreement three months later and enacted the relevant changes in the constitution, along with a set of accompanying laws. The historic document proceeds from five basic principles:

◆ The use of violence in pursuit of political aims is rejected completely and unconditionally. Only peaceful political solutions can ensure a stable and democratic future for Macedonia.

◆ Macedonia's sovereignty and territorial integrity, and the unitary character of the state, are inviolable and must be preserved. There are no territorial solutions to ethnic issues.

◆ The multiethnic character of Macedonia's society must be preserved and reflected in public life.

◆ A modern democratic state in its natural course of development and maturation must continually ensure that its constitution fully meets the needs of all its citizens and comports with the highest international standards, which themselves continue to evolve.

◆ The development of local self-government is essential for encouraging the participation of citizens in democratic life and for promoting respect for the identity of communities.[12]

The agreement addresses and adjusts a broad range of ethnic Albanians' grievances since the country's independence. On certain matters, it goes farther than their initial claims. Thus we have gone a long way since UNPREDEP's modest efforts in good offices and initiatives which, short of violence and in a process of gradual change by peaceful means, could have led to similar solutions. In a way, then, the circle has closed.

Does this mean then that the Framework Agreement rewards violence? Many Macedonians still think so. At the same time, it should be remembered that the accord had been arrived at by democratically elected representatives of the country and based on President Trajkovski's plan to address the crisis, endorsed by the government of Macedonia. It avoided what surely would have become a much larger and much bloodier civil war with thousands of victims. The agreement has preserved the unitary character of the state, its territorial integrity, and its sovereignty; its constitutional amendments had for the first time been voted upon and approved by ethnic Albanians. In short, Ohrid was a national roundtable, arriving at a social contract for Macedonia that was reaffirmed by the country's parliament. Genuine national reconciliation is still far off on the horizon, though, for as long as the country's political and intellectual elites on both sides of the ethnic divide fail to put aside their differences and the riddle of Kosovo is not satisfactorily solved, the Damoclean sword of instability will continue to hang over Macedonia. Equally disquieting is continued criticism of the Framework Agreement: While some ethnic Macedonians believe it is too much of a concession, more radical ethnic Albanian politicians consider it to be only the first step in their quest for changes.[13] Clearly, both views do not bode well for the future of national reconciliation.

Amidst intense concern, Macedonia's citizens went to the polls on September 15, 2002. The elections proved to be free and fair, with very few incidents. The coalition "Together for Macedonia," consisting of several parties led by the SDSM, emerged as an unquestionable victor, winning half of the one hundred twenty seats in the National Assembly. The ruling coalition, headed by VMRO-DPMNE, won thirty-three seats. Not unexpectedly, the ethnic Albanian electorate gave the newly established Democratic Union for Integration (DUI), under the leadership of former NLA leader Ali Ahmeti, as many as sixteen seats. The remaining eleven ethnic Albanian MPs come from three other political parties: DPA, PDP, and the NDP. Proceeding from his consistent belief that the Ohrid agreement must be respected, Prime Minister Crvenkovski invited DUI to join his coalition government and accept five ministerial posts. In forming the new government, he made a reassuring and, indeed, obliging statement to the effect that "we shall work much differently than we did last time, until 1998, and I hope we shall not repeat some of the mistakes we then made. If we do, we do not deserve to be a government."[14]

In the spring of 2001, a former colleague in Skopje, Kannan Rajarathinam, sent me a brief e-mail message: "The problem with preventive peacekeeping is that peace has to be breached for it to be vindicated—in retrospect." Indeed, two years following UNPREDEP's termination, peace in Macedonia was breached; by a stroke of bitter consolation, preventive peacekeeping was vindicated—too late. The lethal shots had been fired and the whole country had almost been set aflame. While students of history will have much to ponder as to what had really happened in and around Macedonia at the beginning of the new millennium,[15] the lessons of the international community's initial response to Macedonia's external and internal instability should not be forgotten: prevention is indeed less costly and less disruptive than cure. This small but strategically significant Balkan country had been able to stave off for quite a while what most observers agreed was impending mass violence, the sources of which were by now quite familiar to those who studied the region. But now, in the first few months of 2001, Macedonia suffered a deep and bloody wound along its society's ethnic integument. The "cure" in this case will take perhaps a long, long while. In the meantime, the country must heal.

NOTES

Preface

1. In addition to a host of other authors who have covered an extensive range of issues that I need not return to here, I have in mind particularly the invaluable writings by Alice Ackermann, *Making Peace Prevail: Preventing Violent Conflict in Macedonia* (Syracuse, N.Y.: Syracuse University Press, 2000); Michael S. Lund, *Preventing Violent Conflicts. A Strategy for Preventive Diplomacy* (Washington, D.C.: United States Institute of Peace Press, 1996) and other of his published works; Stephen Ostrowski, "Preventive Deployment of Troops as Preventive Measures: Macedonia and Beyond," *Journal of International Law and Politics* 30, nos. 3–4 (Spring/Summer 1998); James Pettifer, ed., *The New Macedonian Question* (London: Macmillan, 1999). Hugh Poulton, *Who Are the Macedonians?* (Bloomington: Indiana University Press, 2000); the unpublished manuscript of Lieutenant Colonel Ilkka Tiihonen (ret.) of Finland, "Preventive Deployment of the United Nations Forces: The Case of the United Nations Preventive Deployment Force in the Former Yugoslav Republic of Macedonia" (1997); and Abiodun Williams, *Preventing War: The United Nations and Macedonia* (Lanham, Md.: Rowman and Littlefield, 2000).

1. A New Meaning for an Old Axiom

1. For the relevance of this metaphor see Boutros Boutros-Ghali, "The Challenges of Preventive Diplomacy: The Role of the United Nations and Its Secretary-General" (lecture at the symposium on preventive diplomacy, "The Therapeutics and Mediation," New York, April 23–24, 1996); and Kofi Annan, "The Peacekeeping Prescription," in *Preventive Diplomacy: Stopping Wars Before They Start,* ed. Kevin M. Cahill, M.D. (New York: Basic Books and The Center for International Health and Cooperation, 1996), 174–90.

2. Henryk J. Sokalski, "Towards a Century of Prevention," in *Politica Criminal, Derechos Humanos y Systemas Juridicos en el Siglo XXI: Homenaje a Pedro David* (Buenos Aires: Editorial Depalma, 2001).

3. *Encyclopedia Britannica,* 15th ed., s.v. "Diplomacy."

4. Germany, the United Kingdom, France, and Italy concluded the agreement on September 30, 1938, which allowed Nazi Germany to annex the Sudetenland in what was the former western Czechoslovakia. The agreement became a symbol of appeasement in the face of totalitarian territorial claims.

5. The Soviet Union and Germany concluded the pact on August 23, 1939, just a few days before Germany's invasion of Poland and the outbreak of World War II, as a German-Soviet nonaggression pact. It had a secret protocol annexed to it which allowed the USSR to take over a sizeable portion of eastern Poland. Accordingly, Soviet troops invaded Poland on September 17, 1939. Similar action followed against Finland (November 30, 1939) and the Baltics—Latvia, Lithuania, and Estonia—in the summer of 1940. On June 22, 1941, German troops attacked the Soviet Union.

6. Some other provisions of the UN Charter have contained an explicit or implicit call for support of the collective effort of prevention, including Article 1 (1): ". . . to take effective collective measures for the prevention and removal of threats to the peace . . . and adjustment or settlement of international disputes or situations which might lead to a breach of the peace"; Article 2 (2): "All Members, in order to ensure to all of them the rights and benefits resulting from membership, shall fulfill in good faith obligations assumed by them in accordance with the present Charter"; Article 2 (5): "All Members shall give the United Nations every assistance in any action it takes in accordance with the present Charter, and shall refrain from giving assistance to any state against which the United Nations is taking preventive or enforcement action"; Article 6: "A Member of the United Nations which has persistently violated the Principles contained in the present Charter may be expelled from the Organization by the General Assembly upon the recommendation of the Security Council"; Article 25: "The Members of the United Nations agree to accept and carry out decisions of the Security Council in accordance with the present Charter"; or Article 33: "1. The parties to any dispute, the continuance of which is likely to endanger the maintenance of international peace and security, shall, first of all, seek a solution by negotiation, enquiry, mediation, conciliation, arbitration, judicial settlement, resort to regional agencies or arrangements, or other peaceful means of their own choice. 2. The Security Council shall, when it deems necessary, call upon the parties to settle their dispute by such means."

7. UN Press Release SG/SM/4124 (April 20, 1988), 7–8.

8. See Lilly R. Sucharipa-Behrmann and Thomas M. Franck, "Preventive

Measures," *New York University Journal of International Law and Politics* 30, nos. 3–4 (Spring/Summer 1998): 500.

9. Henryk J., Sokalski, "Preventive Action: The Need for a Comprehensive Approach," in *Preventive Action in Theory and Practice,* ed. Jeremy Ginifer, Espen Barth Eide, and Carsten Rønnfeldt (Oslo: Norwegian Institute of International Affairs, 1999), 62.

10. Hammarskjold died in a plane crash on September 12, 1960, during his fourth peacemaking trip to the Congo.

11. UN General Assembly, Fifteenth Session, Official Records, *Annual Report of the Secretary-General on the Work of the Organization, 16 June 1959–15 June 1960.* UN Doc. A/4390/Ad.1, Supplement no. 1A (New York: United Nations, 1960), 4.

12. See the note by the president of the Security Council, UN Doc. S/23500 (January 31, 1992).

13. According to some experts, "contrary to conventional wisdom, most research indicates that civil wars have decreased in both the number and magnitude from 1992 to 1998. A slight rise since 1998 may be an anomaly in a post–Cold War decline, or it could suggest that the mid-1990s decrease is actually an aberration in an overall upward trend recorded since 1945." They point out that in the last decade of the twentieth century, 30 percent of conflicts ended with peace agreements—more than during any other decade in the latter half of the century. See "From Reaction to Prevention: Opportunities for the United Nations System in the New Millennium" (report of the International Policy Conference organized by the International Peace Academy, New York, April 13–14, 2000).

14. Adopted on December 5, 1988 as annex to UN General Assembly Resolution 43/51, and on December 9, 1991 as annex to UN General Assembly Resolution 46/59.

15. UN Doc. S/23500.

16. Boutros Boutros-Ghali, *An Agenda for Peace* (New York: United Nations, 1992).

17. It should be noted that neither Article 33 of the Charter nor *An Agenda for Peace* would exhaust the list of traditional international measures with a preventive potential. Lilly R. Sucharipa-Behrmann and Thomas M. Franck discuss a series of other measures, including disaster relief, supervised self-determination, peacemaking, promotion of human rights, promotion of economic development and environmental monitoring and protection. See Sucharipa-Behrmann and Franck, "Preventive Measures," 486–92.

18. See in particular statements by the president of the Security Council of

June 30, 1992 (UN Doc. S/24210); October 29, 1992 (S/24728); November 30, 1992 (S/24872); December 30, 1992 (S/25036), January 28, 1993 (S/25184); February 26, 1993 (S/25344); March 31, 1993 (S/25493); April 30, 1993 (S/25696); May 28, 1993 (S/25859); May 3, 1994 (S/PRST/1994/22); July 27, 1994 (S/PRST/1994/36); November 4, 1994 (S/PRST/1994/62); February 22, 1995 (S/PRST/1995/9); June 19, 1997 (S/PRST/1997/34); September 25, 1997 (S/PRST/1997/46); September 16, 1998 (S/PRST/1998/28); September 24, 1998 (S/PRST/1998/29); September 29, 1998 (S/PRST/1998/30); November 30, 1998 (S/PRST/1998/35); July 8, 1999 (S/PRST/1999/21); September 24, 1999 (S/PRST/1999/28); November 30, 1999 (S/PRST/1999/21); November 30, 1999 (S/PRST/1999/34); March 23, 2000 (S/PRST/2000/10); July 20, 2000 (S/PRST/2000/25); February 20, 2001 (S/PRST/2001/5); and March 22, 2001 (S/PRST/2001/10). See also UN Security Council Resolutions 1170 (1998) of May 28, 1998; 1196 (1998) of September 16, 1998; 1197 (1998) of September 18, 1998; 1208 (1998) of November 19, 1998; 1209 (1998) of November 19, 1998; 1265 (1999) of September 17, 1999; 1296 (2000) of April 19, 2000; 1318 (2000) of September 7, 2000; 1325 (2000) of October 31, 2000; 1327 (2000) of November 13, 2000; and 1366 (2001) of August 30, 2001.

19. By mid-2002, forty-five thousand military personnel and civilian police from eighty-seven countries, as well as some thirty-eight hundred international and seventy-seven hundred national staff members, were serving in fifteen UN peacekeeping operations. From 1948 to 2001, as many as 1,738 UN peacekeepers lost their lives in the line of duty.

20. UN Doc. A/50/60–S/1995/1 (January 25, 1995).

21. Statement by president of the Security Council, UN Doc. S/PRST/1995/9 (February 22, 1995).

22. Ibid.

23. See, for instance, Lund, *Preventing Violent Conflicts,* 35–36. The author lists four reasons in support of his thesis: (1) such an equation would risk dispersing the energies of preventive diplomacy; (2) although basic socio-economic, political, or psychological conditions may lay the groundwork for violence, they do not necessarily produce it; (3) many societal conditions giving rise to disputes should not necessarily be eliminated from human experience, even if they could be; (4) policies aimed at transforming basic social and political conditions can themselves foster violent conflicts rather than prevent them.

24. For details, see UN Doc. S/2001/82 and annex of January 25, 2001.

25. See the Provisional Verbatim of the 4272nd meeting of the Security Council, UN Doc. S/PV/4272, pp. 2–4.

26. UN Doc. S/PRST/2001/5 (February 20, 2001).

27. Stephen John Stedman, "Alchemy for a New World Order: Overselling

'Preventive Diplomacy,'" *Foreign Affairs,* May/June 1995, 14–20; and Michael S. Lund, "Underrating Preventive Diplomacy," *Foreign Affairs,* July/August 1995, 160–63.

28. Edward N. Luttwak, "Give War a Chance," *Foreign Affairs,* July/August 1999, 36–44.

29. Ibid., 36.

30. Ibid., 38.

31. UN General Assembly, Fifty-First Session, Official Records, *Report of the Secretary-General on the Work of the Organization to the Fifty-First Session of the General Assembly.* UN Doc. A/51/1 (New York: United Nations, 1996), para. 652.

32. See also Hugh Miall, "Preventing Potential Conflict: Assessing the Impact of 'Light' and 'Deep' Conflict Prevention in Central and Eastern Europe and the Balkans," in *Impact of Conflict Prevention Policy: Cases, Measures, Assessments,* ed. Michael Lund and Guenola Rasamoelina (Baden-Baden, Germany: Nomos, 2000).

33. See UN General Assembly Resolution A/RES/47/120A (December 18, 1992).

34. Lund, "Underrating Preventive Diplomacy."

35. Stedman, "Alchemy for a New World Order."

36. Boutros-Ghali, "The Challenges of Preventive Diplomacy"; and idem., "Challenges of Preventive Diplomacy: The Role of the United Nations and Its Secretary-General," in Cahill, ed., *Preventive Diplomacy,* 18.

37. Lund, *Preventing Violent Conflicts,* 37.

38. Michael S. Lund, introduction to *Impact of Conflict Prevention Policy,* by Lund and Rasamoelina, eds., 13 (note).

39. See Boutros Boutros-Ghali, *An Agenda for Development* (New York: United Nations, 1994).

40. Bruce W. Jentleson, "Preventive Diplomacy: Analytical Conclusions and Policy Lessons," in *Opportunities Missed, Opportunities Seized: Preventive Diplomacy in the Post–Cold War World.* Report of the Carnegie Commission on Preventing Deadly Conflict, ed. Bruce W. Jentleson (New York: Rowman and Littlefield, 2000), 348.

41. Margaretha Ugglas, "Conditions for Successful Preventive Diplomacy," in *The Challenges of Preventive Diplomacy: The Experience of the CSCE* (Stockholm: Ministry for Foreign Affairs, 1994).

42. *Preventive Diplomacy and Japan's Role: An Action Menu* (Tokyo: Japan Forum on International Relations, February 1998), 4.

43. Ibid., 10.

44. Ibid., 4.

45. Swedish Ministry of Foreign Affairs, *Preventing a Violent Conflict–A Swedish Plan of Action* (Stockholm: Regeringskansliet, 1999).

46. Carnegie Commission on Preventing Deadly Conflict, *Perspectives on Prevention, Preventive Diplomacy, Preventive Defense, and Conflict Resolution.* Report of Two Conferences at Stanford University and the Ditchley Foundation (New York: Carnegie Corporation of New York, October 1999).

47. Carnegie Commission on Preventing Deadly Conflict, *Preventing Deadly Conflict: Final Report* (Washington, D.C.: Carnegie Commission on Preventing Deadly Conflict, 1997).

48. Subsequently, the UN Security Council emphasized in Resolution 1366 (2001) of August 30, 2001, "the importance of a comprehensive strategy comprising operational and structural measures for prevention of armed conflict. . . ."

49. UN Press Release SG/SM/6218 (April 23, 1997).

50. See, for instance, "Secretary-General's address to the Forum on the Final Report of the Carnegie Commission on Preventing Deadly Conflict," UN Press Release SG/SM/6454 (February 5, 1998).

51. UN Docs. A/52/1 (September 3, 1997) and A/54/1 (August 31, 1999).

52. UN Press Release SC/6892 (July 20, 2000).

53. UN Doc. A/54/2000 (March 27, 2000).

54. Ibid., paras. 198–203.

55. UN Doc. A/RES/55/2 (September 8, 2000).

56. UN Security Council Resolution 1318 (2000), September 7, 2000.

57. UN Doc. A/55/305–S/2000/809.

58. Ibid., para. 32. The issue of state sovereignty should also be viewed in the context of another penetrating study, *The Responsibility to Protect: Report of the International Commission on Intervention and State Sovereignty* (Ottawa: International Development Research Center, 2001). The comprehensive nature of the report and its new notion of "responsibility to protect" have shed a new light on the concept of prevention.

59. UN Doc. A/54/1 (August 31, 1999), para. 23.

60. Identical letters dated August 21, 2000 from the secretary-general to the president of the General Assembly and the president of the Security Council, UN Doc. A/55/305–S/2000/809 (August 31, 2000).

61. UN Security Council Resolution 1318 (2000), September 7, 2000.

62. UN Docs. A/55/502 (October 20, 2000) and A/55/977 (June 1, 2001).

63. UN Doc. A/55/985–S/2001/574 (June 7, 2001).

64. Lund, *Preventing Violent Conflicts,* 34

65. Boutros Boutros-Ghali, *Unvanquished, A U.S.–UN Saga* (New York: Random House, 1999), 37.

66. Dimitris Triantaphyllou, *The Albanian Factor* (Athens: Hellenic Foundation for European and Foreign Policy, 2000), 11. The author quotes material from the Economist Intelligence Unit, *Economies in Transition/Eastern Europe and the Former Soviet Union: Regional Overview* (First Quarter, 1997), 23.

67. See Michael E. Brown and Richard N. Rosecrance, eds., *The Costs of Conflict: Prevention and Cure in the Global Arena.* Report of the Carnegie Commission on Preventing Deadly Conflict (Lanham, Md.: Rowman and Littlefield, 1999).

68. See Ackermann, *Making Peace Prevail,* 3.

69. Lund, *Preventing Violent Conflicts,* 38.

70. Johan Galtung, *Peace by Peaceful Means: Peace and Conflict, Development and Civilization* (Thousand Oaks, Calif.: SAGE Publications, 1996), 31–33.

71. See *Preventive Diplomacy and Japan's Role,* 5.

72. Statement in the Security Council on November 29, 1999 by Ambassador Marjatta Rasi. Text circulated by the Permanent Mission of Finland to the United Nations.

73. For more on the preventive role of the principal organs of the United Nations, see Secretary-General Kofi Annan's report, *Prevention of Armed Conflict,* UN Doc. A/55/985–S/2001/574 (June 7, 2001).

74. "United Nations Declaration on the Prevention and Removal of Disputes and Situations Which May Threaten International Peace and Security and on the Role of the United Nations in this Field," UN General Assembly Resolution 43/51, annex.

75. For more on the role of the Secretary-General in conflict prevention, see Annan, *Prevention of Armed Conflict,* paras. 51–60.

76. The G-8 includes Canada, France, Germany, Italy, Japan, the Russian Federation, the United Kingdom and the United States. The group's important program on preventive action is contained in "G8 Miyazaki Initiatives for Conflict Prevention," adopted at the Kyushu-Okinawa Summit Meeting, July 12–13, 2000; http//www.g8kyushu-okinawa.go.jp/e/documents/html/initiative.html. The Balkans "Contact Group" includes France, Germany, Italy, the Russian Federation, the United Kingdom, and the United States. Areas of the group's current interest in conflict prevention can be found in the communiqué of the Contact Group following its Paris meeting on April 11, 2001; http//www.

france.diplomatie.fr/actualite.gb/article.asp?cat=3&th=0&ar=622. For more on the "Friends of the Secretary-General," see Carnegie Commission on Preventing Deadly Conflict, *Preventing Deadly Conflict: Final Report,* 134; and Boutros Boutros-Ghali, *Supplement to An Agenda for Peace,* UN Doc. A/50/60–S/1995/1 (January 3, 1995), published in idem., *An Agenda for Peace 1995,* 2d ed., with the new Supplement and Related UN Documents (New York: United Nations, 1995), 30 (paras. 83–84).

77. See, for instance, the report presented to the Nice European Council by the Secretary-General/High Representative and the European Commission, "Improving the Coherence and Effectiveness of European Union Action in the Field of Conflict Prevention," European Commission Press Release 14088/00, November 30, 2000. See also "Open Debate on the Presidency Work Program— Conflict Prevention" (paper by the Swedish Presidency of the European Union, Stockholm, Ministry of Foreign Affairs, January 10, 2001).

78. Jentleson,"Preventive Diplomacy: Analytical Conclusions and Policy Lessons."

79. See Brown and Rosecrance, eds., *The Costs of Conflict,* 227–29.

80. For instance, the UN secretary-general has pointed out in his *Report on the Work of the Organization* for the fifty-fourth session of the General Assembly that "the prospect of closer association with the European Union has served as a powerful tool for promoting tolerance and institutional reforms in several East and Central European countries, but few if any counterparts exist at the global level." Some organizations, as a rule, will not admit new members unless they first settle disputes with their neighbors. See UN General Assembly, Fifty-Fourth Session, Official Records, *Annual Report of the Secretary-General on the Work of the Organization,* UN Doc. A/54/1 (August 31, 1999), para. 55.

81. Michael S. Lund, "Improving Prevention by Learning from Experience," in Lund and Rasamoelina, eds., *Impact of Conflict Prevention Policy,* 74. In the same volume, Hugh Miall ("Preventing Potential Conflict," p. 29) constructs a set of qualitative indicators relevant to Central and Eastern European and Balkan states "such as human rights performance, quality of democratic governance, independence of media, quality of development of civil society, independence of the judiciary, degree of professionalization or politicization of local government, and so on. Although these indicators are not by themselves signifiers of violence, they do signify something about proneness to violence."

82. *Developmental Assistance as a Means of Conflict Prevention* (Oslo: Norwegian Institute of International Affairs, February 1998).

83. See note 18.

84. For details, see *Cooperation Between United Nations and Regional Organizations/Arrangements in a Peacekeeping Environment: Suggested Principles and*

Mechanisms (New York: UN Department of Peacekeeping Operations, March 1999).

85. The secretary-general convened previous meetings of heads of regional organizations in August 1994, February 1996, and July 1998. The 1998 meeting discussed conflict prevention.

86. Compare UN Doc. S/2001/138 (February 14, 2001) and UN Press Release SG/SM/7708 (February 7, 2001).

87. For more on this important aspect of conflict prevention, see Annan, *Prevention of Armed Conflict*, paras. 148–50.

88. For more on the fund, see Kofi A. Annan, *Annual Report on the Work of the Organization, 2001* (New York: United Nations, 2001), paras. 26–262. The subject of cooperation between the United Nations system and the private sector has been extensively covered in the book by Jane Nelson, *Building Partnerships* (New York: UN Department of Public Information, 2002).

89. See Boutros-Ghali, *Supplement to An Agenda for Peace*, in *An Agenda for Peace 1995*, 2d ed., 33 (para. 89).

90. According to the UN Development Program's *Human Development Report 1994* (New York: Oxford University Press, 1999), at the beginning of the twentieth century, 90 percent of casualties from wars were military, while less than one hundred years later, 90 percent of casualties were civilian.

91. George MacLean, "The Changing Perception of Human Security: Coordinating National and Multilateral Responses" (paper prepared for the conference of the United Nations Association in Canada, "The United Nations and the New Security Agenda," Ottawa, Ontario, May 8, 1998).

92. Kofi Annan, "Address to the Foreign Policy Association in New York," March 21, 2001; UN Press Release SG/SM/7747 (March 22, 2001).

93. An interesting set of principles on education for peace is found in the "Declaration on the Preparation of Societies for Life in Peace," UN General Assembly Resolution 33/73 (December 15, 1978). Another pertinent set of measures on behalf of peace can be found in the organization's "Declaration on a Culture of Peace," adopted as UN General Assembly Resolution 53/243 (September 13, 1999).

94. Allan James, "Preventive Diplomacy in a Historical Perspective," in Ginifer, Eide, and Rønnfeldt, eds., *Preventive Action in Theory and Practice*, 42–59.

95. Letter dated November 23, 1992 from the secretary-general to the president of the Security Council, UN Doc. S/24851 (November 25, 1992).

96. Paragraph 28 of *An Agenda for Peace* reads: "United Nations operations in areas of crisis have generally been established after conflict has occurred. The time has come to plan for circumstances warranting preventive deployment, which could take place in a variety of instances and ways. For example, in conditions of national crisis there could be preventive deployment at the request of the government or all parties concerned, or with their consent; in interstate disputes such deployment could take place when two countries feel that a United Nations presence on both sides of their border can discourage hostilities; furthermore, preventive deployment could take place when a country feels threatened and requests the deployment of an appropriate United Nations presence along its side of the border alone. In each situation, the mandate and composition of the United Nations presence would need to be carefully devised and be clear to all."

2. The Balkan Rectangle

1. *Report of the International Commission to Inquire into the Causes and Conduct of the Balkan Wars* (Washington, D.C.: The Carnegie Endowment, 1914).

2. For more on the subject of "the Balkan character," see Joseph Montville, *The Psychological Aspects of Political Conflict* (Washington, D.C.: Winston Foundation for World Peace, 1996), 21–24.

3. Poulton, *Who Are the Macedonians?*, 6.

4. George F. Kennan, introduction to *The Other Balkan Wars: A 1913 Carnegie Endowment Inquiry in Retrospect* (Washington, D.C.: Carnegie Endowment for International Peace, 1993), 11–12.

5. Richard Holbrooke, *To End a War* (New York: Random House, 1999), 125.

6. Ibid., 115.

7. *Report of the International Commission,* 15.

8. Misha Glenny, "The Birth of a Nation," *New York Times Book Review,* November 16, 1995, 24–28.

9. Poulton, *Who Are the Macedonians?*, iii.

10. Jovan Pavlovski, *Macedonia Yesterday and Today,* 2d ed. (Skopje: MI-AN, 1998), 22.

11. See Article 23 of the Treaty of Berlin.

12. One of the giants of the nineteenth-century national Macedonian renaissance, Krste Petkov Missirkov, writes in his book *On Macedonian Matters* (Skopje: Macedonian Review Editions, 1974 [1903]): "The reason why the Uprising failed is perfectly clear: From the very outset it was established on the wrong basis— instead of being a general Macedonian Uprising, it was a partial insurrection with Bulgarian overtones. . . . The intelligentsia, not only of other Macedonian nationalities but also of the Macedonian Slavs themselves, did not figure among the leaders of the Revolutionary Committee. The Committee, as a secret organization, feared to accept on an equal basis members belonging to the other nationalities" (p. 55).

13. President Boris Trajkovski, "Address at the Observance of the Ilinden Anniversary on August 2, 2000," *Macedonian Information Agency Newsletter,* August 3, 2000.

14. See Julie Kim and Carol Migdalovitz, *"Macedonia" (Skopje) Recognition and Conflict Prevention* (Washington, D.C.: Congressional Research Service, January 11, 1993), 2.

15. See Poulton, *Who Are the Macedonians?,* 88.

16. Trajkovski, "Address at the Observance of the Ilinden Anniversary."

17. Republic of Macedonia, *Independence through Peaceful Self-Determination: Documents* (Skopje: Balkan Forum, November 1992), 11.

18. The term derives from the notion of autonomous existence of an ancient Balkan tribe whose members, the Albanians claim, were their forebears. Today, the term has become synonymous with the aspirations of some ethnic Albanians in Macedonia to be granted autonomy.

19. Vladimir Milcin, "Sofia, Skopje, and the 'Macedonian Question,'" *War Report,* July/August 1995. Mala Prespa is a small region of nine villages on the Albanian side of Lake Prespa that is inhabited exclusively by ethnic Macedonians. Both Lake Prespa and its neighboring Lake Ohrid in southwestern Macedonia are shared by the two countries.

20. Formerly, the Party for Democratic Prosperity of Albanians/National Democratic Party (PDPA/NDP). The two parties merged in July 1997 to consolidate the radical elements in the ethnic Albanian community. For a long time, the party could not be registered under its new name as the Constitutional Court had objected to the Albanian symbols on its emblem.

21. Keith Brown, "Balkan Brokers: Culture and Conflict in Southeastern Europe" (paper presented at the United States Institute of Peace, Washington, D.C., June 8, 2000), 22.

22. Republic of Macedonia, *Independence through Peaceful Self-Determination,* 7.

23. See ibid.

24. The EC's original conditions for states seeking diplomatic recognition were contained in the December 16, 1991 declaration of the community's ministers for foreign affairs, entitled "Guidelines on the Recognition of New States in Eastern Europe and in the Soviet Union." A separate declaration on Yugoslavia of the same date spelled out a number of questions to which the Yugoslav republics had to respond in the affirmative for their applications for recognition to be considered.

25. For a detailed discussion of the role of the Badinter Commission, see Steve Terrett, *The Dissolution of Yugoslavia and the Badinter Arbitration Commission* (Burlington, Vt.: Ashgate/Dartmouth Press, 2000). See also the full text of the commission's Opinion no. 6, "On the Recognition of the Socialist Republic of Macedonia by the European Community and its Member States" in Republic of Macedonia, *Independence through Peaceful Self-Determination,* 39–43.

26. "Declaration on the Former Yugoslav Republic of Macedonia," EC Doc. P.53/92 (May 4, 1992).

27. The European Council is an organ of the European Union, established to discuss the union's affairs at the highest political level, including issues of foreign policy. The Council comprises heads of state or government and foreign ministers of the EU, as well as the president of the European Commission.

28. Republic of Macedonia, *Independence through Peaceful Self-Determination,* 47–48.

29. Ibid., 50.

30. European Council, "Conclusions of the Presidency, Part D: External Relations," Document 92/8, December 11–12, 1992.

31. The editor-in-chief of *Dnevnik* must have had good reasons to conclude that "Macedonians, like all the other people of the Balkans, are suspicious of foreigners and trust their words less and less. They still remember how the international community's resolute support for the survival of the Yugoslav federation melted away when it began to break up." Branko Geroski, "NLA Harms Albanian Aspirations," *Balkan Crisis Report,* no. 228 (March 21, 2001).

32. Kim and Migdalovitz, *"Macedonia,"* 8.

33. Republic of Macedonia, *Independence through Peaceful Self-Determination,* 53–55.

34. Notes on the meeting between President Gligorov and Secretary-General Boutros-Ghali, New York, February 3, 1992. Gligorov had publicly advanced these views on some earlier occasions.

35. UN Security Council Resolution 817 (1993), April 7, 1993, recommending to the General Assembly Macedonia's admission to membership in the United Nations. The General Assembly followed the recommendation through Resolution 47/225 (April 8, 1993).

36. Poulton, *Who Are the Macedonians?,* 177–78.

37. Dimitar Mircev, "Foreign Policy of Macedonia," in Pettifer, ed., *The New Macedonian Question,* 216–17.

38. Macedonia's major initiative, concerning the "[d]evelopment of good-neighborly relations among Balkan States," was advanced as early as the forty-eighth session of the General Assembly. See UN General Assembly Resolution 48/84 (December 15, 1993).

39. Kim and Migdalovitz, *"Macedonia,"* 10–11.

40. Macedonia attained full membership in the OSCE on October 12, 1995.

41. The country's admission to the Council of Europe on September 27, 1995 was considerably delayed because of its insufficient legislative reforms regarding the judiciary, self-government, and freedom of the media.

42. According to the March 2, 2001 issue of *MILS News,* during President Trajkovski's visit to Paris the day before, President Chirac reiterated that "this dispute is to be solved in accordance with Macedonian state interests." In his opinion, Macedonia had completely legitimate demands.

43. In an interview for the Belgrade daily *NIN* on September 24, 1993, Prime Minister Branko Crvenkovski recalled that whenever Macedonia "leaned toward one Balkan neighbor, it would end up with tragic consequences."

44. Interview with Kiro Gligorov in *Borba* (Belgrade), June 26–27, 1993.

45. Macedonian foreign minister Aleksandar Dimitrov, "Foreign Policy of the Republic of Macedonia" (address at the Foreign Policy Association, Copenhagen, March 21, 2000).

46. Address by Minister Aleksandar Dimitrov before the fifty-fifth session of the UN General Assembly, September 18, 2000.

47. Personal interview with the author, September 13, 2000, Skopje.

48. On June 15, 1998, eighty-five aircraft from thirteen NATO states participated in "Determined Falcon," an air exercise conducted over Macedonia and Albania, to demonstrate the alliance's capacity and readiness for rapid reaction and to put pressure on the protagonists of the Kosovo crisis to start negotiations. In 1999, the foreign policy issue confronting Macedonia's voters was NATO air strikes against the FRY.

49. For details of the agreement, see UN Docs. S/1996/250 (April 8, 1996) and S/1996/291 (April 17, 1996).

50. UN Doc. S/1996/250 (April 8, 1996).

51. "No Gambling with Identity," interview with President Gligorov, *Puls,* March 5, 1998. The president was referring to his meeting with Slobodan Milosevic on Crete in early November 1997 during the Inter-Balkan Summit.

52. The PDP parliamentary group explained that the method of defining the border was not in question; rather, that the negotiating partner was inappropriate because Belgrade had no competence to negotiate the Kosovo segment of the border. *MILS News,* March 2, 2001.

53. Milena Mahon, "The Macedonian Question in Bulgaria," *Nations and Nationalism* 4, no. 3 (1998): 400–401.

54. As reported in the daily *Nova Makedonija* (Skopje), September 22, 1991.

55. See Risto Lazarov, "Old Burdens and New Impulses in Macedonian-Bulgarian Relations," *Balkan Forum* 2, no. 1 (March 1994): 249–58.

56. *Dnevnik* (Skopje), November 28, 2002.

57. See Vlado Ivanovski, *Macedonia in the Struggle against Fascism* (Skopje: Committee on the Commemoration of the Fiftieth Anniversary of the Victory over Fascism, 1995); Frederick B. Chary, *The Bulgarian Jews and the Final Solution: 1940–1944* (Pittsburgh: University of Pittsburgh Press, 1972); and Poulton, *Who Are the Macedonians?*, 112–13.

58. Poulton, *Who Are the Macedonians?*, loc. cit.

59. On his official visit to Macedonia, July 13–14, 1995, President Suleyman Demirel of Turkey reassured his hosts: "There is no single political problem between Turkey and Macedonia. . . . Macedonia is a heart of the Balkans. . . . The sacred objective is to enable a multiethnic and multicultural community to live under one flag, thus enabling the people to live in a peaceful and secure environment. The Macedonian Turks, loyal citizens of Macedonia, also give their contribution to these values and to our mutual relations, by making a bridge of friendship between our two countries."

60. See Poulton, *Who Are the Macedonians?*, 16, note 10.

61. Constitution of the Republic of Macedonia (English-language version), Skopje, 1994.

62. John Shea, *Macedonia and Greece: The Struggle to Defend a New Balkan Nation* (London: McFarland, 1997), 300.

63. Robert Lee Wolff, *The Balkans in Our Time* (Cambridge, Mass.: Harvard University Press, 1956), 202.

64. According to Albanian sources, five thousand ethnic Macedonians live in Albania. Macedonian sources claim that there are as many as sixty thousand ethnic Macedonians in Albania. See Todor Dzunov, "Macedonian Minorities in Neighbouring Countries: Opportunities for National Expression Have Been Taken Away," *The Macedonian Times,* May 1995.

65. *Platform for the Solution of the National Albanian Question* (Tirana: Academy of Sciences of Albania, October 1998), 33.

66. Interview with President Kiro Gligorov, "Macedonia's President Mulls Future," *Features* (newsletter of the Transnational Foundation of Peace and Future Research), October 28, 1999.

67. At the time, Albania became a major supplier of weapons to Kosovo. According to most estimates, close to eight hundred thousand pieces of arms had been looted from Albania's army stocks. Only less than 10 percent might have been returned.

68. Interview with Macedonian minister of defense Lazar Kitanovski, *Vecer* (Skopje), September 20, 1997.

69. *New York Times,* March 19, 2001.

70. One of the most skillful politicians in the Balkans, Arben Xhaferi would soon tell Timothy Garton Ash: "The Albanians are not peaceful people by nature. They are warriors." See Ash's interview with Xhaferi in "Cry, the Dismembered Country," *New York Review of Books,* January 14, 1999. Earlier, Xhaferi had remarked that "the Albanians are more loyal to their ethnicity than to the state," as quoted in *The Macedonian Times* (Skopje), May 1996, 14.

71. As reported in *Dnevnik* (Skopje), April 3, 1999; and *Vecer* (Skopje), April 3–4. 1999.

72. As reported in *Dnevnik* (Skopje), April 7, 1999.

3. From Autocracy to Democracy

1. See Violeta Petroska-Beska, "Early Warning, and Preventive Action: Macedonia," in *Vigilance and Vengeance: NGOs Preventing Ethnic Conflict in Divided Societies,* ed. Robert I. Rotberg (Washington, D.C.: Brookings Institution Press, 1996), 135.

2. Magarditsch A. Hatschikjan, "Macedonia: Variable Balances, Fragile Structures," *Balkan Forum* 4, no. 3 (September 1996): 130.

3. Ibid., 131–32.

4. Ibid., 132–33.

5. For instance, during the national Ilinden and ASNOM anniversary observances on April 2, 1997, a holy day for all Macedonians, some one thousand supporters of VMRO-DPMNE booed and whistled during President Gligorov's address. One supporter of the demonstration trampled on the national flag. Conversely, for more than a year since President Boris Trajkovski's election, the SDSM leadership had not addressed him by a name other than "citizen Trajkovski" in protest of his victory over the SDSM candidate, former National Assembly speaker Tito Petkovski. Lines of division had also run across the successive ruling coalitions.

6. The April 16, 2001 issue of *Business Week* carried an article under a revealing title "A Delicate Economy Is Threatened. . . . But Does the West Even

Care?" It read in part: "During the Kosovo crisis in 1999, Western leaders promised Macedonia hundreds of millions of dollars in aid and fast-track negotiations for NATO and European Union membership. In return, Macedonia supported the bombing of Yugoslavia, which cost it major trade losses, and took in a quarter-million ethnic Albanian refugees. Only about 20 percent of the aid arrived, and NATO hasn't thrown a backward glance. The alliance put the peacekeeping base it promised Skopje in Greece instead. The European Union has behaved little better. While it took Romania, a ruined economy, into the fold as a formal accession partner, it relegated Macedonia to a level with pariah Yugoslavia and anarchic Albania. . . . One can only hope that, if the West finally upholds its commitments, it won't be too late."

7. The law provoked long-lasting demonstrations against provisions allowing the Albanian and Turkish languages to be used more extensively in training teachers for ethnic Albanian and ethnic Turkish schools in Macedonia.

8. National Assembly, Document 08-937/1 (March 18, 1997).

9. Texts of statements released by the Cabinet of the President on October 23, 1997; February 11, 1998; and April 3, 1998.

10. The 1994 census has shown that national minorities in Macedonia represent 31.5 percent of the population.

11. European Commission against Racism and Intolerance, *Second Report on "The Former Yugoslav Republic of Macedonia"* (Strasbourg: ECRI, April 3, 2000), 15.

12. For details of the 1994 census, see *Biannual Report of the Co-Chairmen of the Steering Committee on the Activities of the International Conference on the Former Yugoslavia,* paras. 26-30, annex to the letter dated December 29, 1994 from the secretary-general of the United Nations to the president of the Security Council, UN Doc. S/1994/1454. See also "Report of the Secretary-General pursuant to Security Council Resolution 947 (1994)," UN Doc. S/1995/222 (March 22, 1995), para. 41.

13. European Commission against Racism and Intolerance, *Second Report,* 17.

14. For more on the subject from the perspective of a Macedonian scholar, see Petroska-Beska, "Early Warning," 133–44.

15. Reporting on an April 1, 2001 meeting in Tirana between Arben Xhaferi and Ali Ahmeti, the leader of the so-called National Liberation Army (NLA), the April 6 edition of the Albanian-language daily *Fakti* (Skopje) noted that both politicians declared themselves against the idea of Macedonia's federalization. They did agree, however, to strive for the recognition of ethnic Albanians in Macedonia as a state-forming nation.

16. The International Crisis Group's report, *The Macedonian Question: Reform or Rebellion* (Skopje/Brussels: ICG, April 5, 2001), notes that "both sides

feel that their essential concerns and fears cannot be freely discussed, because the attempt to do so would open the door to extremist demands and reactions" (p. 15).

17. Other smaller ethnic groups have often pointed out the need for a broader platform of negotiations and their inclusion in discussions on the future of the country. This was particularly evident in April 2001, when President Trajkovski initiated a dialogue with leaders of the ethnic Albanians. The president of the Democratic Party of Turks, Erdogan Sarach, declared that his party disapproved of the solely Macedonian-Albanian dialogue imposed by the international community and the Macedonian government. The party insisted on the participation of the Turkish community in Macedonia in the shaping of a new future for the country. The Democratic Party of the Serbs in Macedonia expressed similar sentiments and urged President Trajkovski to include all political parties in the discussions on the future. See *MILS News,* April 4, 2001.

18. Michael Lund, "Preventive Diplomacy for Macedonia, 1992–1999: From Containment to Nation Building," in Jentleson, ed., *Opportunities Missed, Opportunities Seized,* 203.

19. Dimitris Christopulos, "Minority Protection: Toward a New European Approach," *Balkan Forum* 2, no. 1 (March 1994), 157.

20. See UN Doc. E/CN.4/Sub.2/1993/34, paras. 45–48.

21. Adopted as UN General Assembly Resolution 47/135 (December 18, 1992).

22. Francesco Capotorti, "Study on the Rights of Persons Belonging to Ethnic, Religious, and Linguistic Minorities," UN Doc. E/CN.4/Sub.2/384. A slightly changed version of this definition was offered eight years later by Justice Jules Descheness of Canada, also a member of the subcommission, and read: "A group of citizens of a state, constituting a numerical minority and in a non-dominant position in that state, endowed with ethnic, religious or linguistic characteristics which differ from those of the majority of the population, having a sense of solidarity with one another, motivated, if only implicitly, by a collective will to survive and whose aim is to achieve equality with the majority in fact and law" (UN Doc. E/CN.4/Sub.2/1985/31).

23. European Commission for Democracy through Law, *The Protection of Minorities* (Strasbourg: Council of Europe Press, 1994), 12.

24. For more on the subject, see Nigel S. Rodley, "Conceptual Problems of Protection of Minorities: International Legal Developments," *Human Rights Quarterly* 17 (1995): 48–71.

25. See, for instance, a general comment on the interpretation of Article 27 of the Covenant, contained in UN Doc. CCPR/C/21/Rev.1/Add.5.

26. See, among other sources, Article 13 of the International Covenant on

Economic, Social, and Cultural Rights, adopted as UN General Assembly Resolution 2200 A (XXI), December 16, 1966; Articles 2 and 4 of the Convention on the Elimination of All Forms of Racial Discrimination, adopted as UN General Assembly Resolution 2106 A (XX), December 21, 1965; Article 30 of the Convention on the Rights of the Child, adopted as UN General Assembly Resolution 44/25 (November 20, 1989); Article 2 of the Convention on the Prevention of the Crime of Genocide, adopted as UN General Assembly Resolution 260 A (III), December 9, 1948; Article 5 of the UNESCO Convention against Discrimination in Education, adopted on December 14, 1960; or Article 5 of the UNESCO Declaration on Race and Racial Prejudice, adopted on November 27, 1978.

27. UN Doc. CCPR/C/74/Add.4.

28. For the full text of the committee's concluding observations, see UN Doc. CCPR/C/79/Add.96.

29. Preamble to the Constitution of the Republic of Macedonia, English-language version, Skopje, 1994.

30. *Fakti* (Skopje), April 2, 2001.

31. Interview in the Institute for War and Peace Reporting's *Balkan Crisis Report,* no. 236 (April 6, 2001).

32. In his proposed work plan for meetings of political party leaders on April 10, 2001, President Trajkovski remarked that "the constitution and most people in the Republic of Macedonia refer to 'nationalities' within the state, a concept unknown in Western constitutional law and deriving from Leninist thinking. Should we modernize our terminology?" (Direct quotation obtained through informal contacts.) An interesting and innovative assessment of some aspects of Macedonia's constitution can be found in an article by Ambassador Ivan Toshevski, "Change of the Constitution," *Dnevnik* (Skopje), April 23, 2001.

33. Following the 1998 elections, the PDP has had fourteen and the DPA eleven seats in the parliament.

34. As the only major political party in Macedonia, the PDP refused to send its leaders to Luxembourg to witness the signing of the Stabilization and Association Agreement between the European Union and Macedonia on April 9, 2001. Leaders of both parliamentary and nonparliamentary political parties from the ruling coalition and opposition attended the ceremony, which signified a historic event in Macedonia's relations with the European Union. Protesting "the repressive methods applied by the government coalition—VMRO-DPMNE and DPA," the PDP also announced its intention to freeze its relations with, and participation in, state institutions, including parliament. This protest would continue "until the government is willing to initiate an honest and open dialogue with international mediation." See *MILS News,* April 9, 2001.

35. During my September 8, 2000 interview with Arben Xhaferi in Skopje, I asked him how would he explain the sudden change of his party's approach to joining the government coalition while similar action on the part of PDP used to be called "treason and collaboration." His response was brief: "Because, when joining the coalition, we got what we wanted." He then went on to list a number of specific measures the new government had taken to meet some of the ethnic Albanian grievances.

36. See Articles 48 and 78.

37. Council of Europe, *European Charter for Regional or Minority Languages.* Document ETS, no. 148 (November 5, 1992).

38. Figures based on a March 2000 background summary provided by government spokesman Antonio Milososki. See also Infomac Daily News Service, March 20, 2001; and *MILS News,* April 5, 2001.

39. In the opinion of the Albanian Democratic Alliance (ADA) and its president, Asllan Selmani, the number of ethnic Albanians in high schools has been insufficient. Out of eight thousand ethnic Albanian pupils graduating elementary schools each year, only some four thousand manage to enroll in high schools. ADA asks what happens with the rest of them. *Fakti* (Skopje), April 18, 2001.

40. According to the "Call for Expression of Interest" in the March 10, 2001 issue of *The Economist,* the South-East Europe University, "while being committed to the Albanian culture, language and population, will define itself in a broad international perspective and in a multilingual approach to teaching and research." The entire project will cost more than U.S. $21 million, raised from the international community, including the European Union and the OSCE.

41. For the background on the "nonpaper," see the web site of the Democratic Party of the Albanians, http://www.pdsh.org.

42. Article 171 of the 1974 Constitution of the Socialist Federal Republic of Yugoslavia, for instance, provided for the use of the languages and alphabets of other nationalities "before the relevant state organs and organizations," including republican parliaments.

43. Compare the constitution of the Socialist Republic of Macedonia with amendments I to LVI, *Grafichko-izdavachi zavod* (Skopje: Goce Delcev, 1989).

44. Interestingly, when asked about the specific proposals of his party regarding changes in the constitution, Arben Xhaferi replied: "I think it is still early to talk openly about these issues, because of the danger of creating internal antagonisms in the society. First, we are trying to create an awareness among different factors of the need of transformations and in this regard we have a global mechanism carried out through the Stabilization and Association Agreement between Macedonia and the European Union." Interview with Radio Free Europe, as quoted by the Macedonian Information Agency, April 19, 2001.

45. See the statement by the UN secretary-general before the fifty-fifth session of the Commission on Human Rights, April 9, 1997 (UN Press Release SG/SM/6201-HR/CN/792, April 10, 1997).

46. All citations in this section come from the U.S. Department of State's *Country Reports on Human Rights Practices* for the years 1992 to 2000.

47. During his early February 1996 meeting with Elizabeth Rehn, special rapporteur of the Commission on Human Rights, President Gligorov made a proposal that a comparative study be prepared by the United Nations on the human rights situation of minorities in the Balkans. In her March 14, 1996 report to the commission, Rehn welcomed and supported the proposal made by the president to initiate such a comparative study in the various Balkan countries under the auspices of the United Nations (UN Doc. E/CN.4/1996/63, para. 198). Ethnic Albanian leaders conveyed some concerns to Rehn about the initiative, claiming that there had been an ulterior motive behind the president's proposal—namely, a hope that the report would demonstrate that the human rights of ethnic Albanians in Macedonia were more respected than elsewhere in the Balkans.

48. UN Doc. E/CN.4/1998/12 (September 30, 1997), para. 51.

49. Ibid., para. 65.

50. The republics of the former Yugoslavia used to consume more than 70 percent of Macedonia's trade. From independence to 1995 alone, output fell by 45 percent because of the loss of Macedonia's traditional markets. In November 1997, six years after independence, Macedonia's foreign trade deficit amounted to U.S. $517 million, with exports totaling U.S. $1,069 million and imports U.S. $1,586 million.

51. The Macedonian Bureau of Statistics notes that the country's industrial production in 2000 marked a 3.5 percent growth compared to the previous year. *MILS News,* February 1, 2001.

52. Immediately after independence, the annual inflation rate ran as high as 2,000 percent; in the mid-1990s, per capita income in Macedonia was 50 percent lower than in 1991. According to the National Bank of Macedonia, in the past few years the country has used some U.S. $200 million in medium- and long-term credits annually. In 2001 alone, the country was expected to settle U.S. $187 million in foreign claims and pay U.S. $68 million in interest. *Vecer* (Skopje), February 2, 2001.

53. According to research by Freedom House, as reported in the February 15, 2002 issue of *Dnevnik* (Skopje), some 40 percent of foreign investors in

Macedonia had to bribe customs officials or inspectors in order to operate without obstruction.

54. International Monetary Fund, "Former Yugoslav Republic of Macedonia: Recent Economic Developments." Staff Country Report, no. 00/72 (Washington, D.C.: IMF, July 10, 2000), 77–79.

55. *Business Week,* "A Delicate Economy Is Threatened."

56. Also compare *The Future of Macedonia. A Balkan Survivor Now Needs Reform.* Special Report, no. 67 (Washington, D.C.: United States Institute of Peace, March 23, 2001), 5.

57. The pact was adopted in Cologne, Germany on June 10, 1999, at the initiative of the European Union. It includes some forty partner countries: member states of the EU and European Commission; the countries of the region and their neighbors (Albania, Bosnia-Herzegovina, Bulgaria, Croatia, Macedonia, Hungary, Romania, Slovenia, Yugoslavia, and Turkey); members of the Group of Eight (Canada, France, Germany, Italy, Japan, the Russian Federation, the United Kingdom, and the United States); other countries (Norway and Switzerland); international organizations (United Nations, OSCE, Council of Europe, UNHCR, NATO, OECD, and WEU); international financial institutions (World Bank, IMF, European Bank for Reconstruction and Development, and European Investment Bank); and regional initiatives (Black Sea Economic Cooperation, Central European Initiative, South-East European Cooperative Initiative, and South-East Europe Cooperation Process).

58. On May 11, 2001, Bulgaria's minister for foreign affairs criticized the Stability Pact, underscoring that "the government of Bulgaria has repeatedly expressed its concern that not all commitments made in the Stability Pact for the Balkans had been kept, and that the evidence of this is destabilization of Macedonia." Radio Free Europe/Radio Liberty, *Balkan Report,* May 15, 2001.

59. David Cortright and George A. Lopez, *The Sanctions Decade: Assessing UN Strategies in the 1990s* (Boulder, Colo.: Lynne Rienner, 2000), 63. On the specific UN sanctions, see, respectively, UN Security Council Resolutions 713 (1991), September 25, 1991; 757 (1992), May 30, 1992; and 1160 (1998), March 31, 1998.

60. See also the "Report of the Secretary-General of the United Nations Pursuant to Security Council Resolution 1027 (1995)," UN Doc. S/1995/65.

61. The issue of the implications of the UN Charter's Article 50 has become particularly topical in the latter half of the 1990s and has inspired debate in a number of UN bodies. The subject has been discussed in the General Assembly and its Sixth (Legal) Committee, the Security Council, the Economic and Social Council, the Special Committee on the Charter of the United Nations and on the Strengthening of the Organization, and the Committee for Programme and

Coordination. Under the topic "Implementation of the Provisions of the Charter of the United Nations Related to Assistance to Third States Affected by the Application of Sanctions," all these organs produced a host of presidential statements, resolutions, and reports that considerably moved forward the development of a possible methodology for assessing the consequences incurred by third states as a result of preventive or enforcement measures. In their Millennium Declaration, the heads of state or government pledged "to minimize the adverse effects of United Nations economic sanctions on innocent populations, to subject such sanctions regimes to regular reviews and to eliminate the adverse effects of sanctions on third parties," UN Doc. A/RES/55/2. Worth noting are also UN General Assembly Resolutions 50/51 (January 29, 1996), 51/208 (January 16, 1997), 52/162 (January 15, 1998), 53/107 (January 20, 1999), 54/107 (January 25, 2000), and 55/157 (January 30, 2001).

62. Boutros-Ghali, *An Agenda for Peace,* para. 41.

63. See the statement by the president of the Security Council, UN Doc. S/25036 (December 30, 1992).

64. UN Doc. A/50/60-S/1995/1 (January 25, 1995), paras. 66–76.

65. Ibid., para. 73.

66. See the statement by the president of the Security Council, UN Doc. S/PRST/1995/9 (February 22, 1995).

67. See Eric Schmitt, "Sanctions Don't Work, U.S. Realizes," *International Herald Tribune,* August 1–2, 1998.

68. Kofi Annan, "Towards Smarter, More Effective UN Sanctions" (address at International Peace Academy symposium, New York, April 17, 2000).

69. See, for instance, UN General Assembly Resolutions 48/210 (December 21, 1993) and 49/21A (December 2, 1994) and UN Security Council Resolutions 820 (1993), April 17, 1993, and 843 (1993), June 18, 1993. Earlier, the General Assembly—in Resolution 47/120B—recognized that "in conditions of economic interdependence that exist today, the implementation of preventive or enforcement measures under Chapter VII of the Charter against any state continues to create special problems for certain other states."

70. UN Doc. S/1995/222.

71. "Report of the Secretary-General Pursuant to Security Council Resolution 1027 (1995)," UN Doc. S/1996/65 (January 30, 1996), para. 24.

72. A prominent Macedonian politician of Turkish extraction, Guner Ismail, will tell Misha Glenny in April 2001: "When the UN placed sanctions on Serbia, and then when Greece, a member of the European Union, placed its blockade on this country in 1993, the state had no option but to criminalize itself in order to survive." Misha Glenny, "Criminal gangs running the Balkans," BBC News, April 28, 2001.

73. Adopted under UN General Assembly Resolution 2200 A (XXI), December 16, 1966.

4. UNPREDEP at Work

1. See the letter dated November 23, 1992 from the secretary-general to the president of the Security Council, UN Doc. S/24851 (November 25, 1992).

2. UN Doc. S/24852 (November 25, 1992).

3. UN Doc. S/24923 and annex (December 9, 1992).

4. Ibid.

5. UN Security Council Resolution 795 (1992), December 11, 1992.

6. See the report of the secretary-general pursuant to UN Security Council Resolution 795 (1992), UN Doc. S/26099 (July 13, 1993).

7. See letter dated June 15, 1993 from the secretary-general to the president of the Security Council, UN Doc. S/2594/Add.1 (June 16, 1993).

8. UN Security Council Resolution 842 (1993), June 18, 1993.

9. Report of the secretary-general pursuant to UN Security Council Resolution 795 (1992).

10. The UN mandates for the Macedonian force's three phases are, respectively, UN Security Council Resolution 795 (1992), December 11, 1992; UN Security Council Resolution 908 (1994), March 31, 1994 (see also the report of the secretary-general, UN Doc. S/26470, September 20, 1993, para. 13); and UN Security Council Resolution 983 (1995), March 31, 1995, and the council's successive resolutions on the extension of the force's mandate.

11. See the secretary-general's report pursuant to UN Security Council Resolution 947 (1994), UN Doc. S/1995/222 (March 22, 1995), paras. 84 and 85.

12. For UN action on the Dayton Accords, see UN Doc. S/1995/999, annex of November 21; UN Doc. S/1995/1021; and UN Security Council Resolution 1031 (1995), December 15, 1995.

13. UN Security Council Resolution 1037 (1996), January 15, 1996.

14. See the report of the secretary-general pursuant to UN Security Council Resolution 1027 (1995), UN Doc. S/1996/65 (January 30, 1996), paras. 20–21. The letter from the president of the Security Council to the secretary-general, UN Doc. S/1996/76 (February 1, 1996), read in part: "The members of the Security Council concur in principle with your recommendation that the United Nations Preventive Deployment Force (UNPREDEP) become an independent mission which will have basically the same mandate, strength and composition of forces." The slight disclaimer "in principle" applied to the pending consideration of the financial implications of the new arrangement by the Security Council.

15. UN Doc. S/1994/300 (March 16, 1994), paras. 37 and 42.

16. UN Security Council Resolution 908 (1994), March 31, 1994.

17. See UN Security Council Resolutions 795 (1992), December 11, 1992; 842 (1993), June 18, 1993; and 908 (1994), March 13, 1994.

18. UN Security Council Resolution 1186 (1998), July 21, 1998. See also UN Security Council Resolutions 1160 (1998), March 31, 1998; and 1199 (1998), September 23, 1998; as well as the secretary-general's reports S/1998/12 (August 5, 1998), S/1998/834 (September 4, 1998), and S/1998/912 (October 3, 1998). While the mission observed many incidents of smuggling, direct evidence of arms smuggling from Albania was obtained only on the eve of UNPREDEP's abrupt termination. Also a few days before, the mission's contingency plan on refugees had been activated for the first time, when some four hundred Kosovars entered Macedonia near one of our observation posts and sought humanitarian assistance.

19. United Nations practice lists several such principles, including legitimacy, consent, impartiality, minimum use of force, credibility, and negotiation and mediation. *Legitimacy* derives from the mission's international support, and adherence to statutory law and conventions as well as the credibility of the force. *Consent* means agreement and cooperation of the main parties involved in a potential conflict. *Impartiality* requires that the force not take sides without becoming part of the conflict it has been mandated to control and resolve. *Minimum use of force* implies that in peacekeeping operations under Chapter VI of the UN Charter, force will not be used to carry out the mandate; minimum use of force does not exclude self-defense. *Credibility* is confirmation of the ability of the peacekeeping operation to accomplish its mandate. *Negotiation and mediation* has enormous potential to de-escalate the conflict, to promote a secure environment, and to develop peaceful and lasting solutions to the conflict. See *United Nations Military Observers Handbook* (New York: UN Department of Peacekeeping Operations, 1995).

20. Addressing similar concerns, the Carnegie Commission has listed several obstacles that preventive diplomacy must overcome in dealing with concerned parties: "One of the greatest challenges is suspicion of the motives of those who would practice it. Another is the charge that much of it is really little more than traditional diplomacy—statecraft and foreign policy that have long been composed largely of diplomatic and political efforts to forestall undesirable results." Carnegie Commission on Preventing Deadly Conflict, *Preventing Deadly Conflict: Final Report* (New York: Carnegie Commission on Preventing Deadly Conflict, December 1997), 48–49.

21. Letter of Minister Ljubomir Frckoski, August 6, 1996; emphasis added.

22. See President Kiro Gligorov's address before the forty-eighth session of the UN General Assembly, September 30, 1993.

23. See the note by the secretary-general, entitled "In-depth Evaluation of Peacekeeping Operations: Termination Phase," UN Doc. E/AC.51/1996/3 (March 22, 1996).

24. Report of the secretary-general, *Renewing the United Nations: A Program for Reform*, UN Doc. A/51/950 (July 14, 1997), para. 119.

25. Ibid.

26. With respect to Macedonia, the secretary-general reiterated the SRSG's comprehensive mandate in his periodic reports on UNPREDEP in UN Doc. S/1996/373 (April 17, 1996), para. 32; and UN Doc. S/1997/631 (August 11, 1997), para. 9.

27. In his periodic report to the Security Council, the secretary-general stated that the "host country does not expect the United Nations to defend its borders and considers the very presence of an international force a deterrent sufficient to discourage potential aggressors," UN Doc. S/1995/987 (November 23, 1995), para. 38.

28. At an informal meeting of the Security Council in May 1996, I briefed its members on the status of implementing UNPREDEP's mandate. In the course of the meeting, a junior member of the Egyptian delegation, substituting for his ambassador, queried whether the operation still fell within the terms of preventive diplomacy under the authority of the Security Council or, because of its comprehensive program of activities, it should rather be handled by the General Assembly. Conversely, a prominent practitioner in peacekeeping rightly remarked that "it is difficult to argue that as long as it is 'the only show in town,' UNPREDEP should ignore, on narrow conceptual grounds, needs which are both evident and easily fulfilled, and which help reify its mandate in the eyes of the citizenry at large." See Shashi Tharoor, "The Concept of Preventive Deployment in the 1990s," in Ginifer, Eide, and Rønnfeldt, eds., *Preventive Action in Theory and Practice*, 15–42.

29. UN Doc. A/52/184, para. 11.

30. Report of the secretary-general on the United Nations Preventive Deployment Force pursuant to UN Security Council Resolution 908 (1994), UN Doc. S/1994/1067 (September 17, 1994), para. 23.

31. Report of the secretary-general on the United Nations Preventive Deployment Force pursuant to UN Security Council Resolution 1058 (1996), UN Doc. S/1996/819 (September 30, 1996); UN Doc. S/1996/961 (November 19, 1996), para. 22; and successive reports.

32. Report of the secretary-general on the United Nations Preventive Deployment Force pursuant to Security Council resolution 1082 (1996), UN Doc. S/1997/365 (May 12, 1997), paras. 19, 20, and 26.

33. Report of the secretary-general pursuant to UN Security Council Resolution 1110 (1997), UN Doc. S/1997/631 (August 11, 1997), para. 21. The European Union's economic reconstruction program, Poland and Hungary: Action for the Restructuring of the Economy (PHARE), is now applied to other countries aspiring to EU membership.

34. Report of the secretary-general pursuant to UN Security Council Resolution 1110 (1997), UN Doc. S/1997/911 (November 20, 1997), paras. 18, 19, and 24.

35. Report of the secretary-general pursuant to UN Security Council Resolution 1142 (1997), UN Doc. S/1998/454 (June 1, 1998), paras. 12–14 and 19.

36. Report of the secretary-general pursuant to UN Security Council Resolution 871 (1993), UN Doc. S/1994/300 (March 16, 1994), para. 42.

37. Report of the secretary-general, UN Doc. S/1994/1067 (September 17, 1994), para. 24.

38. Report of the secretary-general pursuant to UN Security Council Resolution 947 (1994), UN Doc. S/1995/222 (March 22, 1995), paras. 40 and 42.

39. Report of the secretary-general pursuant to UN Security Council Resolutions 981 (1995), 982 (1995), and 983 (1995), UN Doc. S/1995/997 (November 23, 1995), para. 21.

40. Report of the secretary-general pursuant to UN Security Council Resolution 1027 (1995), UN Doc. S/1996/65 (January 30, 1996), paras. 14 and 15.

41. Report of the secretary-general pursuant to UN Security Council Resolution 1058 (1996), UN Doc. S/1996/961 (November 19, 1996), paras. 19, 20, and 21.

42. See the reaction to UN Doc. S/1996/961 in *Dnevnik* (Skopje), November 23, 1996.

43. Report of the secretary-general pursuant to UN Security Council Resolution 1082 (1996), UN Doc. S/1997/365 (May 12, 1997), paras. 22 and 23.

44. The merger resulted in the founding of a new political party, the Democratic Party of Albanians (DPA). For five years, the authorities refused to register the party because of the excessive use of Albania's national elements in its emblems.

45. Report of the secretary-general pursuant to UN Security Council Resolution 1110 (1997), UN Doc. S/1997/631 (August 11, 1997), paras. 16 and 17.

46. Report of the secretary-general pursuant to UN Security Council Resolution 1110 (1997), UN Doc. S/1997/911 (November 20, 1997), para. 20.

47. Report of the secretary-general pursuant to UN Security Council Resolution 1142 (1997), UN Doc. S/1998/454 (June 1, 1998), para. 17.

48. Report of the secretary-general pursuant to UN Security Council Resolution 1186 (1998), UN Doc. S/1999/161 (February 12, 1999), para. 26.

49. Report of the secretary-general pursuant to UN Security Council Resolution 1110 (1997), UN Doc. S/1997/911 (November 20, 1997), paras. 21 and 22.

50. Report of the secretary-general pursuant to UN Security Council Resolution 1142 (1997), UN Doc. S/1998/454 (June 1, 1998), para. 20.

51. Report of the secretary-general pursuant to UN Security Council Resolution 1186 (1998), UN Doc. S/1999/161 (February 12, 1999).

52. Constitution of the Republic of Macedonia, English language version, Skopje, 1994.

53. Meanwhile, Macedonia's four neighbors taken together had 427,000 troops, 7,576 tanks, 1,237 airplanes, and 288 helicopters.

54. See Republic of Macedonia, Ministry of Defense, "NATO Membership of the Republic of Macedonia and Its Contribution to the Defense and Security of the Alliance" (report presented during the Individual Dialogue on NATO Enlargement Study, September 18, 1996).

55. Republic of Macedonia, Ministry of Defense, *White Paper on the Defense of the Republic of Macedonia* (Skopje: Ministry of Defense, August 1998).

56. See the letter dated February 6, 1996 from the secretary-general addressed to the president of the Security Council, UN Doc. S/1996/94 and annex. As a result of this reconfiguration, the entire mission consisted of 1,060 contingent personnel, 35 military observers, 26 civilian police, 73 international civilian staff, and 127 locally recruited staff. Subsequently, the authorized strength of the civilian component was set at 168.

57. United Nations, *Ten Rules, Code of Personal Conduct for Blue Helmets* (New York: UN Department of Peacekeeping Operations, 1997)

58. Howard F. Kuenning, "Preventive Peacekeeping as a Model for the Prevention of War: American Lessons Learned in Macedonia," in *UN Peacekeeping in Trouble: Lessons Learned from Former Yugoslavia*, ed. Wolfgang Bierman and Martin Vadset (Brookfield, Vt.: Ashgate, 1999), 238–352. The author was chief of staff of the UN Preventive Peacekeeping Operation in Macedonia from October 1993 to March 1994.

59. Report of the secretary-general pursuant to UN Security Council Resolution 1046 (1996), UN Doc. S/1996/373 (April 17, 1996), para. 26.

60. Report of the secretary-general pursuant to UN Security Council Resolution 1058 (1996), UN Doc. S/1996/819 (September 30, 1996), para. 10.

61. UN Security Council Resolution 1110 (1997), May 28, 1997.

62. UN Security Council Resolution 1186 (1998), July 21, 1998. For more detailed history of UNPREDEP's reconfiguration, see the reports of the secretary-general pursuant to UN Security Council Resolutions 1046 (1996), UN Doc. S/1996/373, paras. 26–31; 1058 (1996), UN Doc. S/1996/819 (September 30, 1996), paras. 24 and 25; 1082 (1996), UN Doc. S/1997/365 (May 12, 1997), paras. 1, 5, and 6; 1110 (1997), UN Doc. S/1997/631 (August 11, 1997), paras. 1, 3, 22, and 23, and UN Doc. S/1997/911 (November 20, 1997), paras. 3, 4, and 29; 1142 (1997), UN Doc. S/1998/454 (June 1, 1998), paras. 4, 5, and 25, and UN Doc. S/1998/644 (July 14, 1998), paras. 4, 5, 7–9; and 1186 (1998), UN Doc. S/1999/161 (February 12, 1999), paras. 3–6. See also letter dated April 3, 1997 from the secretary-general addressed to the president of the Security Council, UN Doc. S/1997/276 (April 4, 1997).

63. One most notable incident occurred in 1994 on the hilltop of Cupino Brdo. The other one, on the Kudra Fura Hill, was a recurrent dispute since 1993. Thanks to preventive diplomatic action by the military commanders, they were both solved without serious ramifications. See Steve Vogel, "U.S. Peacekeeping Troops in Macedonia Beefing Up Presence," *Washington Post*, May 17, 1994, A14.

64. In his report of August 11, 1997 (UN Doc. S/1997/631, para. 5), prepared pursuant to UN Security Council Resolution 1110 (1997), the secretary-general informed: "In paragraph 4 of my report of 12 May, I drew to the Council's attention the fact that military units of the Federal Republic of Yugoslavia and of the host country had increased the number of patrols in their respective territories up to the old administrative border of the former Socialist Federal Republic of Yugoslavia. Recently, both sides informed the Force Commander that, while they would continue to permit UNPREDEP to patrol on the basis of visible and key features of the terrain—including crossing the administrative border when topographical constraints made this a more convenient way of passing from one part of the former Yugoslav Republic of Macedonia to another—they retained their sovereign right to patrol their respective territories up to the old administrative border. Neither side has expressed any concern as to a danger of armed clashes occurring between their patrols in the border areas."

65. For a comprehensive review of the tasks and role of UNMOs, see *United Nations Military Observers Handbook*.

66. Report of the secretary-general, UN Doc. S/24923 (December 9, 1992), annex and para. 4.

67. Identical letters dated August 21, 2000 from the secretary-general to the president of the General Assembly and the president of the Security Council transmitting the *Report of the Panel on United Nations Peace Operations,* UN Docs. A/55/305 and S/2000/809, annex, para. 39.

68. See *United Nations Civilian Police Handbook* (New York: UN Department of Peacekeeping Operations, October 1995).

69. Report of the secretary-general pursuant to UN Security Council Resolution 795/1992, UN Doc. S/26099 (July 13, 1993), para. 17.

70. *United Nations Criminal Justice Standards for Law Enforcement Officials* (Skopje: Ministry of Internal Affairs, 1997).

71. The secretary-general reported to the Security Council: "In contrast to the earlier practice, the request by the United Nations civilian police monitors to visit Mr. Osmani in the prison had been denied by the authorities." Report of the secretary-general pursuant to UN Security Council Resolution 1142 (1997), UN Doc. S/1998/454 (June 1, 1998), para. 17.

72. Ostrowski, "Preventive Deployment," 823.

73. Kuenning, "Preventive Peacekeeping," 244.

74. Ibid., 245.

75. Report of the secretary-general on control and command of United Nations peacekeeping operations, UN Doc. A/49/681 (November 21, 1994), paras. 6 and 7.

76. Boutros-Ghali, *Supplement to An Agenda for Peace,* in *An Agenda for Peace 1995,* 2d ed., 16 (para. 38).

77. Ibid., para. 41.

78. Captain Leif Ahlquist, ed., "Cooperation, Command, and Control in UN Peacekeeping Operations: A Pilot Study from the Swedish War College" (Stockholm: Swedish National Defense College, Department of Operations, 1996), 46.

79. "Cooperation, Command, and Control in UN Peace Support Operations: A Case Study on Haiti" (Stockholm: Swedish National Defense College, Department of Operations, 1998), 55.

80. Ahlquist, ed., "Cooperation, Command, and Control," 85.

81. Kuenning, "Preventive Peacekeeping," 241.

82. Signed on May 3, 1994. For details see: http://www.fas.org/irp/offdocs.pdp25.htm

83. Boutros-Ghali, *Unvanquished,* 134.

84. Personal communication to the author, May 12, 2001.

85. The census was held from June 25 to July 11, 1994. Official results were announced in November 1994.

86. See the letter dated December 29, 1994 from the secretary-general addressed to the president of the Security Council, UN Doc. S/1994/1454 (December 29, 1994), annex, paras. 28 and 29.

87. Report of the secretary-general pursuant to UN Security Council Resolution 947 (1994), UN Doc. S/1995/222 (March 22, 1995), para. 41.

88. Subsequently, as a result of our frequent bilateral discussions and criticisms from other representatives of the international community in Skopje, these two political parties admitted that boycotting the elections had been a mistake.

89. The Declaration was signed by the DPT Youth Forum, PDP Youth Prosperity, Social Democratic Youth of Macedonia, PCER Youth, DPM Youth, Young Socialists of Macedonia, the Union of Young Forces of VMRO-DPMNE, and Liberal-Democratic Youth.

90. The leaders of the organization said they could not accept textual references to the constitution, which was the root cause of all the problems as it conferred the right of a constituent nation to one party only.

91. *Interethnicity: Turning Walls into Bridges* (Skopje: UNPREDEP, July 1996).

92. *Youth as Bridge-Builders in Multiethnic Communities: The Meaning of International Educational and Linguistic Standards* (Skopje: UNPREDEP, May 1997).

93. The implementing organizations included PDP Youth, Liberal-Democratic Youth, Youth of the Democratic Party of Macedonia, Union of Islamic Youth of Macedonia, and Union of Young Forces of VMRO-DPMNE.

94. "Report of the UN Advisory Committee on Administrative and Budgetary Questions," UN Doc. A/55/676, para. 24.

95. United Nations Press Release PKO/52 (October 22, 1996).

96. Ginifer, Eide, and Rønnfeldt, eds., *Preventive Action in Theory and Practice.*

97. Report of the secretary-general pursuant to UN Security Council Resolution 1046 (1996), UN Doc. S/1996/373 (April 17, 1996), para. 7.

98. Report of the secretary-general pursuant to UN Security Council Resolution 1082 (1996), UN Doc. S/1997/365 (May 12, 1997), para. 7.

99. Report of the secretary-general pursuant to UN Security Council Resolution 1110 (1997), UN Doc. S/1997/911 (November 20, 1997), para. 25.

5. The Human Dimension

1. UN Doc. A/5/985–S/2001/574 (June 7, 2001).

2. Ibid., paras. 7 and 11, respectively.

3. Identical letters dated August 25, 2000 from the secretary-general to the presidents of the General Assembly and the Security Council, UN Doc. A/55/305-S/2000/809 (August 21, 2000), annex, para. 44.

4. Only five years later, eminent experts on the subject would admit that "all peace operations should be given the capacity to make a demonstrable difference in the lives of the people in their mission area, relatively early in the life of the mission. The head of the mission should have authority to apply a small percentage of mission's funds to 'quick impact projects,' aimed at real improvements in quality of life, to help establish the credibility of a new mission." Ibid., para. 37.

5. For an extensive discussion of the OSCE mandate and practice in the human dimension, see *The OSCE in the Maintenance of Peace and Security: Conflict Prevention, Crisis Management, and Peaceful Settlement of Disputes,* ed. Michael Bothe, Natalino Ronzitti, and Allan Rozas (Boston: Kluwer Law International, 1997), especially the chapter by Merja Pentikäinen, "The Role of the Human Dimension in Conflict Prevention and Crisis Management."

6. In his report for the Security Council of February 12, 1999 (UN Doc. S/1999/161, para. 8), the secretary-general summarized: "In pursuing a comprehensive model of preventive action, UNPREDEP has also been involved in a wide range of programs related to good governance and the rule of law, strengthening of national capacity and infrastructure, institution building, and human resources development in the governmental and civil sectors. The mission has worked with many groups in the society to encourage them to contribute to the country's development and to serve as agents of conflict prevention and promoters of democracy and human rights. International expertise has been made available to the host country through long-term programs and activities aimed at enhancing social peace and stability. These programs have been funded from extrabudgetary resources mobilized by the office of the Special Representative, which have now reached nearly U.S. $8 million in cash and kind."

7. Other members of the team included Bob Deacon, Matti Heikkilä, Robert Kraan, and Paul Stubbs.

8. *Action for Social Change, A New Facet of Preventive Peacekeeping: The Case of UNPREDEP.* Report of the Intersectoral Mission on Developmental Social Issues (Helsinki: National Research and Development Centre for Welfare and Health, June 1996).

9. The group's inaugural session took place on January 31, 1997.

10. For the supporting resolutions of these United Nations standards, see UN General Assembly Resolutions 37/51 (December 3, 1982), 46/91 (December 16, 1991), 47/5 (October 16, 1992), 37/52 (December 3, 1982), 48/96 (December 20, 1993), 48/190 (December 21, 1993), 50/124 (December 20, 1995), 50/161 (December 22, 1995), 50/203 (December 22, 1995), 50/81 (December 14, 1995), and 51/240 (June 20, 1997).

11. Ingrid A. Lehmann, *Peacekeeping and Public Information: Caught in the Crossfire* (Portland, Ore.: Frank Cass, 1999), 18–19.

12. Report of the secretary-general pursuant to Security Council Resolution 795 (1992), UN Doc. S/26099 (July 13, 1993), para. 19.

13. Reports of the secretary-general pursuant to Security Council Resolutions 1046 (1996), UN Doc. S/1996/373 (April 17, 1996), paras. 33 and 1110 (1997) and UN Doc. S/1997/631 (August 11, 1997), para. 11.

14. The International Bill of Human Rights consists of the Universal Declaration of Human Rights; the International Covenant of Civil and Political Rights; and the International Covenant of Economic, Social, and Cultural Rights.

15. Music by Vanco Dimitrov, lyrics by Ognen Nedelkovski. English translation and adaptation by Zoran Ancevski.

16. Music by Aleksandar Dzambazov; lyrics by Kiril Mojsiev.

17. Olga Murdzeva-Skarik and Svetomir Skarik, "Peace and UNPREDEP in Macedonia" (paper presented at the Sixteenth International Peace Research Association General Conference, University of Queensland, Brisbane, Australia, December 8, 1996).

18. Lidija Georgieva, "Preventive Deployment: Missing Link between Peace-building and Conflict Prevention—The Macedonian Approach to Peace" (paper presented at the International Studies Association annual conference, Washington, D.C., February 17, 1999).

19. Michael Lund and Guenola Rasamoelina, eds., *The Impact of Conflict Prevention Policy: Cases, Measures, Assessments.* SWP–Conflict Prevention Network Yearbook, 1999/2000 (Baden-Baden, Germany: Nomos Verlagsgesellschaft, 2000), 81.

20. Lund, *Preventing Violent Conflicts,* 171.

21. Ibid., 170.

22. Boutros-Ghali, *Supplement to An Agenda for Peace* in *An Agenda for Peace 1995,* 2d ed., 29–30 (para. 81).

23. The July 28–29, 1998 meeting in New York brought together heads and senior representatives of fifteen regional organizations, including the Caribbean Community, the Commonwealth of Independent States, the Commonwealth

Secretariat, the Council of Europe, the Economic Community of West African States, the European Community, the European Union, the League of Arab States, the North Atlantic Treaty Organization, the Organisation Internationale de la Francophonie, the Organization of African Unity, the Organization of American States, the Organization of the Islamic Conference, the Organization for Security and Cooperation in Europe, and the Western European Union. The presidents of the General Assembly and the Security Council also participated.

24. Progress along this path should be seen in conjunction with the Fourth High-Level United Nations–Regional Organizations Meeting, New York, February 6–7, 2001 (UN Doc. S/2001/138 of February 14, 2001) and its follow-up.

25. Eran Frankel, "International NGOs in Preventive Diplomacy and Early Warning: Macedonia," in Robert I. Rotberg, ed., *Vigilance and Vengeance: NGOs Preventing Ethnic Conflict in Divided Societies* (Washington, D.C.: Brookings Institution Press, 1996), 121. See also Lund, *Preventing Violent Conflicts,* 163.

26. *Report of the Panel on United Nations Peace Operations,* UN Doc. A/55/305-S/2000/809, para. 30.

27. These groups included the International Monetary Fund (IMF), the International Bank for Reconstruction and Development (the World Bank), the Office of the UN High Commissioner for Refugees, the United Nations Children's Fund (UNICEF), the World Health Organization (WHO), and the Office of the High Commissioner for Human Rights (OHCHR).

28. More on the subject can be found in David J. Scheffer, "U.N. Engagement in Ethnic Conflicts," in *International Law and Ethnic Conflict,* ed. David Wippman (Ithaca, N.Y.: Cornell University Press, 1998), 147–76.

29. See the UNPREDEP publication, "Inventory of Action by the Entities of the United Nations System in the FY Republic of Macedonia" (report of the Consultative Meeting of the Entities of the United Nations System on their Activities in the FY Republic of Macedonia, Skopje, March 10–12, 1998).

30. Contributions to the inventory were provided by the United Nations Department of Economic and Social Affairs (DESA), the United Nations Conference on Trade and Development (UNCTAD), the United Nations Environment Program, the United Nations Center for Human Settlements (HABITAT), the United Nations Office for Drug Control and Crime Prevention (UNODCCP), the Economic Commission for Europe (ECE), the Office of the Commissioner for Human Rights (UNOCHR), the United Nations High Commissioner for Refugees (UNHCR), the United Nations Children's Fund (UNICEF), the United Nations Development Program (UNDP), the United Nations Population Fund (UNFPA), the United Nations Office for Project Services (UNOPS), the United Nations Fund for Women (UNIFEM), the United Nations International Crime and Justice Institute (UNICRI), the World Food Program (WFP), the

International Labor Organization (ILO), the Food and Agriculture Organization (FAO), the United Nations Educational, Scientific, and Cultural Organization (UNESCO), the International Civil Aviation Organization (ICAO), the World Health Organization (WHO), the World Bank and IMF, the Universal Postal Union (UPU), the World Meteorological Organization (WMO), the International Fund for Agricultural Development (IFAD), the United Nations Industrial Development Organization (UNIDO), the International Atomic Energy Agency (IAEA), the World Trade Organization (WTO), the World Tourism Organization (WTO), and the Joint UN Program on HIV-AIDS (UNAIDS).

31. For details, see the UNPREDEP publication, "Action Through Partnership. An Interagency Effort" (report of the Consultative Meeting of the Entities of the United Nations System on their Activities in the FY Republic of Macedonia, Skopje, March 10–12, 1998).

32. Ibid., 3–6, and the report of the UN secretary-general pursuant to Security Council Resolution 1142 (1997), UN Doc. S/1998/454 (June 1, 1998), annex I.

33. Unfortunately, the government failed to deliver on its promise because of the opposition of the minister of defense, who insisted that his ministry needed the premises badly for its own use. However, the other recommendations that came out of the consultative meeting have stimulated different forms of activities and fundraising, mainly under the aegis of UNDP. Visiting Skopje in early April 2001, UNDP's director for Europe, Assistant Secretary-General Kalman Mizsei, informed his hosts of new projects to speed up recovery in Macedonia's society, whose primary focus would be at the community level.

34. The decision to establish the mission was made on September 18, 1992, and its modalities approved on November 6 of the same year.

35. UN Security Council Resolution 795 (1992), December 11, 1992.

36. See UN Doc. A/47/361–S/24370, annex.

37. See UN Doc. A/48/185, annex II, appendix.

38. UN General Assembly Resolution 48/5 (October 13, 1993).

39. Report of the secretary-general, "Cooperation between the United Nations and the Organization for Security and Cooperation in Europe," UN Doc. 1/51/489 (October 14, 1996), para. 8.

40. "Survey of OSCE Long-Term Missions and Other OSCE Field Activities" (report of the OSCE Secretariat, Vienna, September 14, 1996), 3.

41. Signed in New York on April 15, 1993 by Under Secretary-General for Peacekeeping Operations Kofi Annan and Ambassador Peter Osvald of Sweden on behalf of the CSCE chairman-in-office.

42. Boutros-Ghali, *Supplement to An Agenda for Peace* in *An Agenda for Peace 1995,* 2d ed., 31–32 (para. 86).

43. See, for instance the report of the secretary-general pursuant to Security Council Resolution 110 (1997), UN Doc. S/1997/631 (August 11, 1997), para. 9.

44. The president shed more light on his reluctance to interfere with the judiciary in his March 5, 1998 interview with *Puls:* "The events in Gostivar will be a burden on relations in the country for some time to come. I was asked by Mr. Arben Xhaferi to use my right to abolish the court sentence against Mr. Osmani. This means an act of complete clemency. If so, then only the question of police intervention would remain pending. I cannot take such a decision. I cannot pass judgment on a court verdict, as I would not like to interfere in court practice. This, however, does not mean that I am not carefully following what is happening and how developments influence the political scene."

45. For a comprehensive and updated report on the work of the High Commissioner, see Walter A. Kemp, ed., *Quiet Diplomacy in Action: The OSCE High Commissioner on National Minorities* (Boston: Kluwer Law International, 2001).

46. Foundation on Inter-Ethnic Relations, *The Hague Recommendations Regarding the Education Rights of National Minorities and Explanatory Note* (The Hague: FIER, October 1996).

47. A creative follow-up to the Hague Recommendations has been further expounded by international experts in the *Oslo Recommendations Regarding the Linguistic Rights of National Minorities and Explanatory Note* of February 1998 and in the *Lund Recommendations on the Effective Participation of National Minorities in Public Life and Explanatory Note* of September 1999. See Kemp, ed., *Quiet Diplomacy in Action,* annexes 5 and 6.

48. See the press release from the High Commissioner on National Minorities, November 6, 1998.

49. The law was passed in the parliament on July 25, 2000.

50. CSCE Helsinki Document 1992, as reprinted in Kemp, ed., *Quiet Diplomacy in Action,* annex 3.

51. OSCE Press Release, May 12, 1999.

52. For a more exhaustive inventory of the Working Group's activities, see Ackermann, *Making Peace Prevail.*

53. See Rotberg, ed., *Vigilance and Vengeance,* 5.

54. Carnegie Commission on Preventing Deadly Conflict, *Preventing Deadly Conflict: Final Report,* 47.

55. For a detailed description of the situation in this regard, see Eran Fraenkel, "International NGOs in Preventive Diplomacy and Early Warning: Macedonia," in Rotberg, ed., *Vigilance and Vengeance,* 113–31.

56. *Search for Common Ground and European Center for Common Ground.* Annual Report. (Washington, D.C.: Search for Common Ground, 2000), 20.

57. Eran Fraenkel, "Preventive Action in Macedonia: The Common Ground Approach." Search for Common Ground, Macedonia office, Skopje, 1995.

58. On the two reports, see, respectively, identical letters dated August 25, 2000 from the UN secretary-general to the president of the General Assembly and the president of the Security Council, UN Doc. A/55/305-S/2000/809 (August 21, 2000); and *The Responsibility to Protect.* Report of the International Commission on Intervention and State Sovereignty (Ottawa: International Development Research Center, December 2001).

6. Preserving a Heritage

1. This view has been widely shared by experts, for example: "In spite of a decreasing external threat due to the normalization of the country's relations with its neighbors, uncertainty over developments in the region and national consensus may justify a continued international presence, and not withdrawal or too large a reduction in its size." Sophia Clément, "Former Yugoslav Macedonia, The Regional Setting and European Security: Towards Balkan Stability?" in Pettifer, ed., *The New Macedonian Question,* 296.

2. Andrew J. Pierre, *De-Balkanizing the Balkans: Security and Stability in Southeastern Europe.* Special Report, no. 54 (Washington, D.C.: United States Institute of Peace, September 1999), 7.

3. Clément, "Former Yugoslav Macedonia," 290.

4. UN Doc. S/1999/161 (February 10, 1999).

5. UN Doc. S/1999/108.

6. UN Doc. S/1999/201.

7. Following the establishment of diplomatic relations between Macedonia and Taiwan on February 7, 1999, the People's Republic of China vetoed a proposed draft resolution extending UNPREDEP's presence in the Balkan state. Earlier, the PRC had suspended all diplomatic and economic relations with Macedonia. President Gligorov strongly disagreed with his new government's decision, while public opinion stood sharply divided on the issue. It should be noted the PRC had recognized Macedonia under the constitutional name as early as October 12, 1993, greatly assisting Macedonia's efforts toward worldwide recognition. Furthermore, the PRC had supported Macedonia's efforts to join the UN and other international organizations. The secretiveness of the Taiwan-Macedonia negotiations—not to mention the sudden recognition announcement—only served to unnecessarily undermine Macedonia's international credibility. These events coincided with a serious deterioration of the situation in the Balkan region, affected by both the Kosovo crisis and a policy reorientation by Macedonia's new government in the aftermath of the PRC veto in the UN Security Council. Two years later, President Trajkovski would decide to put relations with Taiwan "on hold for the time being," and maintain them without an exchange of ambassadors. The president added, "I believe this should be in accordance with the common foreign policy of the European Union, of which membership . . . is one of our strategic interests" (*Washington Post,* February 2, 2001, A20). In mid-2001, the Macedonian government announced that it was reestablishing diplomatic relations with the People's Republic, which occurred on June 18, 2001. Taiwan, in turn, severed relations with Macedonia.

8. For the text of the Chinese statement, see the Provisional Verbatim Record of the Security Council, UN Doc. S/PV/3982, pp. 6–7.

9. *MILS News,* March 9, 2001.

10. For the full text of the Interim Accord, see UN Doc. S/1995/794, annex 1.

11. At one point, Macedonia proposed that Greece might use the name of its own choice in Greek-Macedonian relations, while the rest of the international community would be guided by its constitutional name.

12. *Utrinski vesnik* (Skopje), September 15, 2000.

13. Norman Davies, *Europe: A History* (New York: Oxford University Press, 1996), 634.

14. The extraction force, called "Joint Guarantor," was established in November 1998 in the context of UN Security Council Resolution 1203 (1998), October 24, 1998. The task of the force was to be on standby in Macedonia and extract OSCE verifiers or other designated persons from Kosovo in an emergency.

15. Report of the secretary-general pursuant to UN Security Council Resolution 1186 (1998), UN Doc. S/1999/161 (February 12, 1999).

16. Provisional Verbatim Record of the Security Council, UN Doc. S/PV/3982, p. 7.

17. The International Crisis Group pointed out that "the preventive deployment of the UNPREDEP force in Macedonia was a rare bright spot in the UN preventive efforts during the decade, as was UNTAES in Eastern Slavonia." It should be noted here though that UNTAES was a postconflict preventive operation. See International Crisis Group, *After Milosevic.* ICG Balkan Report, no. 108 (Brussels: ICG, 2001), 285.

18. Provisional Verbatim Record of the Security Council, UN Doc. S/PV/3982, p. 2.

19. Ibid., 4.

20. Ibid., 5.

21. Ibid., 6.

22. Ibid., 8.

23. UN Doc. S/PRST/1999/34. For earlier comments in the Security Council on UNPREDEP's performance, see, among others, Verbatim Records S/PV.3670 (May 30, 1996), S/PV.3716 (November 27, 1996), S/PV.3839 (December 4, 1997), S/PV.3868 (March 31, 1998), and S/PV.3911 (July 21, 1998).

24. Letter of March 12, 1999; unofficial English translation provided by the Office of the President.

25. Kofi Annan, address to the opening ceremony of the International Centre for Preventive Action and Conflict Resolution (ICPACR), Skopje, October 20, 2000.

26. James Pettifer, "The Albanians in western Macedonia after FYROM Independence," in Pettifer, ed., *The New Macedonian Question,* 143.

27. Kiro Gligorov, *Makedonija e se' sto imame* (Macedonia Is All We Have) (Skopje: Izdavachi Centar Tri, 2000), 315.

28. When UNPREDEP ended in early 1999, there were some ten thousand NATO support troops in Macedonia for the Kosovo operation, stationed mainly at Kumanovo, Prilep, Skopje, and Tetovo.

29. Ostrowski, "Preventive Deployment," 828.

30. In one of his reports to the Security Council, the secretary-general concluded: "UNPREDEP is the first preventive force deployed by the United Nations. It has played an important role in helping the former Yugoslav Republic of Macedonia to establish its statehood and to consolidate its security. The country has had to undertake this political and economic transition in difficult circumstances. Continuing turbulence in the region has tended to accentuate the stresses and strains that exist within the country's own body politics. Differences with some of its neighbors have been a further complicating factor, especially as regards the country's economic rehabilitation. In this testing situation the mere presence of a United Nations force has undoubtedly had a reassuring, stabilizing, and confidence-building effect. In addition, the Force's military operations have helped to reduce tensions on the country's borders and to ensure that stability there is impaired neither by unintended military confrontations nor by activities of armed smugglers." Report of the secretary-general of April 17, 1996, pursuant to Security Council Resolution 1046 (1996), UN Doc. S/1996/373, para. 37.

31. See Lund and Rasamoelina, eds., *The Impact of Conflict Prevention Policy,* 43.

32. Ostrowski, "Preventive Deployment," 828.

33. See Bradley Thayer, "Macedonia," in Brown and Rosecrance, *The Costs of Conflict,* 139–45.

34. Annan, address to opening ceremony of ICPACR.

35. *Macedonia: Prevention Can Work.* Special Report, no. 58 (Washington, D.C.: United States Institute of Peace, March 27, 2000), 6. Verbal recognition of Macedonia's contribution came half a year later during the budgetary debate in the U.S. House of Representatives: "The managers note the crucial importance of a democratic, multiethnic Macedonia to stability in the Balkans, as well as the contributions made by that nation during the Kosovo air campaign. In view of these factors, the managers strongly support adequate resources for assistance for Macedonia for fiscal year 2001." Conference Report on H.R. 4811, Foreign Operations, Export Financing, and Related Programs Appropriations Act 2001, 106th Cong., 2d sess., October 24, 2000.

36. Pierre, *De-Balkanizing the Balkans,* 7.

37. For more on democratization and good governance, see the secretary-general's report, "Support by the United Nations System of the Efforts of Governments to Promote and Consolidate New or Restored Democracies," UN Doc. A/55/489.

38. *Aktuel* (Skopje), November 23, 2001.

39. See, for instance, *Kapital* (Skopje), December 17, 2001.

40. According to European Council conclusions of May 17, 1999, conditions for meaningful progress in relations with the European Union and for the start of negotiations on a Stability and Association Agreement comprise "rule of law, democracy, compliance with human/minority rights, including media; free and fair elections and full implementation of their results; absence of discriminatory treatment; implementation of the first steps of economic reform (privatization, abolition of price controls); compliance with the Dayton Accords for Bosnia and Herzegovina, Croatia, and the FRY; conditions for concluding negotiations; substantial progress in achievement of objectives of conditions for opening negotiations; substantial results in the field of political and economic reforms (stable economic environment, liberalization of prices, regulatory framework, competitive banking sector, etc.); and proven results in cooperation and good-neighborly relations (http://europa.eu.int/comm/external_relations/see/sap/index.htm).

41. For the full text of the declaration, see UN Doc. A/55/660-S/2000 /1144 (December 1, 2000).

42. See http://europa.eu.int/comm/external_relations/see/fyrom/ index.htm.

43. Ibid.

44. *Dnevnik* (Skopje), September 12, 2001, 5.

45. Statement by the acting deputy of the Stability Pact Coordinator at the conference on Democratization and Human Rights, Skopje, December 17–18, 2001, in *Nova Makedonija* (Skopje), December 18, 2001.

46. See also Benn Stell and Susan L. Woodward, "A European 'New Deal' for the Balkans," *Foreign Affairs,* November/December 1999, 96.

47. Dimitros Triantaphyllou, *The Albanian Factor* (Athens: Hellenic Foundation for European and Foreign Policy, 2000), 7.

48. Carl Bildt, "Winning the Broader Peace in Kosovo," *Financial Times* (London), January 19, 2000.

Epilogue

1. Radio Free Europe/Radio Liberty *Newsline,* March 12, 2001. Xhaferi also called on fellow Macedonian Albanians to participate in a peace march in the capital the following day.

2. *Vecer* (Skopje), March 6, 2001.

3. Joint Declaration of the Albanian Parties in Macedonia, Macedonian Radio, March 20, 2001, as reported in BBC Summary of World Broadcasts, March 22, 2001.

4. Statement by the president of the Security Council, UN Doc. S/PRST/2001/7 (March 7, 2001).

5. See the comments by Sweden's minister for foreign affairs, Anna Lindh Nyköping, EU Presidency, press release, May 6, 2001; declaration by the EU Presidency on behalf of the European Union on the security situation in the Former Yugoslav Republic of Macedonia's border with the Federal Republic of Yugoslavia, EU Press Release 6924/01 (Presse 101), Brussels, March 9, 2001; and the European Council's declaration on FYROM at its meeting of March 23–24, 2001, available at www.ceps.be.

6. See Radio Free Europe/Radio Liberty *Balkan Report* 5, no. 84 (December 18, 2001).

7. EIU ViewsWire, May 8, 2001. Lord Robertson's statement was quoted in Timothy Garton Ash's essay, "Is There a Good Terrorist?" *New York Review of Books,* November 29, 2001.

8. *Dnevnik* (Skopje), March 6, 2001. See also "Albania Is for Institutional Solution of the Conflicts in the Region," Albanian Telegraph Agency, March 6, 2001.

9. Doris Pack, president of the European Parliament's Board for Southeast Europe, said in an interview with Radio Free Europe on May 30, 2001 that "there is no doubt that the crisis in Macedonia has been previously prepared in Kosovo. The problem lies in the fact that great numbers of terrorists can, without major obstacles, come from Kosovo to Macedonia, which shows that the borders are not uncrossable." Reported by Macedonian Information Agency, May 30, 2001.

10. For more on the subject, see *Dnevnik* (Skopje), March 27, 2001, and "Macedonia Village Is Center of Europe Web in Sex Trade," *New York Times,* July 28, 2001.

11. Joint Press Statement on the Western Balkans, NATO Press Release (2001) 080, May 30, 2001; "More Fighting in Offing as Macedonian Government Closes Ranks," Agence France-Presse, May 30, 2001.

12. The complete text of the Framework Agreement can be found on the web site of Macedonia's presidential cabinet: http://www.president.gov.mk/eng/info/soopstenija.asp?id=90

13. According to Menduh Thaci, "the national aspirations of the Albanians do not end with the Ohrid Framework Agreement. . . . The unification of Albanians as a nation is the only guarantee for the inclusion into Western European standards and values." On the same occasion, Arben Xhaferi said that his party "opposes those political forces or thinkers who believe that the Albanians' aspirations and problems in Macedonia have completely been resolved with the Ohrid Agreement." *Dnevnik* (Skopje), August 7, 2002.

14. *Untrinski Vesnik* (Skopje), October 8, 2002.

15. Such studies have in fact begun. In her informative article, "Macedonia in a Post–Peace Agreement Environment: A Role for Conflict Prevention and Reconciliation" (*The International Spectator,* January 2002), Alice Ackermann, as well as other authors she refers to, offers a penetrating analysis of what happened and what may still come. See also Brenda Pearson, *Putting Peace into Practice: Can Macedonia's New Government Meet the Challenge?* Special Report, no. 96 (Washington, D.C.: United States Institute of Peace, November 2002).

INDEX

BIBLIOGRAPHY

A Force for Peace: U.S. Commanders' Views of the Military's Role in Peace Operations. Washington, D.C.: Peace Through Law Education Fund, 1999.

Ackermann, Alice. *Making Peace Prevail: Preventing Violent Conflict in Macedonia.* Syracuse, N.Y.: Syracuse University Press, 2000.

Ackermann, Alice, and Antonio Pala. "From Peacekeeping to Preventive Deployment: A Study of the United Nations in the Republic of Macedonia." *European Security* 5, no. 1 (Spring 1996).

Action for Social Change. A New Facet of Preventive Peacekeeping: The Case of UNPREDEP. Report of the Intersectoral Mission on Developmental Social Issues, STAKES. Helsinki: National Research and Development Centre for Welfare and Health, June 1996.

Ahlquist, Leif, ed. "Cooperation, Command, and Control in UN Peace Support Operations. A Case Study on Haiti." Stockholm: Swedish National Defense College, Department of Operations, 1998.

———. "Cooperation, Command, and Control in UN Peacekeeping Operations. A Pilot Study from the Swedish War College." Stockholm: Swedish National Defense College, Department of Operations, 1996.

———. "The Legal Framework." Report from a seminar at the National Defense College, Stockholm, 1999.

Annan, Kofi A. "The Peacekeeping Prescription." In *Preventive Diplomacy: Stopping Wars Before They Start,* edited by Kevin M. Cahill, M.D. New York: Basic Books and The Center for International Health and Cooperation, 1996.

Atanasovski, Todor. "The Peace-Keeping Operations and the Republic of Macedonia." *Balkan Forum* 2, no. 1 (March 1994).

Bauwens, Werner, and Luc Reychler, eds. *The Art of Conflict Prevention.* Brassey's Atlantic Commentaries No. 7. New York: Macmillan, 1994.

Benton, Barbara, ed. *Soldiers for Peace: Fifty Years of United Nations Peacekeeping.* New York: Facts On File, 1996.

Biermann, Wolfgang, and Martin Vadset, eds. *UN Peacekeeping in Trouble: Lessons Learned from the Former Yugoslavia.* Brookfield, Vt.: Ashgate, 1998.

Boutros-Ghali, Boutros. *An Agenda for Peace.* New York: United Nations, 1992.

————. *An Agenda for Peace 1995,* 2d ed. with the new Supplement and Related UN Documents. New York: United Nations, 1995.

————. "Challenges of Preventive Diplomacy: The Role of the United Nations and Its Secretary-General." In *Preventive Diplomacy, Stopping Wars Before They Start,* edited by Kevin M. Cahill. New York: Basic Books, 1996.

————. *Unvanquished, A U.S.–U.N. Saga.* New York: Random House, 1999.

Brown, Michael E., and Richard N. Rosecrance., eds. *The Costs of Conflict: Prevention and Cure in the Global Arena.* Lanham, Md.: Rowman and Littlefield, 1999.

Brzezinski, Zbigniew. "Fifty Years After Yalta: Europe's and the Balkan's New Chance." *Balkan Forum* 3, no. 2 (June 1995).

Caca, Gjorgi. "Status and Rights of Nationalities in the Republic of Macedonia." *Balkan Forum* 4, no. 2 (June 1996).

Carnegie Commission on Preventing Deadly Conflict. *Preventing Deadly Conflict: Final Report.* New York: Carnegie Commission on Preventing Deadly Conflict, 1997.

Carnegie Foundation for International Peace. *The Other Balkan Wars: A 1913 Carnegie Endowment Inquiry in Retrospect.* Washington, D.C.: Carnegie Endowment for International Peace, 1993.

The Challenges Project. *Challenges of Peace Operations: Into the 21st Century— Concluding Report, 1997–2002.* Stockholm: Elanders Gotab, 2002.

Chopra, Jarat. "The Space of Peace-Maintenance." *Political Geography* 15, no. 3/4 (1996).

Christopulos, Dimitris. "Minority Protection: Toward a New European Approach." *Balkan Forum* 2, no. 1 (March 1994).

"Citizenship and Prevention of Statelessness Linked to the Disintegration of the Socialist Federal Republic of Yugoslavia." Special issue of *European Series* 3, no. 1 (June 1997).

Coady, C. A. J., *The Ethics of Armed Humanitarian Intervention.* Peaceworks, no. 45. Washington, D.C.: United States Institute of Peace, July 2002.

Constitution of the Republic of Macedonia. English-language version. Skopje, 1994.

Cortright, David, and George A. Lopez. *The Sanctions Decade: Assessing UN Strategies in the 1990s.* Boulder, Colo.: Lynne Rienner, 2000.

Council for Research into South-Eastern Europe. *Macedonia and Its Relations with Greece.* Skopje: Macedonian Academy of Sciences and Arts, 1993.

Cowan, Jane, ed. *Macedonia: The Politics of Identity and Difference.* London: Pluto Press, 2000.

Czubinski, Antoni. *Europa XX wieku* (Europe of the twentieth century). Poznan: Wydawnictwo Poznanskie, 2000.

Department for Economic and Social Affairs, Information and Policy Analysis. *An Inventory of Postconflict Peacebuilding Activities.* New York: United Nations, 1996.

Developmental Assistance as a Means of Conflict Prevention. Oslo: Norwegian Institute of International Affairs, February 1998.

Dimitras, Elias Panayote. "Hate Speech in the Balkan Media." *Balkan Forum* 4, no. 1 (March 1996).

Directory of Nongovernmental Organizations in Macedonia. Skopje: Macedonian Centre for International Cooperation, 1997.

Egelund, Jan. "Preventive Diplomacy: Moving from Rhetoric to Reality." *Balkan Forum* 5, no. 1 (March 1997).

Eide, Espen Barth, ed. *Peacekeeping in Europe.* Peacekeeping and Multinational Operations Series, no. 5. Oslo: Norwegian Institute of International Affairs, 1995.

Eliasson, Jan. "Conflict and Development: Causes, Effects and Remedies." Keynote address delivered at The Hague, March 22, 1994.

Euro-Atlantic Partnership Council. EAPC/PMSC Ad hoc Group on Co-operation in Peacekeeping. "Early Warning and Conflict Prevention." Report by the chairman of the seminar on conflict prevention in Skopje held in Brussels, October 15–17, 1997.

———. "Political/Military Tools for Conflict Prevention within EAPC/PFP." Paper presented at meeting held in Ljubljana, October 12–15, 2000.

European Roma Rights Center. *A Pleasant Fiction. The Human Rights Situation of Roma in Macedonia.* Country Reports Series no. 7, July 1998.

Findlay, Trevor. "Multilateral Conflict Prevention, Management, and Resolution." In *SIPRI Yearbook 1997: Armaments, Disarmament, and International Security.* New York: Oxford University Press, 1997.

————. "The Use of Force in Peace Operations." A report from the workshop organized by the Stockholm International Peace Institute (SIPRI) and the Australian Department for Foreign Affairs and Trade, Stockholm, April 10–11, 1995.

Foundation on Inter-Ethnic Relations. *The Hague Recommendations Regarding the Education Rights of National Minorities and Explanatory Note.* The Hague: FIER, October 1996.

Galtung, Johan. *Peace by Peaceful Means: Peace and Conflict, Development and Civilization.* Thousand Oaks, Calif.: SAGE Publications, 1996.

Ginifer, Jeremy, and Espen Barth Eide. "An Agenda for Preventive Diplomacy: Theory and Practice." Report of a workshop held in Skopje, October 16–19, 1996.

Ginifer, Jeremy, Espen Barth Eide, and Carsten Rønnfeldt, eds. *Preventive Action in Theory and Practice.* Oslo: Norwegian Institute of International Affairs, 1999.

Goulding, Marrack. *Peacemonger.* London: John Murray, 2002.

Gutlove, Paula, and Gordon Thomson. "The Potential for Cooperation by the OSCE and Nongovernment Actors on Conflict Management." *Helsinki Monitor* 6, no. 3 (1995).

Hatschikjan, Magarditsch. "Macedonia: Variable Balances, Fragile Structures." *Balkan Forum* 4, no. 3 (September 1996).

Helsinki Committee for Human Rights. *Annual Report on the conditions concerning the human rights in the Republic of Macedonia.* Skopje: Helsinki Committee for Human Rights, December 1997.

Holbrooke, Richard. *To End a War.* New York: Random House, 1999.

Human Rights Watch. *Police Violence in Macedonia.* New York: Human Rights Watch, April 1998.

Human Rights Watch/Helsinki. *A Threat to 'Stability'. Human Rights Violations in Macedonia.* New York: Human Rights Watch, June 1996.

Ilievski, Done. *The Macedonian Orthodox Church.* Skopje: Macedonian Review Editions, 1973.

Ilievski, Petar Hr. "Position of the Ancient Macedonian Language and the Name of Contemporary Makedonski." *Balkan Forum* 1, no. 2 (March 1993).

International Commission on the Balkans. *Unfinished Peace: Report of the International Commission on the Balkans.* Washington, D.C.: Carnegie Endowment for International Peace, 1996.

International Crisis Group, *Moving Macedonia Toward Self-Sufficiency: A New Security Approach for NATO and the EU.* ICG Balkan Report, no.135. Brussels: International Crisis Group, November 15, 2002.

Ivanovski, Vlado. *Macedonia in the Struggle against Fascism.* Skopje: Committee on the Commemoration of the Fiftieth Anniversary of the Victory over Fascism, 1995.

Jentleson, Bruce, ed. *Opportunities Missed, Opportunities Seized: Preventive Diplomacy in the Post–Cold War World.* New York: Carnegie Commission on Preventing Deadly Conflict, 2000.

Jonge Oudraat, Chantal de. "The Threat and Use of Military Force in the Former Yugoslavia." Paper presented to the conference "UNPROFOR 1992–1995: Lessons Learned," organized by the Lessons Learned Unit, United Nations Department of Peacekeeping Operations, Oslo, April 15–17, 1999.

Kemp, Walter A., ed. *Quiet Diplomacy in Action: The OSCE High Commissioner on National Minorities.* Boston: Kluwer Law International, 2001.

Kofos, Evangelos. *Nationalism and Communism in Macedonia: Civil Conflict, Politics of Mutation, National Identity.* New Rochelle, N.Y.: Aristide D. Caratzas, 1993.

Lape, Vladimir. "NATO in Macedonia for Sure." *The Macedonian Times* (Skopje), November 1996.

Lazarov, Risto. "Old Burdens and New Impulses in Macedonian–Bulgarian Relations." *Balkan Forum* 2, no. 1 (March 1994).

Lehmann, Ingrid A. *Peacekeeping and Public Information: Caught in the Crossfire.* Portland, Ore.: Frank Cass, 1999.

Lund, Michael S. *Preventing Violent Conflicts: A Strategy for Preventive Diplomacy.* Washington, D.C.: United States Institute of Peace Press, 1996.

———. "Underrating Preventive Diplomacy." *Foreign Affairs* (July/August 1995).

Lund, Michael S., and Guenola Rasamoelina, eds., *Impact of Conflict Prevention Policy: Cases, Measures, Assessments.* Baden-Baden, Germany: Nomos, 2000.

Lute, Jane Holl. "Rethinking Development Assistance and the Role of AID in U.S. Foreign Policy." Paper presented at the conference sponsored by the U.S. Agency for International Development and the Woodrow Wilson International Center for Scholars, Washington, D.C., January 8, 2001.

McDermott, Anthony, ed. *Sovereign Intervention.* PRIO Report 2. Oslo: International Peace Research Institute, 1999.

McGoldrick, Dominic, ed. *Documents on the Human Dimension of the OSCE.* Warsaw: Organization for Security and Cooperation in Europe, Office for Democratic Institutions and Human Rights, 1995.

Michailovich, Emelianov Valeri. "Some Aspects of Russian-Macedonian Relations in the Light of the Current International Situation and the Geopolitical Factor." *Balkan Forum* 4, no. 1 (March 1997).

Milcin, Vladimir. "Sofia, Skopje and the 'Macedonian Question.'" *War Report,* July/August 1995.

Minority Rights Group International. *The Southern Balkans.* London: Minority Rights Group International, 1994.

Minoski, Michajlo. "The United States and the Macedonian Issue in 1919." *The Macedonian Times,* September 1995.

Missirkov, Krste P. *On Macedonian Matters.* Skopje: Macedonian Review Editions, 1974 [1903].

Najcevska, Mirjana, and Gaber, Natasha. "Survey Results and Legal Background Regarding Ethnic Issues in the Republic of Macedonia." Skopje: University of Sts. Cyril and Methodius, 1995.

Nelson, Jane. *Building Partnerships.* New York: UN Department of Public Information, 2002.

Nordic UN Stand-by Forces, 4th ed. Helsinki: Nordsamfn, 1993.

Oakley, Robert B., Michael J. Dziedzic, and Eliot M. Goldberg, eds. *Policing the New World Disorder: Peace Operations and Public Security.* Washington, D.C.: National Defense University Press, 1998.

Ostrowski, Stephen. "Preventive Deployment of Troops as Preventive Measures: Macedonia and Beyond." *Journal of International Law and Politics* 30, nos. 3–4 (Spring/Summer 1998).

Pavlovski, Jovan. "Can Greece Call Us a Macedonian-Albanian Republic?" *The Macedonian Times* (Skopje), October 1996.

Perry, William. "Partnership for Peace. Transforming Central, Eastern Europe." *Balkan Forum* 3, no. 1 (March 1996).

Petroska-Beska, Violeta. "Early Warning, and Preventive Action: Macedonia." In *Vigilance and Vengeance. NGOs Preventing Ethnic Conflict in Divided Societies,* edited by Robert I. Rotberg. Washington, D.C.: Brookings Institution Press, 1996.

Pettifer, James, ed. *The New Macedonian Question.* London: Macmillan, 1999.

Pierre, Andrew J. *De-Balkanizing the Balkans: Security and Stability in Southeastern Europe.* Special Report, no. 54. Washington, D.C.: United States Institute of Peace, September 1999.

Post-Conflict Reconstruction: The Role of the World Bank. Washington, D.C.: World Bank, 1998.

Poulton, Hugh. *Who Are the Macedonians?* Bloomington: Indiana University Press, 2000.

———. *The Balkans: Minorities and States in Conflict.* London: Minority Rights Group, 1991.

Prentice, Deborah, and Dale T. Miller, eds. *Cultural Divides: Understanding and Overcoming Group Conflict.* New York: Russell Sage Foundation, 1999.

Preventive Diplomacy and Japan's Role: An Action Menu. Tokyo: Japan Forum on International Relations, February 1998.

Quinn, Frederick, ed. *Human Rights and You: A Guide for the States of the Former Soviet Union and Central Europe.* Warsaw: Organization for Security and Cooperation in Europe/Office for Democratic Institutions and Human Rights, October 1999.

Radin, A. Michael. *IMPRO and the Macedonian Question.* Skopje: Kultura, 1993.

Rehn, Elizabeth. "Situation of Human Rights in the Former Yugoslav Republic of Macedonia." Final report submitted by Special Rapporteur of the Commission of Human Rights, pursuant to resolution 1997/57, UN Doc. E./CN.4/1998/12 (September 30, 1997).

"Report of the Panel on United Nations Peace Operations." UN Doc. A/55/305 –S/2000/809 (August 21, 2000.)

Republic of Macedonia. *Independence through Peaceful Self-Determination: Documents.* Skopje: Balkan Forum, November 1992

––––––. "White Paper on the Defense of the Republic of Macedonia." Skopje: Ministry of Defense, August 1998.

––––––. "General Policy Toward Minorities." Skopje: Ministry of Foreign Affairs, September 1996.

Roberts, Adam, and Benedict Kingsbury, eds. *United Nations, Divided World: The UN's Roles in International Relations,* 2d ed. New York: Oxford University Press, 1994.

Romanienko, Sergei. "Russia in the Balkans. Eternal Allies or Eternal Interests?" *Balkan Forum* 4, no. 3 (September 1996).

Rønnfeldt, Carsten F., Espen Barth Eide, and Dan Smith, eds. *Environmental Conflict and Preventive Action: Report from a Seminar at Lysebu, 23–24 November 1998.* Oslo: Norwegian Institute for International Affairs, 1999.

Ross, Marc Howard, and Jay Rothman, eds. *Theory and Practice in Ethnic Conflict Management.* New York: St. Martin's Press, 1999.

Rotberg, Robert I., ed. *Vigilance and Vengeance: NGOs Preventing Ethnic Conflict in Divided Societies.* Washington, D.C.: Brookings Institution Press, 1996.

Rubin, Barnett R., ed. *Toward Comprehensive Peace in Southeast Europe: Conflict Prevention in the South Balkans.* Report of the South Balkans Working Group of the Council on Foreign Relations, Center for Preventive Action. New York: Twentieth Century Fund Press, 1997.

Sandole, Dennis J. D., and Christopher R. Mitchell. *Capturing the Complexity of Conflict: Dealing with Violent Ethnic Conflicts in the Post–Cold War Era.* New York: Pinter, 1999.

Schmidl, Erwin A. "Police and Peace Operations." *Informationen zur Sicherheitspolitik,* no. 10 (September 1998).

Schmidl, Erwin A., ed. "Peace Operations between Peace and War: Four Studies." *Informationen zur Sicherheitspolitik,* no. 11 (September 1998).

Secretary-General of the United Nations. *We the Peoples: The Role of the United Nations in the Twenty-First Century.* Report of the Secretary-General for the Millennium Assembly of the United Nations. UN Doc. A/54/2000 (March 27, 2000).

———. *Command and Control of United Nations Peacekeeping Operations.* UN Doc. A/49/681 (November 21, 1994).

———. *Implementation of the Recommendations of the Special Committee on Peacekeeping Operations.* UN Doc. A/54/670 (January 6, 2000).

———. *Prevention of Armed Conflict: Views of Organs, Organizations, and Bodies of the United Nations System.* UN Doc. A/57/588-S/2002/1269 (November 5, 2002).

———. *Report of the Secretary-General on the Work of the Organization.* UN Doc. A/54/1. New York: United Nations, 1999.

———. Report of the Secretary-General, prepared pursuant to resolutions 1160 (1998) and 1199 (1998) of the Security Council. UN Doc. S/1998/912 (October 3, 1998).

———. *Report of the Secretary-General on the Prevention of Armed Conflict.* UN Doc. A/55/985-S/2001/574 (June 7, 2001).

Shea, John. *Macedonia and Greece: The Struggle to Define a New Balkan Nation.* London: McFarland & Company, 1997.

Smith, Anne-Marie. *Advances in Understanding International Peacemaking,* vol. 2. Washington, D.C.: United States Institute of Peace, 2001.

Sokalski, Henryk J. "Preventive Action: The Need for a Comprehensive Approach." In *Preventive Action in Theory and Practice,* edited by Jeremy Ginifer, Espen Barth Eide, and Carsten Rønnfeldt. Oslo: Norwegian Institute of International Affairs, 1999.

———. "Towards a Century of Prevention." In *Politica Criminal, Derechos Humanos y Sistemas Juridicos en el Siglo XXI. Homenaje a Pedro David.* Buenos Aires: Editorial Depalma, 2001.

Stawowy-Kawka, Irena. *Historia Macedonii* (History of Macedonia). Warsaw: Ossolineum, 2000.

Stedman, Stephen John. "Alchemy for a New World Order: Overselling 'Preventive Diplomacy.'" *Foreign Affairs,* May/June 1995.

Stern, Brigitte, ed. *United Nations Peacekeeping Operations: A Guide to French Policies.* Tokyo: United Nations University Press, 1998.

Sucharipa-Behrmann, Lilly R., and Thomas M. Franck. "Preventive Measures." *New York University Journal of International Law and Politics* 30, nos. 3-4 (Spring/Summer 1998).

Swedish Ministry for Foreign Affairs. *Preventing a Violent Conflict–A Swedish Plan of Action.* Stockholm: Regeringskansliet, 1999.

Terrett, Steve. *The Dissolution of Yugoslavia and the Badinter Arbitration Commission.* Burlington, Vt.: Ashgate/Dartmouth Press, 2000.

Tiihonen, Ilkka. "Preventive Deployment of the United Nations Forces. The Case of the United Nations Preventive Deployment Force in the Former Yugoslav Republic of Macedonia." Helsinki, March 1997.

Troebst, Stefan. "Macedonia in a Hostile International and Ethnopolitical Environment (Six Scenarios)." *Balkan Forum* 2, no. 1 (March 1994).

———. "Still Unanswered: The 'Albanian Question' at the End of the 20th Century." *Balkan Forum* 5, no. 1 (March 1997).

Trushin, Yuri Petrovich. "A Necessity for a Strategic Course in Central and South-East Europe." *The Macedonian Times,* September 1996.

United Nations Administration on Eastern Slavonia, Baranja, and Western Sirmium (UNTAES). *Lessons Learned: January 1996–January 1998.* United Nations, 1998.

United Nations Civilian Police Handbook. New York: UN Department of Peacekeeping Operations, 1995.

United Nations Criminal Justice Standards for Law Enforcement Officials. Skopje: Ministry of Internal Affairs, 1997.

United Nations Development Program and Republic of Macedonia. *National Human Development Report.* Skopje: Ministry of Development, June 1997.

United Nations Preventive Deployment Force. "Inventory of Action by the Entities of the United Nations System in the FY Republic of Macedonia." Report prepared for the Consultative Meeting of the Entities of the United Nations System on Their Activities in the FY Republic of Macedonia, Skopje, March 10–12, 1998.

———. "Action Through Partnership, An Interagency Effort." Report of the Consultative Meeting of the Entities of the United Nations System on Their Activities in the FY Republic of Macedonia, Skopje, March 10–12, 1998.

———. *Youth as Bridge Builders in Multiethnic Communities: The Meaning of International Educational and Linguistic Standards.* Skopje: UNPREDEP, 1997.

United Nations Preventive Deployment Force and Open Society Institute–Macedonia. *Inter-ethnicity: Turning Walls into Bridges. The Implementation of United Nations Standards and Rights of Persons Belonging to National or Ethnic, Religious, and Linguistic Minorities.* Skopje: UNPREDEP, 1996.

United States Institute of Peace. *The Future of Macedonia: A Balkan Survivor Now Needs Reform.* Special Report, no. 67. Washington, D.C.: United States Institute of Peace, March 23, 2001.

———. *Macedonia: Prevention Can Work.* Special Report, no. 58. Washington, D.C.: United States Institute of Peace, March 27, 2000.

———. *Taking Stock and Looking Forward: Intervention in the Balkans and Beyond.* Special Report, no. 83. Washington, D.C. United States Institute of Peace, February 22, 2002.

van der Stoel, Max. "The Role of the CSCE High Commissioner on National Minorities in CSCE Preventive Diplomacy." In *The Challenge of Preventive Diplomacy,* edited by Staffan Carlsson. Stockholm: Ministry of Foreign Affairs, 1994.

Vesilind, Priit. "Macedonia: Caught in the Middle." *National Geographic,* March 1996.

Williams, Abiodun. *Preventing War: The United Nations and Macedonia.* Lanham, Md.: Rowman and Littlefield, 2000.

Henryk J. Sokalski is an expert on international peacekeeping and preventive diplomacy and has more than twenty-five years of experience in the Polish foreign service and thirteen years of service in the United Nations, where his last position was assistant secretary-general. From 1995 to 1998, Sokalski led the UN's preventive deployment force (UNPREDEP) in Macedonia as the Special Representative of the UN Secretary-General. Prior to that, he coordinated the UN's global program on social development, culminating in the International Year of the Family in 1994. Before joining the United Nations, he served for five years as the deputy director of the Department of International Organizations in Poland's Ministry of Foreign Affairs and as Poland's deputy permanent representative to the UN. Sokalski has written several articles on prevention and peacekeeping, including "Preventive Action: The Need for a Comprehensive Approach," in *Preventive Action in Theory and Practice* (1999). He holds an M.A. from the University of Warsaw and has done graduate work at Dartmouth College.

JENNINGS RANDOLPH PROGRAM FOR INTERNATIONAL PEACE

This book is a fine example of the work produced by senior fellows in the Jennings Randolph fellowship program of the United States Institute of Peace. As part of the statute establishing the Institute, Congress envisioned a program that would appoint "scholars and leaders of peace from the United States and abroad to pursue scholarly inquiry and other appropriate forms of communication on international peace and conflict resolution." The program was named after Senator Jennings Randolph of West Virginia, whose efforts over four decades helped to establish the Institute.

Since 1987, the Jennings Randolph Program has played a key role in the Institute's effort to build a national center of research, dialogue, and education on critical problems of conflict and peace. Nearly two hundred senior fellows from some thirty nations have carried out projects on the sources and nature of violent international conflict and the ways such conflict can be peacefully managed or resolved. Fellows come from a wide variety of academic and other professional backgrounds. They conduct research at the Institute and participate in the Institute's outreach activities to policymakers, the academic community, and the American public.

Each year approximately fifteen senior fellows are in residence at the Institute. Fellowship recipients are selected by the Institute's board of directors in a competitive process. For further information on the program, or to receive an application form, please contact the program staff at (202) 457-1700, or visit our web site at www.usip.org.

Joseph Klaits
Director

AN OUNCE OF PREVENTION:
MACEDONIA AND THE UN EXPERIENCE
IN PREVENTIVE DIPLOMACY

This book was set in the typeface American Garamond; the display type is American Garamond Bold. Cover design by Hasten Design Studio, Washington, D.C. Interior design and page makeup by Mike Chase. Copyediting and proofreading by EEI Communications, Inc., Alexandria, Va. Production supervised by Marie Marr. Peter Pavilionis was the book's editor.